PARLIAMENTARY DEMOCRACY IN NORTH-EAST INDIA

PARLIAMENTARY DEMOCRACY IN NORTH-EAST INDIA

A Study of Two Communities Each from the States of Assam, Meghalaya and Sikkim

Jayanti Alam

KALPAZ

ISBN: 978-93-5128-161-0

Price : ₹ 990

First Published, 2016

Published by

Kalpaz Publications
C-30, Satyawati Nagar,
Delhi – 110052
E-mail: kalpaz@hotmail.com
Ph.: 9212142040

Printed at: G. Print Process, Delhi

Cataloging in Publication Data—DK
Courtesy: D.K. Agencies (P) Ltd. <docinfo@dkagencies.com>

Parliamentary democracy in North-East India : a study of two communities each from the states of Assam, Meghalaya and Sikkim.
pages cm
Includes bibliographical references.
ISBN: 9789351281610

1. Bodo (Indic people)—India—Assam—Politics and government. 2. Karbis (Indic people)—India—Assam—Politics and government. 3. Khasi (Indic people)—India—Meghalaya—Politics and government. 4. Garo (Indic people)—India—Meghalaya—Politics and government. 5. Lepcha (South Asian people)—India—Meghalaya—Politics and government. 6. Bhotia (Tibetan people)—India—Sikkim—Politics and government. 7. Assam (India)—Politics and government. 8. Meghalaya (India)—Politics and government. 9. Sikkim (India)—Politics and government.

DS432.B63P37 2015 DDC 305.800954162 23

Contents

Preface

While travelling in a few States of the North-east studying the religious and social beliefs of the various tribes there (for my earlier book), I felt that their political behaviours are not to be overlooked; each tribe has a powerful political sense because they strongly believe in the greatness of their languages, folk-tales, folklores and their overall cultural traditions and in the hard reality that the freedom to practise those cannot be possible without political and financial powers. It is a truth in case of all economic and cultural groups as well as of the female race. That is why, women of India are continuously struggling for the reservation of at least one-third seats in the legislative bodies both at the Centre and the States. The very large State of Assam that is why, got truncated into Nagaland, Mizoram, Meghalaya and Arunachal Pradesh, etc. This movement for identity has not yet stopped—the Bodos and the Karbis in Assam are agitating for full political and financial powers and the Garos in Meghalaya are demanding special powers to them salves.

This was the time, i.e. during my field studies (for my earlier project, which has later come out as a book) in a few States of North-east India, I got curious to know about the level of political consciousness of a few tribes (it was obviously not possible to study about the myriad tribes of this area); this, I thought, can be done by studying their electoral behaviours and the sort of political parties they create and support. So, I thought of seeking ICSSR's help in doing this study. I am grateful to the Indian Council of Social Science Research, New

Delhi for granting me Senior Research Fellowship for two years.

My thanks go to the librarians and the staff-members of the libraries at Osmania and Hyderabad universities (at Hyderabad), Indian Public Enterprise, Hyderabad (to which I was affiliated as a Fellow of ICSSR, New Delhi), ICSSR library at Hyderabad, ICSSR-NERC library and the North-east Hill University library in Shillong, Omeo Kumar Das Institute of Social change & Development at Guwahati, North Bengal University Himalayan Studies department, Sikkim University Library and Nehru Memorial Museum & Library in New Delhi. The teachers and the students of NEHU (Shillong), Sikkim University (Gangtok) and people from various walks of life have enriched my study. My gratitude goes to the Fellows of OKDISSD, who have helped me not only by enriching my knowledge and understanding, but also by arranging my stay and travel. Similar gratitude goes to the staff and the Vice-Chancellor of Sikkim University & North Bengal University and the Director of ICSSR-NERC, Shillong.

But, this kind of study would not have been possible if I did not get the warm co-operation from the MPs and the MLAs from Meghalaya and Sikkim and the activists of the Bodo and Karbi movements of Assam. Last but not the least, the opinions and the beliefs of the common people from different walks of life have enriched me the most. Unfortunately, I found the women of these regions, viz. the Garo and Khasi women, the Lepcha and Bhutia women and those belonging to the militant Bodo and Karbi communities, are not much interested or active in politics. Thus, unlike my earlier studies, where I had given higher importance to the opinions and lifestyle of the women of the communities (I studied), this project could not be women-centric.

Jayanti Alam
Hyderabad
August 2014

Introduction

Electoral politics has become a major field of study in cotemporary social sciences. Even though India's North-eastern States have been keenly observed by the journalists, the scholars and the policy-makers because the politics of these States seem to challenge some of the major theories of Indian democratic politics, yet serious efforts at electoral analysis of the region have rather been limited. Electoral politics of contemporary North-east have been dominated by the issues of ethnic identity and the study of ethnic conflicts, insurgency, identity politics and the preference for the myriad regional parties upholding the limited but focused interests of the innumerable tribes.

Methodology

The work involves dividing the endeavour into the following—

1. Going through all the reading materials—books and articles and other documents—to form a foundation for my study,
2. Going through the proceedings of the Parliament from 2004 to 2014 (I had decided to cover a period of 10 years since it is not possible within the short span of two years to cover the period right from the beginning of the Parliament),
3. Going through the proceedings of the Assemblies of the 3 States during the period as above,

4. Talking to the Members of the Parliament as well as to the Members of the Legislative Assemblies, representing the communities I have chosen for my study. The communities are the Bodos and the Karbis from Assam, the Khasis and the Garos from Meghalaya and the Lepchas and the Bhutias from Sikkim.
5. Talking to a few members of the two communities from each State; they may be shopkeepers, taxi-drivers, students, teachers, home-makers and big and small entrepreneurs, etc. For this I needed the help/co-operation of those from the communities who have leadership qualities and/or are well aware of the economic condition and political behaviour of the members of the community, particularly the electorates,
6. Talking to a few academics in the universities, the colleges and the schools of those regions; students obviously, could not be neglected since they are the best opinion-givers,
7. Finally, discussing my findings with the people I have talked to earlier.

I went through the day-to-day proceedings of the Parliament at Parliament House Library; unfortunately, those were not useful. North-east is such a neglected part of India that hardly any discussion takes place on it. Only violence—terrorists' or peoples' spontaneous—and movement/demand for secession attracts attention; and I cannot take those as Parliamentary behaviour of the electorates or as an indication of "Parliamentary Democracy."

So, I adopted the method of studying the Assembly proceedings of the three States and talk to the MPs and the MLAs of the constituencies representing the communities. I therefore, chose my favourite and tested method of visiting the particular areas and talk to the various sections of the communities from all strata of life. I deliberately did not chalk out set questionnaires though I took the guidelines from the set questionnaires of Lokniti, New Delhi (known all over India for its more or less accurate election studies). My experiences during the writing of my two earlier books (one on the Tibetan society on both sides of the Himalayas and the other on the Buddhist women of Arunachal Pradesh and Tibet) have been that the communities get suspicious and do not open up when they see papers in my hands. I had to spend two to three days to befriend them and even stay at their homes as a friend and a sympathizer before I could get the required answers through informal conversations and interactions. I did use set questionnaires when I talked to the MPs, MLAs and the political leaders though they mostly used to get so involved in their problems that I had to carry out conversations in an informal way as a friendly chat and move away from the questionuaires. The remarkable thing was that the tribal people are very simple-hearted and believe in plain talking once they realise that I have no political motive and am fully sympathetic, on the contrary. They get very agitated and un-cooperative whenever the talks veer round the government of India or the UPA or the Congress Party. I am not aware of their reactions to Hodi or NDA sence I had carried out research earlier to NDA come to power.

So, I decided to study the Garos and the Khasis from Meghalaya, the Lepchas and the Bhutias from Sikkim and the Bodos and the Karbis from Assam after I completed reading about them in Hyderabad Central University Library, Osmania University Library (in Hyderabad) and Nehru Memorial Museum & Library, New Delhi. I did further reading in the libraries of North-east Hill University, Sikkim University and Omeo Kumar Das Instsitute for Social Change and Development, Guwahati. I had extensive discussions with the university and college teachers and the Fellows of OKDISCD, which were extremely fruitful. My deep gratitude is to all of them.

Chapter I

Democracy

Political systems have usually been categorised on the basis of the locus of the political authority and the extent to which popular voice and sentiments are reflected in the process of political decision-making. The conventional classifications of the political systems as monarchy, aristocracy and democracy may formally continue to be operative. There is a lot of inter-mingling and it is possible to find an aristocratic political system in the garb of democratic polity. But, modern age is the age of Democracy and even in dictatorial regimes the pressure of democratic political processes is greater. It is not surprising, therefore, that even authoritarian regimes call themselves democratic!

No matter what the nature of the political system, it has to grapple with the problems of legitimacy. A political system based on monarchy or aristocracy encounters this problem in lesser intensity since allegiance to the system is habitual. This is not so in case of a democratic political order since the idea of democracy presupposes the demolition or atleast the neutralisation of privileges. Democracy does recognise conflicts, but along with it, it also recognises the necessity of a basic consensus which defines the types of conflicts that can be channelised into and resolved by the ongoing processes of the political system, prescribes the norms that should enter into the resolution of conflicts and in general, circumscribes the nature of political debate.

There are three factors essential for the successful functioning of a democratic polity. First, the citizens must reflect a general commitment to democratic ideals and processes. Secondly, there must exist a body of political leaders who, while competing among themselves for the capture and control of political power, remain dedicated to the democratic rules of the game. Lastly, there must be available an institutional structure to support, channelize and control political processes. Every political system and democratic system in particular, has to define for itself the proper balance between stability and change. The question of stability and change brings into focus the dynamic interaction pattern between political system, social system and the individual. If persistent urges for change are ignored for too long, the political order stands in the danger of losing its legitimacy and may face the threats of rebellion and violence.

A reasonably responsive democracy can exist only if eight institutional guarantees are present, viz.

1. Freedom to Form and Join Organisations
2. Freedom of Expression,
3. The Right to Vote
4. Eligibility for Public Office
5. The Right of the Political Leaders to Compete for Support and Vote
6. Alternative Sources of Information
7. Free and Fair Elections and
8. Institutions for making Government Policies depend on Votes and other Expressions of Preference.

These embody the classic democratic rights of liberty and especially of the freedoms of speech and assembly; they also embody the classic democratic value of equality.

Majoritarian democracy is especially appropriate for and works best in homogenous societies, whereas Consensus democracy is more suitable for plural societies. A government by the majority and in accordance with the majority's wishes comes closer to the democratic ideal than government by and responsive to a minority. It argues that the majorities should govern and the minorities should oppose. And, to exclude the losing groups from participation in decision-making clearly violates the primary meaning of democracy. [W. A. Lewis, "Politics in West Africa," 1965.]

Democracy is a recent phenomenon and not a single democratic government can be found in the 19th. century and it was not until the first decade of the 20th. century that in two countries, viz. New Zealand and Australia, fully democratic regimes with firm popular control of governmental institutions and universal adult suffrage were established. [G. Therborn, "The Rule of Capital and the Rise of Democracy," 1977]. The ratings are based on two sets of criteria, viz.: (i) political rights such as the right to participate in free and competitive elections; and (ii) civil liberties such as freedom of speech and association. [R. D. Gastil, "Freedom in the World: Political Rights and Civil Liberties", 1980.]

An effective Opposition restrains the Party in power from transgressing its financial limits, constantly reminds it of its responsibilities, keeps it responsive to the popular demands and poses a challenge to its position by promising better performance. The Opposition also organises social power to check official power from becoming arbitrary and acts as a vigilance force for the safety of the democratic order. The place of the Opposition in a democracy is both a historic necessity and a political imperative. A viable Opposition thus, is a vital institution that reflects the positive reactions of a society and directs social energy towards preserving democracy as a way of life.

The sturdy nature of Democracy cannot be maintained unless a scrupulous distinction between social power and political power is made. History is full of instances that the use of political power for the purposes of social power has invariably ended in either despotism or totalitarianism. Majoritarian democracy is especially appropriate for and works best in homogenous societies, whereas Consensus democracy is more suitable for plural societies. Government by the majority and in accordance with the majority's wishes comes closer to the democratic ideal than government by and responsive to a Minority or Minorities; this is the essence of the Consensus model. This form appears ideal for India; but there is so much diversity in culture, religion, ethnicities, etc. that consensus is not possible. It is not desirable either; the beauty and greatness of India lies in "unity in diversity" (though lately we are witnessing too many conflicts between the divergent groups).

Illiteracy does not handicap the voter in knowing where his/her interest lies. He/she exercises his/her options with an informed awareness of the issues. It is wisdom that matters, not literacy. That is why Indian elections are vibrant, intense and participatory; they are successful at doing what the elections are expected to do. Democracy, to me, is the only form of government that can ensure India's unity.

Dissent is fundamental to the success of democracy; it is a kind of a revolt against tyranny. We can also say that democracy is born out of dissent and out of democracy dissent emerges. The form of dissent differs depending on the situations. Dissent therein paves way for reconsideration of the viewpoint put forth by the ruling party or rectification of the defects pointed out to evolve the policy or principles to further rule of law. Dissent may also mean a democratic challenge to the legitimacy of an oppressive policy or the suppressions of the legitimate expectations or denials of the equal access to the means of livelihood and/or opportunities. The vested interests may perceive it to be an affront to their entrenched rights or interests and law and order will be used to suppress the dissent which can be highly creative or woefully destructive. In India, both forms of dissent are vying with each other. Under rule of law change is to be made by process of law.

But, dissent is not always disobedience. Ventilation of grievances of the individuals or groups or organisations is not per se against law. Terrorism can be considered an extreme form of dissent. It is necessary to introduce an element of dissent in the process of power itself. Societies oscillate between dissent and consensus; dissent, as mentioned earlier, is a part of democracy which is an ever-evolving process along with the consciousness of the people. The nature of dissent reflects the character of the society and the quality of its leadership. The ideal is to lead the society from the present partisan dissent to non-partisan, selfless and wholesome dissent that can result in social consensus.

Democracy is conceived to reverse absolutism. Opposition is not mere opposition of each and every proposal; its task should be to offer alternative and constructive proposals and discussions of their pros and cons. Expression of dissent, freedom of assembly and association, to remove inequality, injustice, coercion and disparity—socially, economically and politically—are fruits of democracy. Political and economic elites usually dominate and rule and the socially and economically deprived people are usually on the margin. It is a long way to reach the condition of full or proper democracy where all people will be equally benefited and involved.

Dr. Ambedkar, in his closing reply to the debates on the floor of the Constituent Assembly, had said that since India lacks the experience of the working of the political institutions on democratic lines, India needs political morality and should establish conventions which should become a way of life. Unfortunately, that has not happened and the reverse is becoming the order of the day thus eroding people's faith in democratic process and parliamentary form of government. We have to, therefore, initiate necessary steps to strengthen our democratic system with the active involvement of the people and the process must be constitutional, legal and constructive since violence, small or big, is always counter-productive.

Dissent can also be for creative change and to legitimise a healthy and judicious dissent is so necessary for an ever-renewing democracy; it is necessary to introduce an element of dissent in the process of power itself. Civil disobedience is dissent and an appeal to a commonly shared conception of justice, whereas dissent by conscientious objectors is grounded on individual beliefs and a powerful sense of justice.

Terrorism is often confused with dissent though it is not an acceptable form of dissent in a democratic set up. Terrorism is sometimes mistaken for revolution, though a revolution is backed by a large segment of society to displace an oppressive government. We must remember that terrorism does not enjoy social backing. Yet, terrorism may sometimes culminate in a revolution depending on the nature of its appeal and the response it evokes! The freedom fighters of India, who had taken to arms, were called "terrorists" by the British government. The revolutionaries in monarchical France and Czarist Russia were also regarded as terrorists by the anti-people autocrats (of these nations).

One of the most important ingredients of a representative government is the accountability of the representative to the people who elected him/her. Accountability is not to be enforced only at the time of elections, but has to be a continuing feature that should govern the relationship between the elected representative/s and the electorate. Unfortunately, this concept of accountability has not developed adequately in our polity. The reasons chiefly are the large size of the constituencies and the social and educational backwardness of a major part of our electorate. Discussion is fundamental to democracy; the democratic set up is designed to facilitate articulation of different views/points. It is also the atmosphere of free thoughts that matter—not free thought for those who agree but also freedom for the thought that we hate! According to Bertrand Russell,

"Democracy is intended to make men's tenure of power temporary and dependent upon popular approval. In so far as it achieves this, it prevents the worst abuses of power." But, the form of government in any country largely depends on the needs of those classes which are influential enough to challenge the power." Not only that, "wherever there is an ascendant class, a large portion of the morality of the country emanates from its class interests and its feelings of class superiority," wrote J. S. Mill.

The legislature is the immediate repository of a great part of the sovereign power and the Opposition within it is not taken on the party basis, but as an indivisible part of the representative system. Just as popular sovereignty is absolute, pre-eminent and indestructible and the ultimate source of all powers, an elected representative cannot be deprived of his membership of the Legislature on any ground by any authority except as available to his/her constituents. In India, on account of the introduction of democracy in its most up-to-date design, political change has been far ahead of its social development and therefore, the interaction between parties and society, vital to the emergence of a party system has been indefinitely delayed. If circumstances are positive, the multi-party system has been indefinitely delayed. India is yet to develop an integrated secular national society as required by the concepts of democracy. There must be independent legislature and independent judiciary.

Caste is a rather significant factor in India's democracy and brings thousands of hurdles on the road to success. The basic foundation of caste is the concept and practice of inequality and we all know and the discussion above on the nature of democracy has made us believe that inequality is the worst enemy of democracy. Caste is an immutable, irremovable, inescapable thrust upon the Hindu by the simple reason of being born in a particular caste. He/she obviously has absolutely no hold or control over this; caste is like the skin on one's body—totally irremovable. One grows within one's caste, lives, marries, works within his caste and finally, dies one's within its impregnable walls. Death is said to be the leveller, but the death of an untouchable does not eradicate the inequality to which he she has to surrender! Naturally, the most numerous groups being the common masses (even if not untouchable or Dalit) had very little to offer except physical labour; they thus were and are condemned to perpetual servitude. Caste refuses to accept merit based on individual attributes but, assigns merit to an individual merely on the strength of the status of his/her social group. A minority that needs protection is that group of people, who by tradition and history, is isolated at the will of the majority and made vulnerable to its tyranny.

Caste is not an innocuous division of labour as over-simplified by its proponents, it is an inflexible social set up, an inelastic economic order, an inclement political system and above all, a monstrous contrivance that governs and guides the mind of the Hindu—his likes and dislikes and prejudices and perspectives. It strikes at the root of individuality and amounts almost to a denial of personality. It refuses to admit that every individual is, in his nature, universal and that he she has the right to seek his/her own self-expression, to determine his own ambitions and pursue his own interests.

The first empirical approaches to the study of class had begun in Europe. Marx divided industrial societies into bourgeois and proletariat. Therefore, an egalitarian society was possible only if economic statuses were equalised–by political authoritarianism, if need be. Once economic equality was achieved, it was assumed that political democracy would automatically emerge. Max Weber suggested that there is no single social hierarchy, but there were different types of stratifications based on wealth, power and status. He believed that there was a great degree of interplay among these three dimensions. There are two types of societal groupings that need to be considered. One is ethnic groups which are defined largely in terms of birth and ascribed statuses; the other is social classes which are based, to a great extent, on achievements. A comparison of these two kinds of groups define their identities and their boundaries as also the way they handle mobility and stratification can give us some idea of how they structure a society. The cultural distinctive of ethnic groups are of two kinds. First, there are certain basic values to which the members are committed and certain standards by which their behaviours are judged. These may include specific religious beliefs, standards of morality or assumptions about the nature of reality. Secondly, there are cultural signs and symbols such as language, dress, construction of the house, general life styles and specific rites expressing their distinctive beliefs; people show/express their identity through these and the group's survival depends on the preservation and survival of these identities. Ethnic groups may develop a close interdependence upon each other by which they provide important goods and services to each other. In this symbiotic relationship they often draw upon the same natural resources in spite of occupying different social notches. Each may have a monopoly on or responsibility for certain roles and/or means of production. It may look like caste system or class. People who develop an awareness of their identity as a group based on a common rank in a social hierarchy constitute a social class.

Something should be done promptly to curb politicisation of religion and to reduce the effect of appeals on the basis of religious and casteist sentiments. The holding of free and fair elections is a sine qua non of successful and enlightened democracy. The political parties and the participants in the electoral process should remember that when there is a conflict between the national interests and the party interests the duty of a citizen is not merely to vote, but to vote wisely. A government according to the majority's wishes comes closer to the democratic ideal than government by and responsive to the minority.

In a two-party system the voters can make a clear choice between two alternative sets of public policies. The programme of the winning party automatically becomes the government's programme. There are four Leftist vs Rightist party positions on socio-economic policies, viz:

(a) Governmental vs Private ownerships of the means of production,

(b) Strong vs Weak governmental role in economic planning,

(c) Support of vs. Opposition to the redistribution of wealth from the rich to the poor and

(d) The expansion of vs Resistance to the governmental social welfare programmes.

In India where the society has numerous ramifications, multiplicity of parties is but a social reflection. It is the feudal structure of society that generated the psychology favourable for the Congress to maintain its position as the dominant party with its heavy centralisation, its distribution of patronage in return for loyalty, its tutelage over its provincial organisations and the pride and elation; its regional formations derive from their submission to over-lordship especially for the final settlement of the issues. In a social situation as obtaining now in India, there can be further fragmentation of the Left with its predisposition to differ. We have to now wait and watch how much more patronage the Modi government will bestow on the capitalists, foreign direct investment and filling up of the coffers of the rich; we have to also wait and watch if the benefits go to the Hindutva practitioners only. The most important thing to watch will be the influence the Hindutva-vadis will have on the school and college text-books and music, plays, films and other aspects of India's diverse culture, i.e. if India's pride viz. "unity in diversity" will be preserved!

CHAPTER II

Parliamentary Democracy

A.

With the coming into force of the Republican Constitution of independent India on January 26, 1950, a full-fledged parliamentary system of government with a modern institutional framework and all its other ramifications was established. The Constituent Assembly of India became the provisional Parliament of India and functioned as such until after the first General Elections, based on universal adult franchise, in 1951-52. The Constitution of India has effected a radical change in the conception of governmental machinery. The Legislature is the supreme authority to which the Executive viz. The Council of Ministers has been made expressly responsible. The Legislature, by itself, has no executive power, but each and every action of the Executive can be scrutinised and questioned by the Legislature. It can even remove the Council of Ministers by a vote of no confidence. But, these two are not arrayed against each other so as to obstruct and/or evade each other; each is part of the same governmental machinery and if the Legislature is endowed with the right to control the Executive, it has also the duty to see that the country's government goes on as smoothly and as effectively as possible.

Parliamentary form of governance, the most popular mode today of political sovereignty, is uniquely dependent on people's consent. An occidental political concept, it is now widely followed all over the world because central to it is the rational collation of the aspirations, desires and wishes in a majoritarian electoral mandate system. The last quarter of the last century can truly be credited with the introduction of multi-party governance and coalitions.

As in other parliamentary democracies, the Parliament of India has the cardinal functions of legislation, overseeing of Administration, passing of the Budget, ventilation of the public grievances, discussing various subjects like development plans and international relations and policies, etc. The Council of Ministers is collectively responsible to the Lok Sabha; the parliament exercises control over the Executive by having full control over the Finances.

India being a federal country, each of the states has its own legislature and executive and some of the legislatures are bicameral. The Indian Parliament too, is bicameral viz. Council of States or the Rajya Sabha and the House of the People or the Lok Sabha. The Rajya Sabha consists of nominated members also. The actual number of the members of Parliament is determined by the Representation of the Peoples' Act, 1950; this has been amended from time to time for the purpose of proportional representation of the growing number of Indians. The members of the Upper Houses (both at the Centre and in the States) are elected under the system of Proportional Representation by means of single transferrable votes of the MPs; the members of the Lower Houses are elected directly by universal adult franchise.

The Indian Constitution has adopted the system of Parliamentary Democracy and the procedure is like in the British parliamentary system. Like in other parliamentary democracies, the parliament of India has the cardinal functions of legislation, overseeing of Administration, passing of the Budget, ventilation of the public grievances, discussing various subjects like development plans and international relations and policies like Industrial policies, Education policies, etc. Parliament usually sits thrice a year—for passing the Railway Budget and General Budget and also during the Monsoon and winter.

It is more or less the same with the Legislative Assemblies in the States. The members enjoy certain rights and immunities, without which they cannot discharge their duties efficiently and effectively. The most important privileges are the freedom of speech inside the Parliament and the Assembly, immunity from court proceedings and arrests. But this immunity does not extend to preventive detention and criminal cases. If any individual or authority disregards or attacks any of the privileges, rights and immunities, this breach of privileges is punishable by the House. In the British system the Parliament is supreme and sovereign; we cannot call our Parliament supreme and sovereign because its powers are defined and delimited by the written Constitution.

The characteristics of our political system are

(a) Supremacy of the Constitution,
(b) Republican and democratic form of government,
(c) Secular character of the Constitution,
(d) Separation of powers between the Centre and the States and
(e) Federal character of the ruling system

India is a sovereign democratic Republic; there is constitutionally granted equality of status and opportunity, secularism and freedom of conscience and, of course, the Rule of Law. Though, on paper, the Executive is accountable to the Legislature, viz. the Parliament or the State Assembly, in actual practice the latter has been made subordinate to the Executive particularly when the ruling Party has a massive majority in the Parliament/Assembly. Parties with less than 50 per cent votes can and actually do, enjoy massive majority in the House! In a multi-party system, a party can get absolute majority in the number of seats in the Legislatures without getting more than 50 per cent of the total votes! Thus, the will of the majority party need not necessarily be the will of the majority population.

India is a country with a very high degree of pluralism and there are diversities of various kinds which—fortunately or unfortunately—cut across each other. An individual in a majority according to one indicator may be in the minority according to other. Thus, the majorities and the minorities in our country are not in separate water-tight compartments. A person, for example, may belong to a majority religious group and to a minority language or cultural group.

Needless to mention that the political parties play a very significant role in the legislatures—both the Parliament and the Legislative Assemblies—and affect their functionings considerably. They carry heavy responsibilities to the electorates also. But, a healthy political party system is yet to evolve in our country. The parties, like other human institutions in a democratic set-up, cannot be ordered or dictated from above; they have to evolve. But, neither ideology-oriented, nor programme-oriented political parties have been able to evolve. Coalition system has made it more impossible for the parties to stick to an ideology or a programme; somehow or other, what matters is power and not the welfare of the people. Ideally a political party must have (a) a philosophy, (b) an ideology, (c) policy/ies and (d) programme/s. Unfortunately, none of our political parties have all or perhaps, not even one.

Qualifications do not necessarily lead to better quality legislators; mere literacy or degrees do not constitute education. An uneducated may be intelligent, sensitive and with deep understanding and wisdom and the opposite may be found with highly educated legislators! We cannot, therefore, confuse mere literacy or education with knowledge and/or wisdom. Sir Edmund Burke rightly observed "in all forms of government the people/the electorate are the true legislators."

Sometimes, constitutional amendment passed by the Parliament is struck down summarily and the will of the people, expressed through Parliament is not accepted by the Judiciary. The Supreme Court may decide that a particular constitutional amendment is ultra vires. The impasse thus continues till the Parliament gets the next best opportunity to restore the will of the people by another amendment.

B.

There is an urgent need to have a fresh look at the deteriorating moral and ethical standards of our political life. Politicisation of religion and caste needs to be curbed in order to reduce the evil effects of the religious and casteist sentiments of the voters. The holding of free and fair elections is sine qua non of successful and enlightened democracy. The political parties and the participants in the electoral process must remember that there is a conflict between the national interests and party interests. The duty of a citizen is not merely to vote, but to vote wisely. Some believe that a right man in a wrong party is preferable to a wrong man in the right party. The founder-members of the Indian Constitution and the national leaders of our independence movement too, may have thought like this though the question of a wrong person or a wrong party was not there. Increasing corruption, money power and criminalisation of politics gradually devalued the democratic institutions and the commitments. The electoral reforms so far attempted are only piecemeal efforts/measures. It appears as if the national parties do not have the political will and determination to enact legislation which will bring in effective electoral reforms thus enhancing the democratic content in the legislatures.

The involvement of the legislatures in the affairs of a nation manifests itself through limited and incremental actions at a whole variety of levels. We neither can expect all powers for the legislatures, nor should we exclude the possibility of legislative intervention in any field. Intervention takes the forms of influence and participation. A whole variety of points of penetration exists in the political system; the legislators are responsible fully or in part. The degree of involvement and influence of the legislatures depends necessarily on a variety of constraints; these may be narrow if the legislators are afraid to question the Executive, the leadership of the party or the military. Social and economic constraints are of immense importance. For legislatures to be effective at detailed or general levels instruments or procedures appropriate to each level has to exist. The procedure of law-making has become an instrument by which the legislators have tended to meet such problems as (1) helping individual constituents, (2) raising issues in order to obtain administrative change, (3) proposing long-term policy alterations, etc.

Ideally, the legislators must be competent in all matters of public interests; but, this is an impossible goal to achieve and increasingly unrealistic as the polity becomes increasingly complex. The efficiency of the legislature and the legislators depends on the extent to which the assembly as a whole provides an infrastructure which helps members and increases their competence. A wide variety of arrangements, procedures and technical support becomes necessary. For the Executive to be able to reduce the influence of the Legislature, it must have some independent authority—whatever Constitutional curbs are at its disposal. Legislatures are weak

(1) under a strong monarchical system,
(2) where there is a strong personal appeal of a leader,
(3) under a military regime,
(4) when the party system is in a flux; the type of party system, its policies and ideology affect the working of both the Executive and the Legislature.

Internal limitations, the existence of a separate source of authority and in some cases constitutional curbs—all lead to the reduction of the legislature's direct and positive role in many of the nation's affairs. The legislatures of the contemporary world may not be powerful or may not wield legislative supremacy but, a large majority of them are at least meaningful. We know that the role of the legislatures in law-making is likely to be limited to executive influence; it becomes necessary to explore the various aspects of legislative involvement amongst the legislators.

Legislatures do not make laws in the fullest sense of the word; they cannot make constitutions either, though they are slightly better-equipped to do the latter than the former. The laws require an administrative base which the legislatures do not and cannot have. The function of the legislature is to provide a means of ensuring that there are channels of communications between the people and the Executive. This statement/observation is not to run down the importance of the parliamentary system which allows for governments to be overthrown by the members of the Assembly.

C.

India, though regarded as one nation, is the conglomeration of many ethnicities, religions, languages and cultures; we can compare it to the continent Europe. It is perhaps, much more diverse than the different nations of Europe are. The cultural and economic growth/development variations are too stunning and unfortunately, the freedom movement was led by the upper caste and the upper class and therefore, the powerful Hindus and the trend continued and continues through so many elections. The recently concluded elections to the Lok Sabha, where the Hindu chauvinists secured as much as two thirds majority of the seats in the Parliament, is the most dangerous trend which can destroy democracy totally; the Party in power can even destroy India's "secular, democratic" Constitution by bringing in amendments to suit its Hindutva dictatorship!

The preceding governments—mostly coalition—too, did not do anything worthwhile for the backward and the disadvantaged and had brought in American Capitalism that made the rich richer and the poor poorer. A very important component of the Preamble to our Constitution, viz. Socialism, has got successfully destroyed because of the introduction of LPG, i.e. Liberalisation, Privatisation & Globalisation. Indian cultures, food habits, dresses and attitudes to sex and morality have changed drastically. Yet, some semblance of secularism was left and the Indian Judiciary had continued to remain impartial, humanitarian and just; it saved the oppressed and the down-trodden. This group includes not merely the poor, but also the dalits and the adivasis. They could practise their religions and customs without much obstacle. With the coming of Modi's government (who had massacred the Muslims and the Christians as the Chief Minister of Gujarat and yet had come to power with thundering majority in Gujarat and now in India) is definitely going to create more discontent and secessionism amongst the adivasis of the North-east. Secessionism is regarded as the "State-shattering form of self-determination." This is true if the government or the party/ies in power are benevolent and truly democratic; but, can we blame secessionism when the State becomes autocratic and repressive? So, we have to now change our thinking about the adivasis under our study, viz. the Garos, the Khasis, the Bodos, the Karbis, the Lepchas and the Bhutias in the States of Meghalaya, Assam and Sikkim.

D.

Regional and/or self-determination movements could not be all that successful because more often than not, the leaders get won over (by money) or co-opted (with false promises and personal benefits). Yet, a semblance of movement is kept up because how can they continue to be leaders if the people start suspecting them or losing faith in them? For example, the Karbi leaders and politicians I had talked to appeared ungrudging and peaceful; yet, they tried to keep the common people agitated against both the Assam and the Central governments so that their leadership does not get questioned; they tried to remain in the good books of both the people and the governments so that money and power could flow into their hands. More or less same was the case with the Garo leaders and the MLAs and the MPs.

Sikkim was a great exception because of the selfless pro-people work done by the single party of Shri Pawan Chamling. He did not have to appear to be pro-people because the people were truly and totally pro-Sikkim Democratic Front (thus, with no Opposition in the Assembly at all). The Chief Minister's unfailing dedication to the people, without making any distinction between the different tribes, and his truly pro-people work had created such a unique situation in Sikkim. Mr. Chamling, himself a Nepali, made no discrimination at all among the various other tribes like the Lepchas and the Bhutias; we must also note here that about 70 per cent of Sikkim's population is Nepali and yet there is no majoritarianism! The majority Nepalis do not look down upon the Minorities in the slightest! They do not even want to join the Gorkhaland movement of Darjeeling in spite of belonging to the same racial, language and religious group!

But, in the recently concluded election to the Sikkim Assembly, strangely a few seats went to the newly formed party named Sikkim Krantikari Morcha. It was a single member party 2013 when I had gone to Sikkim to study the political behaviour of the people there. People were making fun of it. But, in the recent elections of May 2014, this party won as many as 12 seats! This shows that there is a group of voters who do not like the endless rule of one party, headed by a Nepali (which is the largest community in the State). This new trend in Sikkim's electoral politics shows that there is a section of the Minorities, viz. the Lepchas and the Bhutias, who wanted another regional party though they did not like the Congress or any other national party.

E.

The leaders, organising people of a region for a separate State (like Telengana, Bodoland, Gorkhaland, etc.), do not have a coherent view of Indian identity; once, immediately after independence, the Indian leaders and the people were proud of "unity in diversity" or a bouquet of variant Indian cultures. But, the absence of solution of growing economic problems and with the expanding gap between the rich and the poor, the common people are becoming more and more restive and intolerant of the power-hungry leaders/rulers and are becoming excessively identity-conscious. The trend is becoming more and more powerful with the rulers are failing miserably. The results of the just concluded general election is a clear proof of the utter desperation of the voters; they are so fed up of corruption, misrule and absence of development and the extracting mentality of the rich and the powerful that they voted for an alternative. I do not believe that the overwhelming majority of the Hindus have become Hindutva-minded and anti-Muslim, they are just desperate and utterly frustrated with the misrule of the successive UPA governments.

The voters think that self-rule will be better than to be ruled by the corrupt State and Central governments. But, unfortunately, both "democratic" India and authoritarian China have rejected the method of plebiscite. In a multinational country, plebiscite is the best method; issue-wise decisions can solve the problems better than the elected representatives taking up matters in the legislative bodies without knowing the views and pulse of the voters. The farmer never look back to their constituencies once they get elected, nor do they have a coherent view of the Indian identity (since in matters of culture they are parochial). Elections can even be called auctions for the sale of governmental powers! They use patronage to enhance their power-base, which, in turn, gives them leverage within political party for and positions in the government. That is how democracy without referendum has become a grand failure in India even though democracy is supposed to be a system based on separation of powers, free press, liberties of forming associations, universal suffrage as well as individual rights.

F.

The modern elections require at least 4 sets of beliefs that we had not found in the beginning of Parliamentary Democracy; they are (i) a specific kind of public arena, (ii) a set of actors with given role definitions, (iii) a purpose that orients the entire set of activities and (iv) some agreed upon rules of the game. Elections are important because notwithstanding robust media which routinely conducts opinion polls, the elections disseminate political ideas/ideologies and people's views most effectively and those are supposed to gauge political/people's opinion correctly. But, with so much of illiteracy and absence of political education, elections in India have become mere farce just as the recently concluded election showed.

First, with widespread corruption amongst the vote-seekers, the voters are at a loss; to them all the myriad political parties are equally corrupt and power-hungry and all that the voters can do is experiment with a change! Besides, in a multi-party system the party winning the overwhelming majority of the seats may not necessarily get the majority of the votes. Thirdly, (as mentioned earlier), once elected, the MPs and the MLAs forget about their constituencies altogether and concentrate on gaining more and more economic and political powers. The demands of the voters and the promises made during the election campaigns are totally forgotten and there is a strong tendency towards populism rather than substantive politics so as to deliver long-time benefits in areas particularly of health and education. (Let me point out here that capitalism did not become anti-people in China because during the socialist regime highest attention was paid to universal education and health—the most important infrastructure of any economy particularly if it is nascent and backward). As mentioned above, Referendum is thus the only way a citizen can express his/her views and demands; every bill taken up in the Parliament/Assembly should come down to the voters.

Then only true freedom of expression—the strongest pillar of democracy—can be established.

G.

The extent to which a government is accountable depends on the (a) personal objectives of the government officials, (b) perceptions of the citizens or other watchdog agencies, (c) mechanisms by which the citizens and the agencies can exert pressure or remove governments they find non-accountable. If citizens of a particular group (region, caste or class) are less aware or less willing to sanction or pressurise the government, the latter naturally, is less likely to be responsive or beneficially active. Such governments hardly ever care for the less educated and the socio-economically backward.

CHAPTER III

Coalition Politics in India

A Coalition situation arises when an election fails to throw up a party with a majority of seats in the Parliament or any Assembly and for this reason no party singly is able to form a government. Some like-minded parties or even parties of different or opposing views may then enter into an agreement to form the government. In such a situation, the Opposition too, usually is a coalition like it was at the Centre (till BJP won with two-thirds majority in the just-concluded election) and the in the State of Meghalaya (though Congress got many more seats than it usually does in 2013 Assembly election). There are instances of Minority government being formed like that led by P. V. Narsimha Rao (1991-96); the Aam Admi Party in Delhi assembly election was another example of Minority government since Congress was not joining the government but, was giving support from outside. Such situations cannot be avoided in a nation with multifarious nationalities and divergent views and demands which opens the space for the formation of almost innumerable number of parties and even States; the role of regional parties with the demands of various linguistic-cum-cultural groups is of no minor significance. The demand for proportional representation leads to multi-party system.

Coalitional governments at the State levels are much older than at the central level because of the reasons mentioned above. Coalition government had started in Kerala as early as in 1950s and in a few North Indian States after a decade or so. Those were extremely unstable and the governments used to fall much before the stipulated five years because the only bond among them was non-Congressism. The first example of a very stable coalition government was the Left Front governments; elections after elections it won in West Bengal. In Kerala, anti-incumbency factor works powerfully; the coalition governments change with every election.

Majoritarian politics has revolutionised democratic consensus and governance and had introduced egalitarian ethos in large measure; but, the growing incompatibilities inherent in the representation process have raised obstacles to its growth. The growing complexities of elections and consensus mechanisms are becoming the governing legislative motif everywhere and coalition politics is one of the emerging realities of democratic systems and may be construed to be the mainstay of majoritarian representation system.

Coalitions fit the bill because they have catered invariably always as vehicles for making governments formation possible when the electorate is not satisfied with the existing government or is dissatisfied with one single party ruling for a long time. Coalitions may be likened to a framework within which multi-level adjustments, bargaining, negotiations, power-sharing—both express and implicit—take place. Almost all European democracies have been governed by some coalition or other at some period or other; coalitions have not been strange to Indian political conditions either. It seems that coalitions are going to be the trend more and more because there is no end to new parties coming up every now and then; these have no ideology or clear vision about what is good for the electorate. The recent election broke the tradition of the voters' dissatisfaction with the bickering of the various partners in a coalition and Indian democracy thus has gone back to the early years of Indian politics; Congress used to be the party with simple majority (election after election); now it is the BJP—the opposite pole of Congress both in ideology, practice and attitude to the ruled.

Politics has been defined as the art of the possible. Political systems are contrivances to make possible what may not be achievable otherwise; coalitions are justifiably thought of as via media to make governance possible, what otherwise, will appear impossible. There is a growing complexity in the election process when the formation of a traditional one-party government becomes impossible or popular governments fail to deliver democracy. Very few democracies remain untouched by the phenomenon of coalition and India is no exception to that. The first coalition government at the Centre was in March, 1977 till July, 1979. That was because Congress for the first time had become unpopular as a result of the imposition of Internal Emergency by the then Prime Minister Indira Gandhi. The next significant coalition had come to power in 1989 under the leadership of V. P. Singh; for the first time voice was raised against corruption, autocracy (of Congress) and dynastic rule of the Nehru family.

As mentioned earlier, Narassimha Raó's was a Minority government and the disgruntlement against Congress autocracy led to United Front government under Deve Gowda (1996) and later under I. K. Gujral. Then there were the coalition governments under Vajpayee known as NDA or National Democratic Alliance (though the governance was far from being democratic) and later, till the election of April-May, 2014, under Manmohan Singh known as UPA or United Progressive Alliance.

Such forms of governments are increasingly becoming popular and inevitable because the parties do not stick to their ideologies or manifestoes or pre-election promises; so, the electors are confused, disappointed and therefore, undecided; they have no option but to go on experimenting with various parties or candidates. Quite often there is negative voting and the minds of the voters are anti-incumbency; the best examples are Kerala and Himachal Pradesh. The victory of Trinamool Congress in West Bengal after a very long stint of Left Front (coalition) and the recent victory of Aam Admi Party in Delhi can be perhaps, taken as positive voting because people voted with hope and trust for the new parties since they felt that the existing coalition (in West Bengal) and the Congress Party (in Delhi) had failed in their promises; they wanted the end of autocracy and corruption.

Absence of a majority party may also be due to the dysfunctionality of the election procedure; coalition has thus been accepted almost worldwide as the contrivance for governance in democracies, where a crisis of legitimacy has occurred. The salience of the local factors such as ethnicity, caste, linguistic and religious sensitivities, etc. form a major part in the formation of coalition governments. These are pre-modern traditional loyalties transferred to modern settings and working within the modern space of constitutional democracy; these are much more of primordial importance than mere ideology.

We must remember that we had always co-existed as a society with the system of coalition—be it formal or informal—even before the coalitional systems began in the Indian federal union as alternative government models, they became a part of the political process informally. The Congress system had experienced ascendancy in the few decades after India's independence due to successful manipulation and effective management of the oppositional forces and power process. In the 70s floodgates for the resurgence of the regional forces into the mainstream got opened. It was only after 1967 that the Indian party system transformed itself into a competitive party system; the Congress could manage such a position in the Indian politics because of it not taking a position of either the Left or the Right and maintained a high level of plurality. But, it failed to solve the ground level problems of the common people. So, the voters started experimenting with new parties, particularly the regional ones, because the local/regional problems were of primary importance in a country of varied interests and needs.

1. Coalition involves political activities that involve individual/group engaged in collective activity in interaction with more than one another.
2. Coalition involves the exercise of powers, the use, organisation and application of resources to gain certain ends.
3. Coalition involves the area of human affairs in which no solutions of pure conflict or pure co-ordination obtain.
4. Coalition is inherent to social action and social integration; there is no other way of forming a collectivism. Coalition ministries are short-lived compared to homogenous governments. A Cabinet can form persistent policies with firmness and effect only when it can rely for support on a compact and faithful majority.
5. An administration led by a coalition of parties is weak because the candidates and the parties whose professed principles differ are likely to be entangled in inconsistencies and unstable compromises. The fewer and stronger are the parties, it is better. The politics of coalitions are more pervasive than the frequency of actual coalition governments.
6. Each party has to find out which parties coalitions can be successful in the game of politics and political power; they also have to understand well what kind of coalition will pay off in getting ministerial seats. This involves complex and confounding calculations. The longer the coalition-bargaining process lasts the more is the pressure for some Cabinet to be formed. If no "majority" solution can be reached, a "minority" government has to be formed with the party getting the single largest number of seats with "outside"

support from the other like-minded parties. A proper coalition with a majority of seats may emerge later

7. Crucial to the entire exercise is the availability of a set of parliamentary parties, who are willing to bargain. This willingness determines the general range in which the coalitional status of the cabinet falls. This range can vary and that variance depends on the degree of information certainty that exists within the parliamentary bargaining area. If parties can properly estimate the relative strength of all other parties they will unite to form the minimum winning coalitions.
8. Opportunistic policies tend to prevail in societies without clear party divisions along an ideological line; in the centrist Congress-dominated political system, the parties with ideologies like the Left parties and the parties of the Sangh Parivar have traditionally played a small role, though the trend towards split in the parties and the formation of new and new regional parties has increased since 1967 and is ever-growing. Coalitions in present India are thus an important mechanism through which caste, class and religious cleavages and regional or territorially-based identities are sought to be put in a cohesive frame even in the absence of shared ideologies. Thus, coalition becomes not merely a political requirement in a federal Constitutional system but also an important medium of assertion of the pluralities that constitute the Indian State. It forms an important forum of articulation of various concerns, demands, requirements, grievances that remain unattended or unaltered by the political process. Coalitions can even rectify historical wrongs like the caste inequities, class discrimination, political neglect and alienation from the mainstream.
9. 1967 marks a change in Indian politics which led to change in the character of the party system in India; the number of seats held by the dominant Congress

Party dropped to 54 per cent from 72 per cent. It lost majority in as many as Nise States viz. Punjab, Haryana, Uttar Pradesh, Madhya Pradesh, Bihar, West Bengal, Odisha, Tamil Nadu and Kerala. This brought in a completely new situation in Indian politics whereby the non-Congress parties experimented with coalition politics.

10. In the North-east, in Manipur, Meghalaya, Mizoram and Nagaland, unstable two-party or multi-party alliances came up and in the Centre an alliance of four parties, the Janata Party comprising Congress (O), Bharatiya Lok Dal, Socialist Party and the Jana Sangh came up. According to some this was the result of a negative vote like it has happened in West Bengal where the ruling coalition with CPI (M) at the head lost to the regional party Trinamool Congress. But according to others it was an upsurge of suppressed democratic regional forces. Janata Party also claimed that it achieved victory of democracy over authoritarianism. But, it was a hastily assembled coalition with the sole purpose of defeating the autocratic Indira Gandhi; otherwise, Jana Sangh could not have been the part of the coalition. Therefore, natural divisions among them emerged sooner than later. After the Emergency of 1975 Jagjivan Ram walked out of Congress by managing to get the support of a large section of the untouchables who were trying to establish a powerful political movement by calling themselves Dalits. BLD was a party of the middle and small peasant proprietors of North India and wanted the re-allocation of the national resources from the urban to the rural and from the industrial to the agricultural sectors. The Socialist Party was truly socialist and its support base was the rural and urban poor and the Minorities; it used to support the trade unions also. Yet, this unwieldy coalition served a much-needed purpose of that time—the end

of one-party hegemony and the beginning of consensual democracy (however squabble-ridden it was). The failure of the Janata Party, though not unexpected, was significant. It brought into focus the importance of better co-ordination in coalitional government; six coalitional governments had come to power since then—

11. National Front coalition under the leadership of V. P. Singh (1989–90)
12. United Front coalition under H. D. Deve Gowda (1996-97)
13. BJP-led minority government under A. B. Vajpayee (1998–99)
14. National Democrtic Alliance of as many as 24 parties under the leadership of Vajpayee again (1999-2004)—the longest running coalition till UPA came to power
15. United Progressive Alliance I of 16 parties (2004-2009)
16. United Progressive Alliance II of (pre-poll) 10 parties (2009–2014).

The election of 2014 changed the entire picture again; it went back to the days of Congress in the beginning of Indian democracy with a remarkable change though. It is now the hegemony of the BJP—the most reactionary and communal party with the goal of establishing Hindu rashtra with all the unbearable dogmatism of orthodox, non-tolerant Hindutva.

Coalitions are thus a way of power-sharing when the views and ideologies are so diverse and where the smallest groups also want power. But, in spite of coalition governments as a kind of solution, it is/was not possible to make every group happy or a participant in the political process. It has been noticed that the diverse opinions do form a coalition front for the sake of contesting elections, but; most unfortunately, there is no "coalitional" mentality or endeavour when it comes to welfare of the people or solving the problems of particular groups! Interestingly, yet, people had voted the

UPA back to power 2009 and gave it another chance because it was headed by the Congress Party and most Indians blindly associate this party with the greatness of Gandhi and Nehru!

People perhaps, had given up hopes and did not find much difference between one-party rule or 10-party rule because in reality and for all practical purposes it is the President and the Vice-President of the majority coalition party who ruled. The same was the case with the Left Front coalition of West Bengal; in reality it was the rule of the majority party viz. CPI (M). It became horribly obvious after the Nandigram incident when the CPI (M) had neither taken the other coalition partners nor the peasants into confidence. In Meghalaya the electorate is bothered only about the candidate and not the party he belongs to; we may perhaps, call the system oligarchic democracy!

According to Granville Austin coalition governance has certain obvious advantages for democracy. In a situation of multitudinous diversity (as in India), a coalition or joining hands of parties with varied beliefs and interests can bring in stable government (we saw two UPA governments ruling for two full terms in spite of rising disgruntlement among the electorate). The stresses within society—classes, castes, tribes, minorities—strive for a bigger piece of national pie, force coalition members to act in concert and otherwise, get driven out of office. Hence coalitions have to respond to the demands of the time and the requirements of the people who are its sovereign power.

The future of coalitions surely hinges on the spirit of accommodation and toleration which may give a stable economic base and a truly federal structure. Challenges from the varied strata of people or voters may make the coalition partners amicable and people-centric.

Before the 1957 General Elections, there was a coalition of Praja Socialist Party (PSP), the Socialist Party (SP) and the Communist Party of India (CPI) in Assam. There were local pre-poll alliances too. There was also a time when the PSP and the Revolutionary Socialist Party of India (RCPI) did not enter into alliance against CPI in Gauhati constituency. In Ramguri, CPI and PSP did not set up candidate against RCPI. Thus, we see a confusing political situation where ideology did not play much role; it was the local convenience and political interests which were of importance. The only goal of these parties was to defeat Congress. The opposition coalition was named United Opposition Front and the composition varied from election to election; All-Party Hill Leaders Conference (APHLC) also had become part of the coalition Opposition in pre-Meghalaya Assam. In 1967 general election, the Opposition parties improved their position by doubling their numbers over 1962 performance. But, there came up two Opposition coalitions, viz. United Legislature Party and United Democratic Front! The APHLC had failed to get the Opposition status by securing only half of the required seats. The Opposition in Assam could have easily exploited the position of the Congress Party in Assam if not for a powerful Congress government at the Centre. The Assam Congress had to fight a sort of warfare within its ranks.

During 1969-71 there was a split in the Congress Party at the Centre itself. The party got defeated at the Centre in 1977 when the Janata Party coalition came to power (as we already know); as a result, in 1978 Assembly election no party could command a majority. The Congress got reduced to a minority party notwithstanding three decades of unquestioned rule in Assam. Splits after splits came into the Congress Party at the Centre during this period; there were Congress (Indira Gandi), Congress (Devraj Urs), Congress (Brahmananda Reddy) and Congress (Swaran Singh). By 1981, however, Congress (I) was declared as the real Congress by the Election Commission.

The Janata Party split at the Centre had similar effects in Assam. In 1979 Janata (S) group/party was formed in Assam. The second coalition ministry of Golap Borbora was sworn in 1979 with the ministers resigning forthwith. Borbora was accused of misusing administrative machinery and stalling of developmental activities. But, Borbora could still retain 68 members in his party. What sounded Borbora ministry's death-knell however, was local communalism. The next coalition ministry was formed in Assam under the Chief Ministership of Jogendra Hazarika. All Assam Gana Sangram Parishad had started agitational politics against this coalition. Hazarika had to face no-confidence motion, which was luckily defeated. The coalition had consisted mainly of Janata Party and Congress (U); the other parties (in diminishing order) were AJD, CPI (M), Congress (I), Janata (S), CPI, PDF, PTCA, RCPI, SUCI, CPI (ML) and two independents. In 1980 Congress had formed government without absolute majority since it was the single largest party without having attained absolute majority. A few parties supported the ministry from outside without joining as a coalition. Similar situation had arisen in Delhi recently with Congress supporting the Aam Admi Party government from outside (and not joining it in coalition). The CPI (M) too, had supported UPA I from outside or issue-based. The next coalition government in Assam was formed after the 1996 general elections; AGP had a pre-poll alliance with four other political parties in the State.

We all know that the present Meghalaya, comprising of the Garo the Khasi and the Jaintia Hills, was part of Assam State till much after the independence of India and during the colonial period and the tribal leaders used to join the coalition when necessary. The ministry of the Meghalaya Provisional Legislative Assembly was a grand coalition facing no Opposition party or Opposition coalition at all. Meghalaya got a Legislative Assembly of its own under the North-eastern Areas (Reorganisation) Act of 1971 and the first general election to the newly formed Assembly was held in March, 1972. This time there was pre-poll alliances between APHLC and Congress in the Garo Hills though the former got as many as 18 seats and Congress got only six; in the Khasi Hills the APHLC got 25 and Congress got only four; in the Garo Hills yet, alliance with Congress was of importance to APHLC because of Congress' unquestioned power in the Centre. Strangely, APHLC and the Congress fought against each other in the Jaintia Hills.

When APHLC, led by Capt. Sangma, merged with Congress for the first time in 1976, the other APHLC group, led by Lyngdoh, had to sit in the Opposition like HSPDP (Hill State People's Democratic Party). In March 1978 a coalition called Meghalaya United Legislative Party was sworn in with Mr. Pugh as Chief Minister. Later, a coalition, popularly known as "Three-Flag Government", was formed with Congress-led coalition (Meghalaya United Legislature Front) in the Opposition. The 1983 election also could not give one=party majority; the three regional parties with a total of 34 seats, formed the coalition called Meghalaya United Parliamentary Party. Leadership had become the main bone of contention and ultimately, Lyngdoh of APHLC became the Chief Minister. But, there were too much of dissidence and too many defections and the government lasted for 29 days only. At this juncture of terrible crisis Congress-dominated coalition, called Meghalaya Democratic Front, took over and the government lasted till 1988 general elections.

Interestingly, every time the regional parties formed a coalition without Congress could not last long and every time a coalition had Congress in it (with however low number of seats), the government lasted for a reasonable period. 1993 General elections gave the highest number of seats to the Congress though, once again, not the majority. HPU, HSPDP and APHLC got a total of 22 seats while there were as many as 10 independents. So, there had to be coalition government again in spite of Congress becoming the single majority party. Mr. C. Marak of Congress became the Chief Minister and it was the longest-lasting coalition ministry. On the other hand, the Congress (I)-led coalition ministry of S. C. Marak was the shortest—only for 12 days! Another record was the formation of three coalition ministries within a period of barely five months. Thirdly, the MPF coalition government had the largest number of ministers—35 in a House of 60 members!

In the Assembly election of 2013, when the major part of India was suffering from "anti-Congressism," Congress got an unexpected number of seats; it got as many as 29 seats in an assembly of 60—just short of absolute majority by two seats only! How can one explain this? Too many independents won—as many as 13. Thus the regional parties together got only 18 seats.

Chapter IV

North-East India

In the process of nation-building, especially in the Third World countries with colonial legacy, several challenges may be confronted, of which the most complex and the most persisting is the quest for identity. This urge is deep-seated, abiding and universal and can act as a powerful unifying force.

In a multi-cultural country like India it is inevitable that there are several layers of identities—some overlapping and mutually reinforcing—and others exclusive and at times conflicting. When a society is encumbered with national, linguistic, religious, ethnic, caste, class and group identities, it demands utmost vigil for some sort of equilibrium. Imaginative handling is thus necessary for evolving national consensus. Local identities need to be transcended to achieve comprehensive national identity.

As the struggle for gaining recognition as "indigenous people" gains momentum, more and more tribal communities in North-east India have begun identifying or projecting themselves as such. Although no community is officially declared indigenous, the central and the State governments grant Constitutional and political concessions to certain tribal communities in the North-east, thus indirectly recognising their claims to indigeinity. But, there is incessant conflict among the tribes regarding who actually is indigenous.

There is a possibility that the ideology and politics of indigeneity can well become a tool in the hands of the elite among the indigenous people and thus, become an obstacle to understanding the interests of the oppressed native communities and the poor migrants. Decades-long campaign and lobbying by the aboriginal activists groups in the West had attracted the attention of different marginalised and tribal communities in the developing world. The social, cultural and economic conditions of the indigenous communities distinguish them from the other sections of the communities in a nation. The indigenous people are those who have inhabited a piece of land or region before the entry of the very first migrant or coloniser; they also have been cautiously and lovingly maintaining their customs and traditions. They also speak and fondly preserve their indigenous dialect, customary and political institutions and primarily subsistence-oriented agricultural production.

The following are the opinions of a few human/tribal rights activists—

1. Migration from the North-east to the more developed parts of India has certainly picked up in the past couple of decades; there is no doubt, a 'pull' factor (due to better developments in the non-tribal regions/ States) but, there is a strong 'push' factor as well. These States have not witnessed/experienced an economic development of a meaningful kind; neither jobs are created, nor is entrepreneurship stimulated. But, these migrants are facing hostilities—even physical and sexual—because of the belief amongst the mainland Indians that the tribes and especially those from the North-east, are too different and cannot be mingled with! These tribes are believed to be more successful in

the tourism and hospitality industries because of their smart looks, Western clothes and informal approach.

2. The North-east societies are not stratified on the basis of caste and community unlike the rest of non-tribal India. There is no vertical ordering or oppression from the top, once again very much unlike the caste-ridden societies of the majority of Indians. The different tribes co-exist as equals even though their customs and traditions may be different. Their culture has absorbed the varied influences from China and the other geographically contagious countries as well as from the West. They quite often become targets of the Indians who are too traditional, conservative and sexually repressed. So, there is tremendous distrust and fear of the mainland Indians. Besides, these tribal people see the Indians more in military uniform enforcing torturous laws on them. That is why, the States of the North-east has got very little of the kind of governance which can be called 'democratic'. In spite of many shortcomings the rest of India enjoys the type of government it votes for.
3. Peoples, whose social, cultural and economic conditions distinguish them from other sections of the national community and whose status is regulated wholly or partially by their own customs and traditions or by special laws and regulations and also to peoples who are regarded as indigenous because of their descent from populations that inhabited at the time of conquest or colonisation or when people of different cultural and ethnic groups arrived. They had preserved the customs and the traditions of their ancestors almost intact and are marked by isolation from other segments of the country's population. Their civilisation is also marked by the presence of customary political and social institutions and primarily subsistence-oriented

production and some of them also survive by hunting, food-gathering and shifting cultivation.

Thus, they live in close association with Nature. They have been unfortunately marginalised or subordinated by the communities that colonised them. To this day, even after getting States of their own and protected as "Scheduled Tribes" by the Constitution of India, their fight for identity is on and the apathy of the ruling political parties force them to enter into violent agitation even—like the Nagas and the Mizos were and the Bodos and the Karbis are. The Sixth schedule of the Constitution has granted them Autonomous District Councils and later full-fledged States like Meghalaya and the other States of North-east India.

Despite the Bodos, a plains tribe of Assam, not being majority in the district they claim to be their homeland, the Union government created the Bodo Territorial Council in 2003 under the Sixth Schedule and bestowed considerable autonomy and powers to them. Such concessions to powerful tribal groups have led to further autonomy to even the smaller tribal communities. Even communities not listed as STs have started demanding indigenous status for themselves. They insist that they were the very first settlers. We all know ancient India was a civilisation without written or documented history. Then, there is the insurmountable problem of too many invasions and migrations. The Bodos claim that their civilisation started from the days of the Mahabharata; but, who lived in this area before the days of Mahabharata nobody knows! This problem never arose in the countries like USA, Canada and Australia.

4. According to the Anthropologists, an overwhelming majority of the settlers in the North-east of India were Mongoloids coming mainly from North-west China. It does not make much sense trying to find out which

tribes/migrants were the very first or indigenous. In Sikkim too, the Lepchas claim indigenous status; but there is no history to prove that. Most communities have gone through a process of conflict, displacement and accommodation. Even the more advanced communities like the Koch, Ahoms and the Meitis were also tribal at one time. In the course of time, having mostly lived in the plains, got Hinduised and even built kingdoms with feudal characteristics (which practice is totally non-tribal). Their chieftains were called "rajas" by the British colonialists. But no community was as big or strong as to occupy or control the entire North-east.

It was not true that all migrant communities were economically and culturally superior to the locals. The adivasis who were forcibly brought from other areas to work in tea and other plantations or the Bengali Muslim peasants who were forced to migrate due to dire absence of agricultural land and poverty, were no exploiters in any sense. Barring Tripura, which experienced a large-scale influx from East Pakistan and present Bangladesh, the tribals remain a majority in all hill areas and the States that were formed as a result of their demands. The indigenous youth from these States often experience racial discrimination and even sexual violence in the non-tribal regions of India; (we keep reading about this injustices in the newspapers every now and then). These tribals do not turn vindictive; such is the nature of the tribal culture and morality. The British too (we already know) had been unfair to them; they followed a policy of exclusion, no administration and no proper road connectivity. (But, to this day, even in non-colonised independent India, the condition of the roads and transport is very poor; a tourist can compare the road leading to Shimla and that leading to Shillong (both very popular tourist spots); the former is so good and well-maintained because it does not fall under the ever-neglected North-east! Secondly, the tribals are usually deprived of jobs in the education and service sectors because the absence of good schools and colleges stop them from achieving as well as the non-tribals do. (This kind of discrimination or disadvantage has not been faced by the indigenous people of USA, Canada, Australia and New Zealand; it is very difficult now to find out in these countries who was indigenous originally and who is a migrant. Of late the Anthropologists have started differentiating between indigenous and "autochthonous"—the first are the communities that are truly primitive, marginalised and discriminated while the second are those who have established superiority in the region but are apprehensive of future domination by more powerful groups and communities. Who knows some from the former category may occupy this place!

We already know that non-tribals from Bihar and Bengal had been imported in this region by the British colonialists. Added to this are the migrants from Bangladesh. Besides, these non-North-eastern people control the region's business and trade apart from taking away so many jobs and so much land (because of which the North-easterners have no option but to migrate to various parts of India in search of employment). Substantial government spending is diverted to the private contractors who have migrated from other non-tribal parts of India. A combination of all these factors has created a stereotype of the "ugly Indian" amongst the tribals.

Good or truly democratic governance in this region is not possible so long as draconian military laws are enforced. The Army has to quit and peace talks got to be started seriously and sincerely. Engagement with the civil society should be promoted to ensure absence of fear and alienation. Trade and communication have to be promoted.

Literary works in translation and research on their histories can be one way of bridging the divide. The region does well in sports and more such facilities should be extended. And, of course, tourism should be much better developed with better roads, better transport system and organised markets for the sale of the typical tribal art and other products. The supply of water and electricity too need to be improved. Many jobs can be created in handicrafts, tourism and hotel management.

The volatility of the present ethnocentric crisis in Assam can be gauged by the fact that most of the tribes have already rejected the proposal to become part of an Assamese identity. While some communities like the Karbis and the Bodos are demanding separate States, others like the Tiwa, the Mishing and the Rabhas demand only autonomy under the Sixth Schedule. (The Karbis and the Bodos are already enjoying that status.) Interestingly, the same tribe, living in the hills are considered tribes and those living in the plains non-tribal! The latter do not thus, enjoy political freedom and rights. The Ahoms ruled over this region for more than 600 years and have slowly adopted Brahminical Hinduism. So they cannot be regarded STs. Before the advent of the Ahoms history speaks of Kamarupa kingdom and though called "Assam", the kingdom included territories which now are northern Bengal and Bangladesh! (The written history of Kamarupa is available from 7th century AD); thus, a powerful caste-based structure came up with the Brahmins owning land and power and full control over the non-Brahmins; the former had the added advantage of knowledge and the ability to read and write and formulate whatever laws and dicta suited them. The feudal socio-economic order failed to incorporate the various indigenous ethnic communities. Strangely but, this kind of socio-economic order did not create any antagonism between the tribes and non-tribals!

Slowly a tiny but well-educated tribal middle class emerged and the leaders started speaking out on different occasions on the indifferent attitude of the caste-Hindu Assamese leadership and the sufferings of the ethnic population. However educated and politically conscious this non-Assamese leadership was, they found it difficult to gain much advantage in the economic and political arenas; they had to compete and fight with caste-Hindu Assamese leadership in a deeply caste-ridden structure of India in general.

The term "tribe" was alien to the Indian subcontinent prior to the advent of the British; classical Sanskrit had words like "Aranyavasi," "Kiraṭa," etc. and they were derided for not following the Aryan customs and beliefs like the caste-system and so many other anti-human behaviours. But, those words are not considered equivalent to the word "tribe" in Anthropology and this was borrowed by the British administrators for convenience. Thus, it may not be wrong to say the government of independent India should have got rid of the colonial notion about the tribes and had paid the right kind of attention to the aspirations of the tribal people and thus avoid the tension in the tribal areas (which are becoming worse and worse).

Chapter V

Assam

A

In the process of nation-building, especially in the Third World countries with colonial legacy, several challenges may be confronted, of which the most complex and the most persisting is the quest for identity. This urge is deep-seated, abiding and universal and can act as a powerful unifying force.

In a country like India it is inevitable that there are several layers of identities—some overlapping and mutually reinforcing—and others exclusive and at times conflicting. When a society is encumbered with nationalistic, linguistic, religious, ethnic, caste, class and group identities, it demands utmost vigil for some sort of equilibrium. Imaginative handling is also necessary for evolving national consensus. Local identities need to be transcended to achieve comprehensive national identity. Assertions of other types of loyalties relating to race and religion are also normal.

Identity syndrome has deeply affected the Assamese. There have been streams of migration over centuries in Assam; it is a melting pot of different religious, ethnic and linguistic identities and the intermingling with the original inhabitants has been so perfect that it is now difficult to know who are the original

Assamese. Apprehensions and misgivings have spread among the Assamese people. Some scholars believe that there has been this kind of intermingling from the days of the Mahabharata. They also believed that in the Brahmaputra valley Hindu-Muslim communal problems were unheard of particularly due to the influence of Shankara Deva; he had given an egalitarian and humanitarian angle to the Assamese culture. Terrorism and riots, which marked Assam's politics in the late 20th century, were never a part of Assamese culture therefore. Folk culture is very important because in this region there are so many tribes. Nehru, the first Prime Minister of India, had rightly thought that the immigrants should get assimilated; otherwise they become foreign bodies always creating trouble. According to 1971 Census the tribes constituted 11 per cent of the total population and this was before Meghalaya was carved out of Assam. Even as distant a State as Mizoram was carved out of Assam.

B.

In a pluralistic society like India consolidation of national identity is not an easy process. Assertions of regional identities and several other sub-national, sub-regional identities would come to surface demanding recognition. It is not often fully realised that the people of the North-eastern States, including Assam, suffer from a serious feeling of alienation. Until the Treaty of Yandabo in 1826, Assam was outside the British orbit of influence and the Assamese were proud that they could resist the Moghul invasions; this makes Assam's stance against the "foreigners" and the "intruders" understandable. Even the educated Indians misunderstand Assam as outside the periphery of Indian culture! The Assamese can scarcely be blamed for regarding the rest of the Indians as equally "foreign"! Migration into Assam has been taking place since the latter half of the 19th century. Tea gardens were the main attractions; the landless and the unemployed from other poor States of India flooded into Assam as 'coolies'. As per 1931 Census, 1.4 million workers were described as coolies. About

12 Per cent of the cultivators were also immigrants from Bengal in the 'char' land of the Goalpara district; slowly they had spread to the other parts of Assam.

Bhawani Singh, in his book "The Politics of Alienation in Assam," has suggested that a solution to the foreigners' issue may be to divide Assam further. He further points out that every urge for preserving ethnic identity is neither divisive nor secessionist; rather it is a complementary force which unites and integrates. Some have pointed out that the Assam agitation was an inspiration to the Gorkhaland and Uttarakhand movements. On the other hand, AASU seems to have been inspired by the DMK and Akali Dal agitations. Assam's geographical location in proximity to densely populated Bengal and the policies of colonisation and land developments pursued in the pre-independence period were responsible for the steady stream of immigrants/foreigners to Assam. Along with the sharp rise in population came shrinkage of the territory following frequent truncation of the State to carve out new States and Union Territories; the Assamese thus, started feeling increasingly apprehensive about preserving their identity; the various tribes had started getting this fearful feeling since centuries ago. Marques de Marcia had commented "there are more storms within ourselves than over land or sea." It was not merely AASU or other regional parties like the Purbanchaliya Lok Parishad, Assom Jatiyatabadi Dal, etc. who voiced apprehensions about the presence of the 'foreigners' or the non-Assamese and their nefarious designs, these feelings/fears were found in almost all who claimed to be original Assamese.

The nationalist parties like the Jana Sangh, the Lok Dal and the Janata Party also added fuel to this fire. Another factor that fuelled misgivings was the growing political power of the Muslims. The number of Muslim MLAs suddenly went up in the election of 1967; it became 20 from 14 in the next election and the number swelled to 28 in 1978. Thus religious fear got added to the already existing language-cum-cultural fear in the minds of the 'original' inhabitants. Immigration from Bangladesh became an overpowering factor of disgruntlement in the Assamese mind. This fear or anger was not absent in the minds of the supporters of AASU, which was known to be a secular organisation. We keep watching anti-Muslim (Bangladeshi) unrest every now and then in Kokrajhar (the district headquarters of the so-called "Bodoland"); it happened during the election campaign of 2014. Better economic opportunities in India acted as a pull factor from across the borders. There were immigrants from Nepal also. A major number of refugees from East Pakistan had come to West Bengal, Tripura and Assam because of linguistic and other cultural affinities. Refugees had gone to Uttar Pradesh, Madhya Pradesh and the Andaman and Nicobar Islands also. According to Scott Buchanan, "every human being has a responsibility against injustice anywhere in the community."

According to Chhabra, the Assam agitation on foreigners' issue had many dimensions—the most important being identity. One of the features of the 'identity' syndrome is to achieve aggregation of numbers through selective exclusion and the "sons-of-the-soil" theory becomes the all pervasive touchstone for determining eligibility and acceptability; this is not always in consonance with the one 'common citizen' principle enshrined in our Constitution. Carlyle had aptly said, "I grow daily to honour facts more and more and theory less and less." The eight-point demand of AASU to the Union government included

- (i) Foreign nationals must be detected and deported and their names scrapped from the electoral rolls
- (ii) Inclusion of foreign nationals' names in the future should be made impossible
- (iii) Borders must be fully and effectively sealed
- (iv) Constitutional safeguards should be provided to the North-east region since all the States are vulnerable to foreign infiltration.

(v) The 1961-71 entrants should be disenfranchised and taken outside Assam and settled in other parts of India; but, post-1971 migrants should be deported and their names deleted from the electoral rolls.

A few hardliners suggest that the process of identifying foreigners should begin from 1826; that was the time when the territories comprising Assam was ceded to the British government by Burma. The Congress (I) and the Left parties were opposed to these demands of AASU and since CPI(M) held sway in West Bengal and Tripura, its support for the Bengali community, settled in Assam, was suspected as part of a grand design to carve out portions of Assam to form a Greater Bengal! Some believe that identity requires space not in the geographical sense, but on several planes living in the same society. Accommodation of these urges by creating space on the multi-dimensional plane is what the restructuring should be about and not merely by redrawing of boundaries and carving out areas of exclusive influence for diverse ethnic and linguistic groups.

C.

It was widely feared that the Central government would soon announce a Gorkhaland pattern to the Bodos and confer autonomous status to the North Cachhar Hills and the Karbi-Anglong areas. The ethnic minorities were feeling restive and began voicing their demands in an aggressive manner and Bodo militancy was threatening to go out of control. The AGP government found itself besieged with a host of strident demands from the different sections of the pluralistic society of Assam leading to further fragmentation of the polity as an aftermath of Assam agitation. In 1990 President's Rule was imposed with the allegation that the AGP was not able to control the violent activities of the ULFA. The various regional parties competed with each other to endear themselves to ULFA by making strident demands for autonomy. The AGP sought an amendment to the Seventh Schedule of the

Constitution so that the States could be vested with all powers barring Defence, Foreign Affairs, Currency and Communication.

The failure of the ruling AGP to deliver to the satisfaction of the masses, the 11th Assembly polls of 2001 was not an uncertain game. The bad governance of the AGP gave it only 20 seats and the most shocking was Prafulla Mahanta's defeat in his own constituency (Dispur); he finished third. BJP's position was as bad because it had aligned with AGP. In 1999 election the BJP-led NDA had come to power. None of the Left parties got a single seat when in 1996 the CPI and CPI(M) had three and two seats respectively. The Congress was successful in the Panchayat elections also.

D.

The Asom Gana Parishad took up the following issues for the 2004 Lok Sabha elections:

1. It pledged to fight for greater autonomy and decentralisation and devolution of more power to the States.
2. It renewed its call for separate economic zone to facilitate growth of trade and commerce amongst the North-eastern States and even amongst the South-east Asian nations.
3. The party wanted 100 per cent job reservation for the locals in the grade III and grade IV categories of all public sector industries in the State.
4. It wanted the Tea Head Office to be shifted from Kolkata to Guwahati and promised to take up the problems of the small growers.
5. The party believed that the aspirations of all the ethnic groups can be taken care of by giving them rights over their Natural resources. The Centre has been minting money with Assam's oil resources, which should actually go to the Assamese people only.

6. The Left parties demanded the status of Special Category State to Assam and put up their candidates in Silchar, Barpeta, Diphu, Tezpur, Dibrugarh and Lakhimpur promising to reinvest 50 per cent of the annual turnout from the Natural resources of the State in the State itself; the State is rich in oil, gas, coal, wood and, of course, tea. Other promises were (i) regenerating the sick industries in the public and co-operative sectors, (ii) declaring the floods and other Natural calamities as national disaster and make the Centre bear the costs of dealing with the insurgents. It also promised to, (iii) safeguard the interests and the needs of the ethnic groups, (iv) solve the problems of women and last but not the least, (v) to safeguard the interests and the future of the Minorities. Asom Gana Parishad (AGP) also believed in this and its Chief Minister Gogoi had said, "We too, believed in harmony, and Hinduism has never believed in communal violence of the BJP type."

The NDA had tried peace efforts in Assam and Vajpayee's "peace deal" with the Bodo Liberation Tigers was much propagated and complimented. At that, the AGP questioned "why not peace talks with ULFA? The party further commented "it (meaning the Central Government) made efforts to bring peace in Nagaland through talks, but applied coercive methods vis-a-vis ULFA!"

According to 2001 Census the Muslims constituted almost 32 per cent of the population in Assam and it is the only community that backs Congress regularly and wholeheartedly. On the other hand, P. A. Sangma had already created the platform for the consolidation of anti-Congress and anti-Left forces in the region. In 1999, the AGP-BJP combine could keep Congress at bay. A few Congress MPs joined AGP having been denied tickets from the Congress. But, unlike the AGP, the BJP did not succeed in increasing its vote share significantly. Instead, its vote share decreased from 30 per cent in 1999 to

23 per cent in 2004 in spite of aligning with JD (U) and few other insignificant local parties. Even the cultural icon Bhupen Hazarika lost to Congress! In a democracy the Minorities cannot be sidelined however much the political parties may get the votes of the Majority community.

E.

The Students' Body asked all political parties to clarify their plan of action for the implementation of the Assam Accord, signed in 1985, and sealing of the Bangladesh border to check infiltration. The parties were also asked to clarify where they stood with regard to 100 per cent reservation of seats in the panchayats, local bodies, etc. and reservation of jobs for the indigenous Assamese. But, all the parties, viz. the Congress, BJP and AGP, refused to answer. On the other hand, Jamait-Ulema-e-Hind's national President threatened to overthrow Tarun Gogoi-led Congress government unless its 18-point demands, including reservation of jobs for the Muslims as well as reservation of seats in the Assembly and the Parliament, were fulfilled. It was quite a grave threat since the Muslims constituted 30 per cent of the total population of Assam.

F.

According to Girin Phukon, 'parliamentary democracy' is essentially a bourgeois democracy as it seeks to protect and reproduce socio-economic systems based on private property. There is a logical connection between capitalism and liberal democracy. The defence of democracy therefore, appears to be defence of 'bourgeois interests'. Under Indian situation bourgeois democracy is not expected to be 'revolutionary socialism' but counter-revolutionary authoritarianism.

The parliamentary democracy and the representatives of the people are expected to reflect the will of the people and respond to the needs of the people at least, to a certain extent. In a developing country like India where political awareness is limited and public opinion is unable to assert itself effectively, the democratic process suffers from many inherent maladies. In the last half century Indian democracy has demonstrated unhealthy political culture emanating from insurgency, secessionism, terrorism, communal riots, ethnic conflicts and excessive use of force and authoritarianism of the State (on the other hand). There are rampant corruption and political-criminal nexus, highlighting the role of money and muscle powers. This has led to a sharp decline in social and political values thus, challenging the credibility of the State apparatus. As a result, new social groups have entered the political arena and pressed newer demands. That is how there are demands for growing regional autonomy and divergent forces. The sub-national forces like caste, religion, language, issues of the Minorities and the backward classes thus stand in the way of successful functioning of the Parliamentary democracy. Different social groups feel that they are entitled to a share in political power and national economy not any more as a matter of concession, but as a matter of right. Violence and intimidation are threats to parliamentary democracy. Strangely, growing process of democratisation and social reform have accelerated the pace of social change by mobilising new groups into political arena thereby considerably enhancing both the volume and intensity of social conflict. Conflict was always there; what has happened now is that the character of conflict has changed. In Assam, thus, ethnicity has emerged as a major instrument of social consciousness, political activity, re-allocation and re-distribution of resources and share of political power. Political demands were articulated at a higher pitch over various periods of time and socio-cultural identities were used to articulate these demands.

Some feel that with the decline in political power of the Congress Party, there is a growing organisational vacuum at the core of India's political space, which has not been offset by the coming into existence of sundry other political parties. Regionalism and the consciousness of being 'natives" have been the ideology of the dominant section of the Assamese.

The caste-Hindu-oriented petty nationalism of AGP had endangered the social co-existence of different communities in Assam; it lost grip over the political situation that is why. The dominant Assamese middle class had not been prepared to share power with the parties representing other ethnic and caste groups which became articulate and assertive. Thus, numerous social groups had their presence felt and the numerous tribal groups like the Bodos, the Karbis, Misings, Rabhas, etc. have become politically conscious and active with the growing process of democratisation. The "other backward classes" like the Ahoms, Chutias, Koch, Rajbonshi, etc. and the tea-tribes, who used to be ignored by the elite-dominated Congress, have also lately thrown their weight in the politics of the State.

Most of the ethnic groups have concentrated in certain areas which they regard as their own and in order to protect their economic interests and cultural identities they do not want any "outsider" to settle there. It is significant to note here that unlike the hill tribes, the plains-tribes strongly feel that they have been denied the benefits of autonomy!

G.

The following are the chief demands of the politicians of Assam (which have been dealt with earlier at relevant places)—

1. The continuous infiltration across the border has to stop and the Central Government must take the necessary steps to seal the border (with Bangladesh).
2. The names of the "foreigners" (immigrants i.e. mainly Bangladshi Muslims) should be forthwith deleted from the electoral rolls in accordance with the existing electoral laws.

The RSS thinking was behind these demands; it propagated that the Muslims were silently 'invading' Assam to make it a part of the Islamic world and therefore, wanted that they should be deported from Assam and the Hindus (whom they called "refugees") should be made to stay back in Assam.

(They were unclear about the Bengali Hindus, but even though the upper-caste-class Assamese too, wanted to drive them out.) The Jamat-e-Islami Hind tried to do exactly the same with the Hindus which the RSS wanted against the Muslims. Due to reasons not yet clear, the CPI(M) held the same view as the supporters of the Assam Movement! But, the exact number of "foreign" nationals could not be estimated; it varied from 2 lakhs to 77 lakhs the so-called immigrants were so nicely mingled with the supposed-to-be pure Assamese Muslim population! According to AASU the number was 45 lakhs, of whom the names of 15 lakhs were in the electoral rolls. Percentage of foreign nationals thus, varied from 10 per cent to 50 per cent!

Even the members of AASU or the other agitators could not agree amongst themselves about this number! The leaders of the Assam Movement threatened bloodbath if elections were held without removing the names of the infiltrators/ foreigners. This was the situation most suitable for engineering genocide, looting and killing. Assam was never before exposed to such an orgy of vicious civilian violence against civilians. In spite of large-scale violence resisting election in 1983, Congress (I) came to power with as many as 91 out of 109 seats; (elections could not be held for 17 seats). But, we must not forget that the voter turnout was abysmally low in the Brahmaputra valley. The immediate task facing the new Ministry was to engage seriously in providing rehabilitation and relief to the large number of victims of election violence. According to a report in The Statesman more than 4,000 people had died. However the Central government realised the importance of having a serious talk with the leaders of the Assam Movement. It is important to recall that a petition was filed in the Supreme Court to stop the election. The leaders had filed another petition in the same court seeking that the election should be declared null and void.

The Assam movement emerged very strongly in the Brahmaputra valley (the traditional homeland of the

Assamiyas) and gained character in the latter part of 1979; the movement failed to penetrate into the Barak valley and in the hill districts. The response of the tribes to the Assam movement was weak and the movement failed to penetrate into the remaining two hill districts of Assam (the other districts had been taken away to form Meghalaya). AASU, that is why, demanded the Constitutional facilities given to the Scheduled tribes. It even proposed to issue citizenship certificates to the 'genuine' people of Assam.

The Assamiya Hindus mainly composed of the Brahmans, Gonaks, Kayasthas and Kalita and the dominant majority of the Assamese middle class consisted of the businessmen, contractors and small capitalists. They also dominate the State administration, police, bureaucrats, professionals, educationists apart from press and media. They, though small in number, supported and strengthened the movement; thus, the movement also reflected the biases of the powerful in a multi-racial, multi-religious and multi-linguistic society. A French social scientist had observed that without opposition a movement does not exist or, in other words, a movement exists because certain ideas are not recognised. It is therefore, equally important to identify the opponents as to identify the defendants of the idea or ideology.

H.

The Assamiya Muslims were with the movement from the very beginning; but later, they became apprehensive because of AASU's friendship and coalition with BJP and RSS. The Nellie massacre, killings at Chaulkhowa Chapori and the bomb-blasts at Balatu Bazar near Hajo forced Assamiya Muslims to rethink on their continuous support to the AASU movement. They were, as a result, expelled from AASU and this was understood to be on the provocation of the RSS. The support of the non-caste Assamiyas like the Ahoms and the Koch-Rajbonshis of upper Assam was also lukewarm; the movement, for obvious reasons, did not receive any support from the Hindu Bengalis and nor from the Nepalis.

The Punjab violence had made the Government of India nervous and so it entered into "Assam Accord" in 1985. Significantly, this was signed on the morning of August 15. The then Prime Minister Rajiv Gandhi announced this historic accord from the ramparts of Red Fort. All political parties and the Press hailed it as historic. But, the leadership of the 6-years movement signed the Accord with hesitation and confusion.

A new political party, known as Assam Gana Parishad (AGP) was formed in October, 1985 with Prafulla Kumar Mahanta as the Chief of the Presidium. Prominent leaders of AASU had joined this new party. AASU once again declared its commitment to remain apolitical. Two regional parties, viz. AJD and PLP, also joined this new party. The leaders and the supporters of the counter-movement (to AGP) formed United Minorities Front (UMF) with Kalipada Sen as the President. They had felt let down by the Congress which was insisting on 1971 as the cut-off year when UMF was asking for 1966.

The AGP Ministry however, failed to give representation to all sections of the inhabitants of Assam; the Hindu Bengalis and the Na-Asamiya Muslims felt left out though a few Asamiya Muslims could become Ministers even. It looked like a party of the high-caste Assamese. It could not fulfil the major demand of driving out the "foreigners" even after Five years of its existence in power; only about 1,000 foreigners were deported whereas in the mid-sixties Congress government had managed to deport 1,93,000 foreigners. During only one-and-half years of its rule, the Janata Party had managed to deport as many as 8,000 foreigners or Bangladeshis. AGP could not even stop new infiltrations successfully. But, the positive gains of the Assam Accord were restrictions on political activities had stopped and the civilians could indulge in democratic political activities. The masses came out on the roads fearlessly to listen to their leaders and participated in large numbers in the elections that followed.

I.

The demand of the hill people of Karbi Anglong and North Cachar hill districts for an autonomous State in Assam is rooted in the long history of similar movements in the North-east, which had led first, to the separate State of Nagaland, then Mizoram and then to the Constitutional experiment with an autonomous tribal State called Meghalaya. According to some such demands are the result of the decline of Congress, erosion of Left forces and the success of the youth-dominated AGP of Assam. The Government of India too, was firmly opposed to further bifurcation of Assam. But the power of the movements of the oppressed and exploited tribes did not become weak since Assam government was not able to fulfil the democratic aspirations due to the limitations of the political and economic structures. The Bodo tribes had also started demanding separate State on the north-western banks of Brahmaputra. Another major area was put under Union government and called North-east Frontier Agency (NEFA). It became an Union Territory called Arunachal Pradesh in 1972.

Historically, the tribes of North-east India were neither a part of India and nor of Assam before colonisation by Britain, though they had trade relations with people of the Brahmaputra valley. They maintained their own distinct tribal culture, traditions, taboos and social systems quite different from those of the people of the valley. The major hill tribes of undivided Assam, viz. the Nagas, the Mizos, the Jaintias, the Garos, the Khasis, the Karbis, the Bodos, etc. had their own small kingdoms with very little outside interference; this was because geographically they were distant from the Brahmaputra valley. They were anthropologically Mongolian; some belong to Austro-Asian and the others to Tibeto-Burmese races. This had happened in very distant past, many centuries ago. The British had tried to follow the "divide and rule" policy with these tribes as they had tried with the Hindus and the Muslims. The tribal leaders felt that independent India should recognise them not as 'subordinates,' but as friends with sovereign power in internal matters within their territories. The chief cause of the various tribal insurgencies is this demand and expectation; tradition, culture, language and their own history (which is never taught in India's school text-books) are of great value to the tribal mind.

J.

Nagaland became a full-fledged State with a population of mere five lakhs (which is less than the total population of many districts of India). The demand for Statehood from the other tribes of this area thus became much more powerful. In 1966, Mizo Liberation Army captured Aizwal. The Indian Air Force was sent to quell the violent agitation but, with no success; so finally, Mizoram was born as a State. As a protest to continuous diminution of the territory of Assam, All Assam Students' Union (AASU) was formed and tried to adopt violent means to thwart further bifurcation.

But, the movement did not help much and could not stop the formation of Meghalaya—the State for the Khasis, the Garos and the Jaintias. It was called an "autonomous State" under Art. 244A of the Indian Constitution. It was regarded as an extra-ordinary experiment since formerly, there were only two types of component of federal unit—the State and the Union Territory. The State highway connecting Shillong with Guwahati, industries like the Assam Cement Factory at Cherapunji, major irrigation and power projects, law and order except village and town police, supply and distribution of goods and the taxes on electricity were with the Assam government. However, the quantum of tax collected within Meghalaya went to Meghalaya government only. The new State had a population of 10 lakhs over an area of 8,700 sq. miles.

K.

After the formation of Bangladesh, the Government of India went for further re-organisation of Assam and gave full

Statehood to Manipur, Tripura and Meghalaya and renamed NEFA as Arunachal Pradesh. A movement becomes significant only when it succeeds in attaining mass character and this has happened in Karbi-Anglong and Bodoland. The Karbis and the Dimasa-Cacharis are Hinduised whereas the tribes of Meghalaya, Nagaland and Mizoram are overwhelmingly Christian. The Karbis and the Cacharis could not join Meghalaya in spite of geographical proximity because of this religious reason. The nativity ideology propagated by the leadership of the Assam Movements in collaboration with the high-caste dominated Assamese bourgeois press has been successful, to a large extent at least for the time being, to present it as an ideology of liberation of the Assamese nationality.

The large-scale eviction of tribes from the government reserved forest lands without any alternative arrangement and the continuous discriminatory policy and practice in the employment of the tribes had deeply sharpened the process of alienation of the oppressed and the exploited. Then there was the continuous refusal of the AGP to share the fruits of democracy with the other ethnic groups and the Minorities. There was over-representation of the high-caste elements in the Cabinet and the Legislature and disparity in the distribution of patronage and rewards. These had deepened the crisis and the frustrations further.

In the 1960s the plains tribal people of Assam formed the Plains Tribal Council of Assam (PTCA) and launched in 1967 a popular movement with the demand for a new State for all the plains tribal people of Assam. They wanted to call it "Udayachal" on the North bank of Brahmaputra. But, the PTCA gave up agitation for a separate homeland after it joined Janata government in 1978-79. All Bodo Students' Union (ABSU)'s demands were threefold—(a) creation of a separate State of Bodoland, (b) setting up of the District Councils of the tribal areas on the south bank of the Brahmaputra and

(c) inclusion of the Bodo-Cachari of Karbi-Anglong in the Sixth Schedule of the Constitution.

L.

The strategic location and the emerging tribal movements forced the Government of India to reformulate its policy towards the North-east. In January 1967 the Government of India came out with a federal plan to reorganise Assam and thus satisfy the agitating tribes. Unfortunately, both the people of the plains and the hills rejected those proposals and All Assam Students' Union (AASU) particularly opposed it vehemently. It organised protest rallies all along the Brahmaputra valley and they had neither organisational ability nor popularity in the hill areas. But, after the formation of Bangladesh, the Government of India once again declared its plan of further re-organisation of Assam and finally gave full-fledged Statehood to Manipur, Tripura and Meghalaya. The Mizo hills and the NEFA were promoted to Union Territories.

Though the high-caste bourgeois Assamese Press does not provide adequate information about the movements launched by tribal people of Karbi Anglong and North Cachar Hill districts for the creation of an autonomous State within the State of Assam, the movement has now touched the minds of the common masses and has developed its significance by attaining mass character. Over the years the Congress has gradually declined as a political party and movement all over India and Assam is no exception to that. Its tendency towards centralisation and personality-oriented politics at the national level and its nominated leaders at the State and grassroots levels gradually reduced the vitality of the Congress. Since the beginning of the Assam movement the Left forces have been facing a serious erosion of their fragile bases and have been forced to become defensive. Besides, the leadership of the Assam movement have been tacitly using their own movement to crush the Left democratic movement.

The success of AASU and its youth leaders in capturing the political power of the State had given a new impetus to the youth belonging to the other ethnic groups or the tribes. They are all angry, young educated boys, most of them below 30 years of age. It is important to note here that even AGP has several tribal legislators and ministers though they have no influence either in the government or in the Party. In fact, they are quite dissatisfied with the way AGP handles the politics for the tribal communities. Thus, the tribes are becoming increasingly restive. They are extremely backward economically and are therefore, politically frustrated. The degree of dissatisfaction is so high that now they are no longer satisfied with the concept of an autonomous State; they are demanding full-fledged States. There is an obvious discriminatory policy in the employment of the tribal people not only in Assam, but all over India in spite of the SC/ST Act and the reservation of these people in the government jobs! So the tribes feel increasingly exploited and alienated. In spite of getting a distinct ethnic identity politically, they find themselves with a begging bowl vis-a-vis the Central and the State governments.

M.

The election scenario in Assam took a significant turn with the decision of the AGP and the BJP leadership to forge an alliance though the BJP cadre had opposed. There is a danger that AGP-BJP alliance might give a new Hindutva thrust to Assamese nationalism, which was increasingly becoming anti-Muslim because of the unchecked continuous infiltration from Bangladesh. The AGP had lost three of its allies, CPI, CPI(M) and United People's Party (UPP) because of its new alliance with BJP. The UPP, fighting for the rights of the Minorities, now joined hands with Samajwadi Party (SP). It would have been in a more advantageous position if it had forged an alliance with United Minorities Front (UMF). In that case a significant number of Muslims would have supported its politics and thus, its poll prospects would have been better.

The National Congress Party had come to an electoral understanding with seven regional parties, viz. Asom Gana Sangram Parishad (AGSP), Purbanchaliya Lok Parishad (PLP), Asom Jatiya Sanmilan (AJS), Janata Dal (Secular) Revolutionary Communist Party of India (RCPI), Revolutionary Socialist Party (RSP) and Asom Labour Party (ALP). Rampant corruption, economic instability and soaring unemployment have made the voters lose interest in this so-called democratic exercise. They feel that the elections are held on communal and sectarian issues and are ignoring the problems mentioned above.

The social composition of Assam is strongly influenced by two inseparable historical facts—the extraordinary role of the immigrants and the ethnic, cultural diversity of these groups. Assam's indigenous population is also diverse in linguistic, cultural and religious terms. The Hindus form 67 per cent of the population and the Muslims (who are mostly accused of being illegal immigrants) constitute 28.5 per cent of the population. The percentages of the Scheduled Castes and the Scheduled Tribes are 7.4 and 12 respectively. The major linguistic groups are the Assamese (57.8 per cent) and the Bengalis (21.6 per cent); then there are the Nepalese and the tea-garden community (who were brought to Assam from Bihar and even from as far as Madras by the British).

The tribal-dominated constituencies used to be the Congress bastion till 1985 when as many as 85 per cent of the total population had exercised their voting rights. This was the time when AGP started becoming popular and catching the imagination of the people because they felt that the national parties, including Congress, had failed to understand the gravity of the Assam movement. The Lok Sabha election of 1998 saw the rise of militant organisations like ULFA and Bodo Democratic Front which had given call for the boycott of the elections. (The Bodos had done the same thing in the just concluded election of 2014). The Congress changed its track and tried to win over the Minorities and the tea-workers. Besides, ULFA's target was mainly AGP; it ignored Congress.

But, in 1996, Congress too, became ULFA's target! The AGP could neither suppress nor enter into a deal with ULFA. But, when the electoral base of Congress was shrinking in many other States of India, it consolidated its gains in Assam since it has a powerful support-base among the tea-garden community and the Minorities, especially the Muslims, the Bengalis and the Hindi-speaking communities plus a small section of the upper class educated Assamese. In a section called "North-east" in its manifesto the BJP had blamed the Congress for failing to check the entry of the "illegal" immigrants to Assam. It also accused Congress for "lack of political will."

The Assam People's Front, a combination of ASDC, ADSF and CPI(ML), promised to continue with its relentless efforts to form a strong regional force to fight the corrupt AGP, the fascist BJP and also inefficient Congress and thus resist them through a united peoples' movement. Holiram Terang, a Karbi, was the leader. Ethnic identity also was an important election issue. A post-poll survey conducted by CSDS (New Delhi) found that electioneering at this time was at a very low key. There was low intensity of canvassing and voters' participation in the poll campaign. On the whole the mandate was against AGP-led alliance and also indicative of the decline of AGP's support among the scheduled tribes and the scheduled castes. Its support from the Muslims had declined to 13 per cent from 47 per cent. On the other hand, the support for the Congress among the Muslims increased to 75 per cent as against 50 per cent in 1996. The immigrant linguistic Hindu Minority as well as a small number of the indigenous communities voted for BJP. The Hindu polarisation also polarised the Muslims. The rumour about Pakistan's ISI link with the immigrant Muslims created more of antagonism against this community. In addition, there was euphoria over the Kargil war according to a CSDS survey; BJP's vote share thus increased. The same survey shows that 26 per cent of the Congress votes had got shifted to BJP because of the anti-Pakistan mood of the indigenous voters. AGP, however, remained quiet over this issue because it did not want to lose its vote share amongst the Muslim immigrants.

The dominance of the Congress in the tribal-dominated constituencies continued even in the 1998 Lok Sabha election. The massive turnout of voters in spite of a poll boycott call given by the extremist outfits indicated the prevailing assertive behaviour of the tribal electorate and the strength of the mobilisation on ethnic lines; in the post-independence period the Government of India had offered "protective discrimination" to the tribes. Yet, they had continuously faced land alienation, poverty, indebtedness, severe unemployment and all kinds of economic and cultural exploitations. Only a small section amongst them could reap the benefit of this special policy, which appeared benevolent for all. These ST elites, like all elites, paid scant regard for the betterment of the entire community. This is one of the reasons behind the powerful demand for Bodoland, Karbi-Anglong and even Udayachal on the northern bank of the Brahmaputra. The elites, however, continued to be hegemonic forces in their respective communities. In the Karbi-Anglong autonomous parliamentary constituency Shri Jayanta Rongpi got elected for four consecutive terms and his margin over the Congress candidate was quite high. BJP, but, increased its vote share in 1998. In the Bodo area Shri S. K. Bwismuthiary, backed by ABSU, won by polling 25 per cent of the votes while his opponent, the Congress candidate Shri Prem Singh Brahma, got only 12 per cent of the votes. The North-eastern experience of democratic mobilisation clearly suggests that when the educated elite or the educated middle class of a less developed community begins to emerge, it tries to benefit by remaining close to the more powerful and the hegemonic forces. But, when it gains strength, it uses regional or ethnic politics as a bargaining strategy.

N.

The tea-tribe communities of Assam have played an effective role in the electoral politics ever since independence.

The establishment of the tea gardens and tea companies in Assam was a colonising trick of the British. The tea estates were the good avenues for the investment of foreign capital. The industry invited a large number of cheap labour from Bihar, Chhotanagpur (now Jharkhand), Uttar Pradesh and even Madras (now Tamilnadu). At present the community constitutes 21 per cent of the total population of Assam. As many as 30 Assembly seats are controlled by these tea-tribes and they traditionally support the Congress party. Even during the AGP wave of 1985 their allegiance to the Congress did not decline. In fact, Assam Cha Mazdoor Sangha is an affiliate of INTUC, trade union of the Congress, since 1958. AGP's performance was very poor in the 2001 Assembly and Panchayat elections and BJP severed ties with it since it could not do well in spite of NDA being in power at the Centre. In the constituency named Khumtai one-third of the voters was the tea-workers. The bye-election of this constituency was important because of the votes of this tribe in the general election that was coming next year in 2004. The chief issues of the opposition parties were corruption and mis-governance like it is now in almost all States of India. We cannot forget that a totally new party had recently emerged as the governing party in the national capital State on these issues only and was expected to give a tough fight to the long-established national parties in the 2014 general election. But the corrupt forces in our polity are so powerful that AAP had to give up power in mere 49 days and could win only 4 seats (in Punjab only) in total in the general election of 2014. Apparently, the party disappointed those well-meaning honest people by giving up power without even trying to control corruption, forget about eradicating.

Infighting within the Congress is rather well-known since it cares for power by hook or by crook (like the BJP) and does not care for any idealism or ideology. This confuses its workers and the loyal supporters. People were suspicious about the tripartite talks amongst the Government of India, Government of Assam and the Bodo Liberation Tigers though no section openly opposed it. Besides, the dissent within the Congress Party had disillusioned the tea workers also. The Congress government was unable to make its promises constructive. The political tussle between the Ahoms and the tea-tribes of upper Assam has a significant contribution towards the future of Assam politics. The realignment in the relationships among various social groups has made contemporary Assam a virtual laboratory for the politics of ethnicities.

There was no visible wave in 2004 election towards any political party in Assam. There was a triangular contest among the Congress, the Bharatiya Janata Party and the Asom Gana Parishad. Congress' support base among the Minorities remained intact; the immigrant linguistic Hindu Minority supported the BJP and the indigenous people seemed to have rallied behind AGP. The election also marked the revival of AGP though the Congress was found popular even in the autonomous District Council of Karbi-Anglong. The most spectacular victory of the Congress was the defeat of the iconic figure Bhupen Hazarika who had fought on BJP ticket. The AGP's vote share had increased from 12 per cent in 1999 to 20 per cent in 2004.

The Left Democratic Alliance failed to win any seat although its vote share had shown a marked increase. The votes were more for the personal appeal of a candidate than for the party (though the defeat of Bhupen Hazarika cannot be explained). An Independent candidate, supported by ABSU and BJP won the prestigious Kokrajhar seat with the highest margin of votes in the State. The AGP-BJP poll alliance of 2001 Assembly election did not prove fruitful since the presence of "fascist" BJP led to the distancing from AGP of the Left Alliance consisting of CPI, CPI(M) and the United People's Party. Religious minorities and the secular segments among the Ahoms considered this alliance as opposed to the ideology of AGP. It is worth noting that the Gorkha Autonomous Demand Council (GADC) pledged issue-based support to

AGP and in return, the latter promised to work for the good of the former.

O.

The Assam Movement was launched in 1979 demanding detection and extradition of the "foreign nationals." The Union and the State governments failed to take corrective measures. The electoral politics of this State was so intricately related to this issue that it took the form of an incurable endemic disorder. It had become a necessity for the sustainability of vote-bank politics of the ruling cliques. The Congress and BJP have been taking diametrically opposite stands on the question of the rights and interests of the Muslims. The pertinent point of resolving the issue in conformity with the Assam Accord was totally ignored. The Congress has always been opposing the demand for the scrapping of the IMDT Act. This became its poll plank in the Muslim-dominated areas. People belonging to this community, particularly in the border areas, are always apprehensive of their status in this country. In a post-poll survey when the people were asked to give their opinions on the IMDT Act, 21 per cent felt that the Act should be repealed, 11 per cent felt that it should continue while 14 per cent commented that it should be strengthened. Almost 54 per cent seemed to be ignorant about this problem/Act.

The voting behaviour of the Muslim population has become increasingly crucial in the Assam elections because the Muslims are growing in number. Their percentages are 71 in Dhubri, 56 in Barpeta, 55 in Hailakandi, and 50 in Goalpara (1991 Census). The Congress has been the most popular party among them except in 1985 and 1996 when a split in the Muslim vote was inevitable due to the emergence of regional, ethnic and even cultural parties in Assam politics. By opposing the repeal of the IMDT Act along with alloting permanent land 'pattas' and OBC status to the "char" dwellers, the Congress endeared itself to these people; the voting turnout in these areas was significantly high with Congress getting 65 per cent of the Muslim votes compared to only 18 per cent to AGP and mere 7 per cent to BJP (CSDS data). As mentioned earlier the tea workers (who mostly belong to the tribal communities) have always played an important role in Assam electoral politics. About 30 Assembly constituencies have a majority of them. They constitute 21 per cent of the State's population. These too, like the Muslims, are the traditional voters of the Congress, particularly in upper Assam. The AGP had pulled up a surprise when the President of its student body, AASU, won a tea-belt seat by defeating the former General Secretary of Tea-tribe Students Union; he not only defeated BJP, but also Congress. INTUC, the trade union of Congress, played a very important role with the tea-tribes of Assam since 1947. But non-fulfilment of their demands like the land settlement of small tea-growers and the payment of full bonus and wages fixed by the State government might have attributed to the decline of Congress' support base among the tea-garden community (in the 2004 election). It is an enigma why the Left parties could not have any hold with the tea-labour when they are otherwise known for successful trade union activities!

The BJP has an upper hand over Congress among the Hindu upper-caste-cum-upper-class; in certain areas it does even better than AGP by converting Assamese nationalism into Hindu nationalism. The Congress got as many votes from the 'worse-off' than it got from 'well-off'. The richer and more educated the person is, the more he/she is prone to vote for BJP. The Congress performs better than both BJP and AGP in the rural areas .

The dominance of the Congress Party in the electoral history of Assam had continued uninterrupted for three decades beginning with the first election in 1952. The 1986 and 1996 Assembly elections saw its debacle and thus, a new trend was set. Contemporary Assam is characterised by multi-polar competitions and explosion of ethnicities.

P.

With 69.60 per cent turnout in the 2009 Lok Sabha elections, the State saw the turnout of 2004 votes surpassed by 4.9 percentage points. The percentage of women voters had increased from 65 per cent in 2004 to 67 per cent in 2009. But, out of 158 candidates contesting only 11 were women.

2009 was the second time that AGP faltered due to fighting the election in alliance with BJP. The first time was in 2001 Assembly election. The BJP, on the contrary, had managed to consolidate its position better in the Brahmaputra valley where regionalism holds its sway. The Congress however, had continued its alliance with Bodo Peoples' Progressive Front like in the last Assembly election. (The Front was led by Shri Hagrama Mohilary). This party had contested the Kokrajhar seat in alliance with Congress. It is reserved as ST constituency and the high turnout of voters indicate the prevailing assertive behaviour of the tribal voters in whichever part of India they get the right kind of democratic atmosphere.

The multiple sub-nationalities of Assam are immigrant Muslims, Nepali peasants, caste Hindu communities, Scheduled Castes and Scheduled Tribes. Broadly, they can be divided into two main communities, viz. the Hindus (67 per cent) and the Muslims (31 per cent). Then there are Bengalis—both Hindus and Muslims and the latter is found mainly in the lower districts of Brahmaputra valley and Barrak valley and in 6 districts their number is more than 50 per cent. The Congress lost grip over the immigrant Muslim votes; 78 per cent of them had voted for AUDF, the AGP-BJP alliance lost 13 percentage points among the immigrant Muslims though. AGP then realised its mistake about aligning with BJP. The Congress vote bank among the tea-tribes was more or less steady. More than three-fourths of Bangla–speaking Muslims supported the AUDF while the Asomiya-speaking Muslims remained more or less steady with Congress.

The Illegal Migrants' Determination by Tribunals Act of 1983 deals with the procedures to detect "illegal immigrants."

It was applicable only in Assam whereas in other States detection of foreigners is done by Foreigners' Act of 1946. Under the former the onus of proving somebody as foreigner lies with the complainant while under the latter the onus is on the accused. In 2005 the IMDT Act was challenged in the Supreme Court and quashed. Now, all tribunals set up under IMDT are transferred to the Foreigners' Act, which is applicable throughout the country.

"Char" is a local term used for sand bars or river islands which are extremely fertile; there are many such in the Brahmaputra and these are inhabited primarily by the immigrant Muslim population, who are good at cultivation.

The other aspect of Congress' electoral luck was that it was more popular with the illiterates or the semi-educated while the AGP and the BJP got votes from the highly educated. Interestingly, more than half the voters felt that corruption had increased during Tarun Gogoi's rule; yet, there was no ebb in his personality appeal. When asked about the success of the governments at the Centre, 39 per cent thought of UPA while 26 per cent opted for NDA; 13 per cent considered both equally good, while only 5 per cent thought that both were equally bad and about 17 per cent had no opinion. Yet, Aam Admi Party, with its one-track goal of ending corruption and the VIP-culture, could not manage a single seat in the just concluded election of 2014; the equations may have changed if this party could get a few seats at least since "aam admi" or the common man is truly fed up of large-scale corruption and mis-governance.

Q.

Belying the fears of a fragmented verdict in 2011, the mandate of Assam Assembly elections has been clear and decisive. The Congress victory for a third term has been a rare achievement considering the fact that anti-incumbency works in most of the States of India. This election had registered a record 76 per cent turnout. This happened despite allegations of corruption against the Chief Minister Tarun Gogoi. One more advantage for the Congress Party was the alliance with the Bodo Peoples' Front. This partnership was formed during and continued after the 2006 election, which was followed by a coalition government. Congress seat share increased by 25 seats in 2006 while AGP, the main opposition, managed to retain only 10 seats; it suffered due to organisational weakness and internal factionalism. Its seat adjustments with Bodoland Peoples' Progressive Front, the Ganashakti Party and the Autonomous State Demand Committee could not improve its tally. Besides, the AGP leaders' vacillating stand about whether to align with the BJP and AIUDF (All India United Democratic Front) before the election possibly raised doubts in the minds of the religious minorities and the secular segments of voters on the aims and objectives of the party. The advantages secured by the AGP as a result of historical and political exigencies in its endeavour to unite people for forming a cohesive Assamese nationality could not be capitalised by the party this time, i.e. 2009. Its chief mistake was aligning with the BJP or the Left as it found convenient. It had forgotten, as if, its multi-ethnic electoral base. This confusion was definitely to the advantage of the Congress which had already strengthened the process of polarisation among the Muslims—both immigrants and domiciled. It even succeeded in posing a threat to the Congress through the initiation of peace dialogue with the ULFA (United Liberation Front of Assam) in a land reeling under violence for nearly quarter of a century; this proved to be its trump card. People living under the shadow of gun for decades know how valuable even a semblance of peace is.

It is to be remembered that the structural reasons that have produced regional parties in Assam have not disappeared; rather, it may be present in some areas in greater intensity even if it may appear to be dormant. The future of the regional forces in Assam lies not in short-term political alliances for garnering a few seats in the elections, but it works in addressing the desires of the hitherto unrepresented social forces in the State. The regional parties have to create a larger political umbrella that can effectively combine the interests of the minorities and other dominant identities in the State. The Congress, which won three consecutive elections, had failed to address the corruption issue adequately; the regional issues seemed to have greater salience in the Assembly elections. Yet, the Congress or Shri Tarun Gogoi must focus on the issues raised during the election campaigns; those are corruption, illegal immigration, rising prices, grievances of the ethnic minorities and other areas of development, which if left unattended, may snowball into major irritants.

R.

In 1960, the Plains tribal people of Assam formed the Plains Tribal Council of Assam (PTCA) and launched in 1967 a popular movement with a demand for a new State for all the plains tribal people of Assam on the north bank of Brahmaputra calling it "Udayachal." The Congress has gradually declined as a political party and there is movement against it all over India with the mushrooming of any number of regional parties; and Assam, obviously, is no exception. The party's tendency towards centralisation and personality-oriented leadership or 'dynastic' rule at the national level and its 'nominated' leaders at the State or grassroots level are taken as the causes.

The Left movement too, started eroding also due to the same reasons. The movements for tribal Statehoods were much more powerful because of the absence of understanding of their very specific problems by the non-tribal upper-caste leadership. The success of AASU and its youth leaders in capturing the political power of the State had given a new impetus to the youth belonging to other ethnic groups including all tribes. It has become apparent from the composition of the new leadership who are leading the movement for the autonomous States. They are all "angry young" educated boys within the age of 30 years mostly. It is important to note that AGP had a few tribal legislators and ministers; but, they are not powerful. In fact, some of them are thoroughly dissatisfied with the way AGP functions. This has been successfully articulated by the new tribal leadership.

Chapter VI

Bodos in Assam

A.

Mainstream Indians suffer from a prejudice against the tribal people in their ethnocentrism; hence, they fail to understand the tribal movements in their cultural contexts and thus such movements become an enigma to them. They believe that though the tribal movements have their own cultural contexts, they basically are not enigmas. Those become enigmas not because of ethnocentric prejudices, but because of ideological mystifications which are designed to suppress the consciousness of the sordid realities of social exploitations and political repression by the ruling party or parties. The fury unleashed against ordinary Assamese working people and dissident Bodos (who have the same goal differing in the methods of reaching them is suggested by the fact that 160 Bodos themselves have been killed by the Bodo militants till 1989). This is supposed to explain the resistance of the Assamese and the AGP government against the Bodo demand for autonomy. Since the Bodos do not belong to the food-gathering and hunting tribes, the Assamese do not believe that they are a genuine tribal community! As a matter of fact, the Bodos have been an agricultural tribe for centuries though practising 'shifting cultivation' like the other tribes of the North-east.

Even though their implements were primitive like wooden hoes and ploughs, they were regarded as the most skilled agriculturists by the British colonial observers. The latter was particularly impressed by their little irrigation canals, known as "dongs," in a region where the great majority of peasants depended (and depend to this day) on the vagaries of Nature.

The present MP of the Bodos, Shri Bwismuthiary, claimed that the Bodos are the very first indigenous tribe and they are living in their land and culture since the days of Mahabharata and the other tribes, including the Ahoms, came in much later and started ruling thus, turning the Bodos aliens in their own land. He also said that their representative in the provincial Legislative Assembly had urged the colonial rulers to save them from the Assamese! On the eve of independence the Congress leadership in Assam was forced to come to terms with the tribal demands and make certain major concessions. The freedom struggle of India had brought to the fore two concepts of Assamese nationalism at odds with each other. We all know that a large number of tribal groups shared the land of Assam apart from those who claimed themselves to be indigenous Assamese. Later came the immigrant Muslims in large numbers and the Nepalese too. There was thus, the chauvinistic model pushed by the Assamese middle class elite, which took for granted the superiority and the desirability of the Assamese culture for all and called for an eventual assimilation of all the tribal and ethnic elements into the dominant caste—the Hindu Assamese. Even though the Assamese ruling class shows now a kind of a liberal face, it dare not retreat from the chauvinistic model with predictable consequences.

In the 40s, during the freedom struggle of India, there used to be some close link between the tribes and the middle class elite because a number of tribes became martyrs in the movement led by Congress at that time. The leader of Assam Congress Committee, Shri Gopinath Bordoloi, had a better understanding of the problems between the tribals and the non-tribals and therefore, struck a deal with the tribal leaders; this was especially necessary in the backdrop of increasing communal machinations of the Muslim League hand-in-hand with the colonial government. He guaranteed some sort of autonomy to those tribes living in the hills; those living in the plains got some sort of "tribal belts and blocks" to prevent, as much as possible, further alienation. Yet, some popular tribal leaders could not believe him fully and suffered from apprehension which perhaps, was not unfounded. The Sixth Schedule of the Indian Constitution, which the Assam delegates to the Constituent Assembly themselves introduced, hardly saw far into the future. The Bengalis and immigrant Muslims had been allowed to settle down in what was declared as "tribal blocks and belts!" It was nothing but economic exploitation and political domination by the dominant Assamese upper caste elite. There used to be and still are brutal oppression and cruel servitude of the tribal communities. The privileged Assamese elite ride on Assamese nationalism and manipulate it only to wrest concessions for themselves from the Indian ruling elite. It is natural for an oppressed community to oppress others like the oppressed Dalit men oppress their women and children. The complexity of the situation gets increased by the fact that the Bodo militants show ferocity on the field and an indiscriminate hatred. Assamese elite's neglect, oppression and exploitation of the tribes are crimes which only the worst type of stooges can endorse or condone.

B.

Bodos, the largest plains tribe of Assam, had started an armed struggle for a separate State in the mid-1980s. The incident of arson and killing in Bodoland Autonomous Council area in 1994 is part of a chain of events and initiatives, double-dealing and double talks whose origin go back to the very aims and objectives of agitation for the creation of Bodoland and which became murkier after the signing of the Accord.

Hundreds of persons known as East Bengal immigrant Muslims (though their ancestors had, many generations back, immigrated and settled down as part of this nation) have been killed during this incident and thousands were made homeless. A senior police officer and a minister have been named in several of these reports as having incited a section of the youth of "immigrant origin" (meaning the Muslims) to attack Bodo settlements; and the Bodos are believed to have retaliated! (Similar incidents/atrocities took place even two years back when the people of the North-east were running back to their homelands from Bangalore, Hyderbad, etc. fearing repercussions from the Muslims of those cities (in retaliation to what the Bodos did to the Muslims in Kokrajhar, the main town of BAC). But, the single MP from BAC refuted this "accusation" claiming that the immigrant Muslims only had started the violence in Bodoland because they were illegally and unacceptably living in a "foreign" land—a land where only the Bodos have lived from the days of Mahabharata; according to him, not just the Muslims, no other non-Bodo tribe can be or will be allowed where the Bodos have been living from such ancient times. "Unfortunately," he insisted, "the British colonialists changed the map of eastern India and forced the Bodos to get confined in a very small area."

The Chief Minister (of Assam) wanted the Armed Forces to act independently of the civil authorities in all the seven districts that fall under BAC. The Bodo agitation was a separatist (called nationalist by the Bodos) aspiration due to the apprehensions about losing their own land and the compromises that the leadership had to make. The Assam and the Union governments call such moves by the Bodo leadership "opportunistic and unworkable" and the basic intentions of the leaders (as it is found with the leaders of all the tribes, the dalits and the discriminated classes all over India) were self-promotion and cutting to size other leaders of the various (almost endless) factions within the BAC. On the other hand, the State government's indifference to the reasonable demands of the ABSU cannot but be blamed. The memorandum submitted to the Minister by ABSU in January 1984 containing its "long-standing grievances" did not demand separation from Assam, not even political and administrative autonomy! The 46-point memorandum talked of cultural and educational matters. But, demand no. 46 talked of the "influx of the non-tribal immigrants and foreign nationals." In 1994 all tribal belts and blocks have been pushed into a crucial position of being annihilated and extinguished totally by the continuous unchecked encroachments by the non-tribals and the "foreign nationals" (meaning the Muslims—may or may not be from Bangladesh); this process, the agitators insisted, is rendering thousands of tribal people landless and insecure in all spheres of their community life. In March, 1987 there rose a demand for the creation of a separate State (with the status of Union Territory) for the plains tribes in the north of the Brahmaputra valley.

C.

Kokrajhar and the autonomous districts are reserved as ST constituencies and there is a high turnout of voters here indicating a prevailing assertive behaviour of the tribes in support of their ethnic identities. The tribes have perpetually experienced land alienation, poverty and indebtedness, severe unemployment along with economic and cultural exploitations. The sense of alienation came to be expressed in the growth of different tribal organisations, which started demanding political power and social justice. The election results from the constituencies of this region clearly reflect an emerging trend of ethnic polarisation. While the Muslims had shifted their loyalty to the AUDF, the Asamiya-speaking Muslims remained with the Congress; but, more than three-fourths of the Bangla-speaking Muslims remained with AUDF. Of those with higher education about 46 per cent voted for BJP-AGP alliance while 34 per cent voted for Congress in 1999. A change had been observed in SC/ST voting preferences while the Muslims remained more or less constant with AUDF. More than half the voters felt that corruption had increased during Tarun Gogoi's rule even though his 'personal' appeal remained unchanged. According to a CSDS, Delhi survey when the people of Assam were asked "if we compare the present UPA-led government at the Centre with the earlier NDA-led government," 39 per cent voted for UPA and only 26 per cent for NDA; about 13 per cent said "both equally good," 5 per cent said "both equally bad" and 17 per cent had no clear opinion.

The "Illegal Migrants' Determination by Tribunals Act," which was passed in late 1983, deals with procedures to detect "illegal immigrants" and it was applicable only in Assam; in other States on the border this act is done by the "Foreigners' Act" of 1946 under which the onus of proving that he or she is not "illegal/foreigner" is on the accused. The Act was challenged and in 2005 was quashed by the Supreme Court, responding to a petition by Asom Gana Parishad. By the way, the word "char" is a local name for bars/river islands in the very wide river Brahmaputra and is inhabited mainly by the so-called "illegal immigrants."

All Bodo groups had welcomed the proposed formation of the Bodo Territorial Council (BTC) as chalked out during the negotiations between the Centre and the Bodo Liberation Tigers (BLT). The National Democratic Front of Bodoland (NDFB) had indicated its willingness to hold talks with the government if talks with the BLT are successful. The All Bodo Students' Union (ABSU) and Bodo Peoples' Action Committee (BPAC) were no longer keen on launching a fresh movement for the creation of a separate State because most Bodo groups are optimistic that the BTC would fulfil the aspirations of the Bodo people (unlike the BAC, which was formed in 1993 and had no Constitutional validity). BTC, on the other hand, was formed by the provisions of the amended Sixth Schedule of the Indian Constitution.

But, the Bodo groups are fast losing patience since the delay in implementing the Act is due to the opposition by and apprehensions of the non-Bodo people constituting the other tribes like the Koch=Rajbongshis (in particular since they constitute a large proportion of the population within the proposed BTC). The latter had feared and still fear that their existing rights will be ignored or superseded. The second problem was the difficulty in determining the exact territorial limits of the proposed Council. The Bodos constitute the largest Plains-tribal community in Assam (though their MP insists that the Bodos are the original-most indigenous people of Assam and not tribal) but, in the proposed area of BTC they comprise only 40 per cent of the population. Within the 40-member BTC 30 seats were supposed to go the tribals while only 10 to the non-tribals. The State government had therefore, suggested amendments to Art. 332 for the protection of the non-Bodo's political rights, including that to contest elections. But, this amendment will give the right to contest only to the tribal inhabitants of the area. Interestingly, tribal courts were allowed to judge the tribals and, of course, not the non-tribals. Thus the former could have access to both procedures of law. The support of the non-Bodos at the grass-root level was of great importance than the support of the political parties and groups. Reaching an agreement between the tribes and the non-tribals can perhaps, bring in a solution in a spirit of give-and-take in the matters of inclusion or non-inclusion of villages and the new formation.

Conflict research about North-east India tends to focus on ethnicity; internal borders are fundamental to the understanding of conflict dynamics in Bodoland and there are three types of conflicts, viz. pre-conflict, conflict and conflict resolution. Insurgency is an endeavour to re-invent and re-draw these conflict-inducing borders. There are three categories of internal borders—political, structural and symbolic and this has to be kept in mind while analysing the causes of Bodo insurgency represented by Bodo Liberation Tiger Force (BLTF) and National Democratic Front of Bodoland (NDFB). Political borders are the results of a struggle to extend political power and may be deeply embedded in political violence. Structural borders are the results of socio-economic differences and the symbolic borders are closely related to the concepts of ethnic boundaries (as described by Frederick Barth). Invention of traditions and homelands and natural superiority and inferiority legitimise these borders. Borders are therefore, not a static 'given', but can shift and change and can be transformed by individuals and groups, who can force an entry and gain access to them.

D.

We have to now look at the structural or socio-economic borders around the tea estates (of Assam); domestication of the forests by the British colonialists followed by the same colonial mentality of the post-independence governments of India and Assam paved the way to large-scale rebellions and one such was the Bodo insurgency. The colonial project of turning people's jungle into the government's reserved forests had changed the face of Assam and also of what the Bodos claim to be their land. New borders were drawn around the resource base of the tribes, especially the Bodos. Natural/ forest products like the sal wood, rubber and silkworms had to be inventoried. This 'mapping' of the jungle became a political project from 1826 onwards. By 1874 much of the jungles in the tribal areas of colonial India had disappeared and these used to be and still are their homeland and the forest products their food and livelihood. Instead, timber-logging and rubber-tapping used to be done and are still done by the unscrupulous traders, whose access is allowed by the forest guards in return of the bribes. In the colonial period only the zamindars and the local chiefs were granted access. The tribes are not allowed to collect even the broken twigs or the medicinal plants and herbs about which only the tribes have knowledge and those valuable Natural products go waste otherwise. The chief purpose was and still is to keep the local population under control and create hostilities between the forest and village dwellers; this ensured political control over the region and the people.

Violence and political repression were used against the "jhum" cultivators also. (We all know that "jhum" or slash and burn cultivation is very common with almost all the tribes of the North-east). The new forest policies of 1952 and 1980 further strengthened the borders around the reserved forests; two different standards were used for the industrialists, who got logging concessions (though, to be truly democratic, they should be taxed/fined heavily for their anti-Nature activities) and for the local communities, who were arrested as "encroachers," were thus applied. Can we then blame the driven-out forest-dwellers for being anti-government and thus demanding a separate homeland for themselves, where they can prosper under their own laws and if they fail to distinguish between the British colonialists and the governments of independent India? But, in the eyes of the government at Delhi, the ideal villager remained estranged from the forests rather than becoming an integral part of forest management and policy. Biosphere Reserve and UNESCO World Heritage Site were declared without consulting the people who lived there for generations and were ousted due to colonial policies of both pre-independence and post-independence India. Almost half of North-west Assam, the heart of Bodoland thus became a buffer surrounding the "park" and making the use of the forest resources by the forest-dwellers increasingly difficult. The governments' arguments were that the ousted people got enough opportunities to alternative livelihoods. Even the tea plantations in Assam (owned by the British and later by the outsiders) were considered the prime examples of "structural violence". Bonded labour, child labour, malnutrition and high infant mortality were some of the vices that gripped them. The freedom-loving, assertive tribes found wage-labour degrading and that sounded their eco-cultural death-knell further; labour got transported from the economically deficient parts of British India; those were the present Jharkhand, Bihar, Uttar Pradesh and even very far off Madras. As many as three million non-indigenous labour flooded Assam thus. Most of the money earned through tea-producing in Assam got diverted to Kolkata and Delhi and the indigenous Assamese got neither the jobs nor a share in the profits made out of tea-exports all over the world. Apart from the unequal access to the basic infra-structure, the people outside the Estates have land but no money and inside the estates they have money but no land. These structural differences gave birth to strong symbolic divisions which, in turn, strengthened the structural tea plantation borders. A new category of tea-tribes, with their own prides and prejudices, made the distinction still clearer. This distinction was exploited during insurgency. The forests were not the only borders affected by the insurgency; the structural tea plantation borders were also targets so much so that the assassination of tea estate mangers, extortion and blackmail, etc. started becoming regular; even the profits of the tea plantations started getting looted by the insurgents with the argument that these did not benefit the local people at all. (Both the owners and the labour were from outside the Bodo districts as well as the State; they were Tata and Khaitan groups and also the Church groups. Demands from the Assam governments to shift the main offices from Calcutta to Assam, i.e. closer to the tea estates, were ignored by the corporate sector). While political borders can be softened, the structural borders seem to be more rigid; the politically inspired insurgency of the Bodos does not seem to have an impact on the socio-economic set-up of the structural borders. New tea-producing countries like Turkey, China, Malawi, Kenya, Indonesia and Sri Lanka seem to be more threatening (to the tea garden owners) than the hazard of an insurgency. The war in Iraq seemed to have upset the tea industry more than the insurgencies at home; Iraq was the biggest export market for Assamese tea. Only a small part of the profits earned by the tea-estates remains in Assam (where tea is produced) while the bulk travels to outside the State. This had thus, made the estates both the theatre and target of the insurgents.

The suggestion was that the BTC/BTAD could assist the estates in meeting the official standards while the owners of the tea-estates could open the required infra-structure like hospitals, schools, post offices for the workers and partial use by the outsiders. This would not only halt the structural violence between the insiders and the outsiders, but would also help to soften the symbolic boundaries, thus making reconciliation more plausible. We all know that the structural inequalities between the British colonial power and later the Government of India on the one hand and the local communities on the other provided the root cause of present structural violence; the governmental policies mentioned above had denied and are still denying the people (particularly the tribes) of their livelihoods. These were the arguments used to justify the violence. Symbolic violence, often with a nationalist undertone, was often used by the governments to criminalise the forest-dwellers.

Not only did the pressure on available land mount, the structural violence and the flow of the immigrants led the Bodo community to erect strong symbolic boundaries that talked of their glorious past and therefore, a vision of their own homeland. The decision-taking power was not distributed to the Bodos also during the Assam Movement; so the insurgency started attacking both the governments and the "illegal" immigrants. In order to understand Bodo insurgency, some attention must be paid to the erection of symbolic borders around the Bodo community. These would not only facilitate the insurgency, but also form the basis for the post-conflict political and economic projects.

E.

In the beginning the Bodos had supported the so-called Assam Movement which was in protest to the "illegal" immigration of the Bangladeshis during 1979 to 1985; but later, they were estranged by the post-Assam Movement politics, which centred on Ahom Assamese. The Asom Gana Parishad (AGP), which came to power as a result of the above-mentioned movement, had promulgated a law evicting the "unauthorised" occupants of the forest reserves and lands, the way the British and even the post-independence "democratic republic" government has done. (This has been discussed above). The targets of this injustice were naturally the tribal people like the Bodos. They reacted sharply to the "Ahomisation" of the State and their elites started erecting symbolic borders by referring to their traditions. The pioneers of this movement against Ahom chauvinism were All Bodo Students' Union (ABSU) and Bodo Sahitya Sabha and these were non-violent. Deaf ears to the reasonable cultural demands of the Bodos turned them towards violence and created BLTF and NDFB (the full names have already been mentioned elsewhere). NDFB was formerly known as Bodo Security Force (BSF). As mentioned earlier, the Bodos, as a reaction to the Ahomisation, declared themselves as the original inhabitants of this land and therefore, historical and natural heirs to the State of Assam. They quoted 19th century writings about "greater Bodo race." They claimed to have lived in this area much before the Ahoms came (presumably before 1228). According to the Anthropologists and historians the dozen or so branches of the greater Bodo race cannot be taken as a basis of what the Bodo agitation claims. Only a few of the branches of this race speak Bodo language. To regard them as completely separate from the Bengali-speaking and Asom-speaking people of this region does not seem possible now (whatever may have been their history). But, the dozen or so different clans of the greater Bodo race can no longer be seen as one big family; only a part of them still speak Bodo language and practise their religion Bauthism; a large number of them are now Hindus or Christians (with an inborn hatred of the Muslims). Even the Bodo elite found it difficult to completely separate them from the Hindu Bengalis and Hindu Assamese. The demand for Bodoland is roughly in the districts of Kokrajhar, Barpeta, Bongaigaon, Nalbari and a part of Kamrup and Darrang.

According to Bert Suykens, "by looking at the policy options open to the Bodo Territorial Council (BTC), which was formed as a part of the peace agreement, the transformation of political and structural borders as assets is necessary." Bodo Territorial Council (BTC) and Bodo Territorial Autonomous District (BTAD) were formed with this aim and these primarily emphasize ethnicity as the chief driving force behind the conflict. In 2006, approximately 5.3 per cent of the population of Assam was declared as Bodos, who dwell between the north-western bank of Brahmaputra and the foothills of the Himalayas south of Bhutan and though considered tribes, are the indigenous-most people of Assam (as I have mentioned earlier).

The creation of the BTC and BIAD was the outcome of a Memorandum of Settlement (MoS) negotiated between the Government of India and the Bodo Liberation Tiger in 2003. This was giving self determination to the tribes under the Sixth Schedule of the Constitution of India. This law was formed in 1952 to give autonomy to the hill tribes, but was amended to give similar rights to the plains tribes like the Bodos. But Bodos constitute only half of the population of the area/districts they claim as theirs; the non-Bodos feared the possible Bodo domination and monopolisation of political power by the Bodos. The Bengalis (though not all), irrespective of their religion had opposed the BTC/BTAD, contending that the law was originally made for the Hill tribes only. The Muslims particularly regard this concession granted by the Central government as a threat. As the latest attack on the Muslims in Kokrajhar showed, the Muslims were and are extremely fearful of the Bodos though the lone Bodo MP claimed that the attack was started by the "Illegal Bengali immigrants" (from Bangladesh). The Central government had behaved clever enough to keep certain key economic assets outside the control of the Bodos; for example, the oil refinery was made to be located just outside Bongaigaon. Secondly, security was kept by the Centre in its own hands and thus Bodo insurgency could be controlled if and when it became too violent.

In a State like Assam, which is full of Scheduled Tribes, the non-STs feel insecure in the ST-dominated areas; even the STs of the tea gardens, who came from different States (like the Santhals), feel insecure because they do not enjoy ST benefits in Assam even though their counterparts do in Odisha, Jharkhand, West Bengal and Tripura. A great amount of distrust is among the non-Bodos in the Bodo region. Such fears do not seem to be unjustified since in the the Bodo Assembly the Bodos got 30 out of 40 seats and a majority of the seats in the Executive Council are reserved for the Bodos. Kokrajhar, the administrative centre of the BAC is heavily populated by the Bodos only. A sustainable peace-building effort should consider the issues of the three types of borders (as discussed in the beginning of the chapter) and solve the questions of border-making and border-breaking. The first step should be creating a space for the decision-making power to be regionalised; this will make the decisions about the borders at least seemingly easier. Resettlement and re-integration of not only the refugees, but of the entire population are necessary if the BTC/BTAD wants to gain legitimacy. BAC or the Bodo Autonomous Council was created in 1993 as a result of a peace accord between the Bodo militants and the Government of India. But, it is believed that this "peace accord" was not grounded on Constitution and was therefore, rejected by BLTF and NDFB. The distinction between the Plains tribe and the Hills tribe is said to be a product of colonial imagination; the Inner Line system, set up in 1873 drew a boundary between the "backward" and the "primitive" hill tribes and those from the plains; it was believed that the latter could be easily integrated in the process and progress of modern economy.

F.

The Assam movement basically is a movement against foreigners, viz. the Bengali and Hindi-speaking immigrants from East Pakistan (now Bangladesh) as well as other parts of India; it is often difficult to distinguish them from the 'original' inhabitants. The movement dominated much of Assam's political landscape during 1979–1985 and led to the formation of United Liberation Front of Assam (ULFA). The supposed to be ceasefire came into effect in 1999 and kept on being extended again and again until the conclusion of the so-called "peace agreement". This was the result of negotiations among the Government of India, of Assam and the BTC/BTAD. We must note that the NDFB is observing ceasefire since 2004 and is continuing with that till now; the actual peace agreement was concluded in May 2005. Ahom Assamese or ethnic Assamese are people who speak Assamese and do not belong to the tribal or immigrant population. The term "Ahom" refers to the Ahom kingdom, which ruled Assam from the 13th century until colonisation by the British in 1826. It is perceived that the Assam movement benefited the Ahoms only and not various other ethnic groups.

The Bodos are the most important Indo-Mongoloid people in Eastern India and they had migrated from North-west China to North-east India through Tibet and Bhutan centuries ago. But, a large section of them had merged with the Assamese population. Fifty-three per cent of the total population of Assam had identified them as Bodos during the 1991 Census! ABSU had launched its movement in March, 1987 on the basis of 92-point charter of demands and the last demand was the establishment of a separate State for the plains tribes on the North bank of Brahmaputra. The 92-points demand was later condensed to three main political demands, viz.: (i) the creation of a separate State called Bodoland, (ii) the setting up of district councils in the tribal areas of the North bank of Brahmaputra; and (iii) the inclusion of the Bodo-Kacharis of Karbi-Anglong in the Sixth Schedule of the Constitution. But, the last demand was contested by PTCA and even by a faction of the ABSU, though it alienated the Bodos from the Assam mainland.

The Bodos feel that they have been neglected, exploited and thus alienated and discriminated against for decades. The growth of literacy and education among the plains tribes was negligible and thus, the Bodo-inhabited districts of Kokrajhar, Darrang, Lakhimpur and Kamrup are among the least developed. Such attitude towards the Bodos has been found both among the Congress and AGP governments. The British government had not granted permanent land rights to them; so, they had to keep on migrating from place to place in search of fertile land and many of them lost land due to the merciless grip of the money-lenders. They insist that at least 50 per cent of the Bodo land had got transferred to the non-Bodos over the last two decades. Many other tribes are found in a similar situation (as it happens all over India). They naturally, resented the campaigns of assimilation by the majority groups; they were worried about losing their cultural identity also.

The Bodo agitation for a separate Bodoland had started in 1987 in a democratic manner; but, they demanded "divide Assam 50:50" and that could not possibly be accepted by the Assam government or the Government of India. So, ABSU had to take to violent methods attacking PTCA supporters and the non-Bodo government officials. The non-Bodos were asked/ordered to quit the land claimed by the Bodos; the Bodo militants started ethnic cleansing campaigns through targeted violence, extortions, kidnappings, etc. They started attacking even schools, bazaars, public buildings, railway stations, roads, bridges, etc. in order to pressurise both the State and the Central governments. The governments responded equally violently with the help of Army and para-military forces. The problem facing the governments was that the Bodo population did not inhabit a geographically contiguous area.

G.

However, in February 1993 ABSU along with Bodo People's Action Committee (BPAC) signed an Accord with the Central and the State governments to end the violent Bodoland movement. As a result, Bodo Autonomous Council (BAC), comprising "contiguous geographical areas between river

Sankosh and Mazbat" was formed; but, the government was to scrutinise the list of villages submitted by the Bodo activists claiming that those had 50 per cent or more Bodos; but, for the purpose of geographical contiguity even the villages having less than 50 per cent Bodos were included! The government of Assam therefore, had no other option but to declare the Bodoland boundaries unilaterally. As expected, this led to large-scale violence in Kokrajhar, Bongaigaon and gruesome massacre of the non-Bodos in Barpeta in 1994. ABSU complained of non-implementation of the Accord and in 1996 revived the demand for a separate State. The Bodo Liberation Tigers (BLT) emerged with armed struggle. The National Democratic Front of Bodoland (NDFB) also became very active. But, there were revenge killings by the Santhals and the Bengalis also. Both the groups had agreed for unilateral ceasefire of July 1999 and in February, 2003 the BLT signed a new Accord with both the governments (i.e the State and the Centre) for the creation of "Bodoland Territorial Council" (BTC) under the modified provisions of the Sixth Schedule of the Constitution.

The BTC was to comprise 4 new districts viz. Kokrajhar, Baksa, Siring and Udalgiri, to be created by reorganising the existing ones; initially, the BTC comprised of 3082 villages, where the Bodos are in majority. The BTC had even legislative and financial powers apart from administrative and executive powers. The Council had 40 elected and six nominated members; five from the non-tribals and five from the general category were allowed. The BTC had power over 10 major socio-political areas; these were over land, forests (including reserved forests), canals or water course for the purposes of agriculture or shifting cultivation apart from the establishment of town and village committees, appointment of headmen of the villages, inheritance of property and conducting marriages and divorces and other sundry local customs. The Bodo language also was supposed to be the official language of the BTC though Assamese and English also were allowed. However, such laws needed the consent of the Governor of

Assam, who could even dissolve the Council on the recommendations of the Committee (formed by him/her to report on the functioning of the BTC). The BTC had representatives of the Central & State governments plus from the BLT. The villages having 50 per cent or more Bodo population automatically became the constituents of the BTC. The first challenge before the BTC therefore, was to instil confidence in the minds of the non-Bodos (living within a particular BTC). Reservation in jobs and education was allowed for the non-Bodo Minorities. The non-Bodos however, falsely argued that only 25 per cent of the population within a BTC was Bodo and therefore, the "Minority" Bodos had no right to rule over the "Majority" of the non-Bodos. But, the NDFB, a rival of BLT, was fighting violently for the creation of a "separate and sovereign" Bodo nation.

Inspired by the above-mentioned armed struggles, the adivasis, the Koch-Rajbongshis and even the Bengalis had been preparing to start armed struggle for similar rights; the KLO (the outfit of the last) started getting training under NDFB and ULFA! The BTC would become violent again if the above processes are not stopped. In spite of the granting of the BTC, many non-Bodos are still living in the 54 government-run relief camps as refugees; in 2003 there were 33,255 non-Bodo refugees but also 6,089 Bodos! They are living in these camps since 1996 and some since 1990. So, it is the immediate duty of the BTC to rehabilitate the refugees in their original places and give them land and jobs since the latter had lost everything when they ran to the relief camps. Let me remind my readers at this point that the Sixth Schedule of the Constitution deals with the provisions of administration of the tribal areas in Meghalaya, Tripura and Mizoram also apart from Assam.

H.

Ethnicity and identity have been the key issues of mobilisation in the entire North-east (of India). The region has a long history of being marginalised, its inclusion within the Indian nation has been seriously challenged by the original inhabitants and therefore, identity politics has shaped the politics of resistance; the struggle for freedom, both economic and political, was mostly bloody. The failure of the Sixth Schedule to deliver led to contest over land and resources, the lack of development and the fear of disempowered smaller groups are all tangled in the web of electoral politics of the ruling classes/parties. Violence therefore, has been endemic in Assam and it is difficult to forget the horrendous Nellie massacre of 1983 of the so-called illegal immigrants/the Bangla-speaking Muslims in Kokrajhar a few years ago though the Bodos claim that so many of them had to leave their homeland due to a pervasive atmosphere of mistrust and fear. This tension had spread all over Bodoland Territorial Areas District (BTAD) viz. Kokrajhar, Chirag, Baksa, Udalgiri, Dhuburi, Sonitpur, Barpeta, etc. and there have been about 60 incidents of violence in which at least 75 were killed, hundreds injured and 4 lakhs displaced/turned homeless; a majority of them are still living in the relief camps. All Assam Tribal Sangha (a body of the plains tribes) had criticised the Assam government for mishandling the situation. The President of the ABSU and the Chief Executive Member of the BTC blamed "the miscreants from Bangladesh" for these violences. The BJP had joined them in this blaming game. The action and reaction of the Congress-led Assam government were extremely slow and it termed the incidents as efforts to destabilise the Tarun Gogoi government. The AGP, along with BJP and AIUDF had called these as "communal" clashes and thus demanded immediate action with regard to the immigrants' issue. The media had compared this with what had happened in Gujarat in 2002 and who knows whether such violences will start again with the mastermind of the Gujarat massacre as the Prime Minister now!

The Bodo educated elites and intelligentsia have been articulating their divergence from the Assamese caste Hindus and highlighting issues like land alienation along with social and economic backwardness. Just after the Assam Accord of 1985 the Bodo leadership felt betrayed within a very short period of two years and started a movement demanding "divide Assam 50:50." Prior to the ABSU movement, during the colonial period, the Bodos used to participate in representative politics within the ambit of the Tribal League. In the 1950s the Plains Tribal Council of Assam (PTCA) was formed to give leadership to the tribes of the Brahmaputra valley. It demanded the formation of a separate State called Udayachal on the north bank of Brahmaputra. But, ABSU's demand was a Bodoland State for the Bodos and it was a shift from the earlier stand for "pan-tribal unity." As the movement progressed, violent methods were adopted attacking bridges, roads, railways, government offices and even schools. The Bodos started attacking the non-Bodo tribes also thus demolishing the idea of "pan-tribal unity/community." Finally, in 1993 the Bodo Accord was signed by the ABSU and the governments of Assam and India leading to the formation of BTC (which I have discussed in details above).

By 1996, within a period of less than three years, the Bodo agitation restarted with the demand for full-fledged Statehood (like Assam is). Peace talks started again in 1999 between the BLT and the governments and in 2003 BTC was established with 93 Bodo-majority villages; (the powers and duties of which have been discussed above). In 1996 the BLT faction of the movement declared ceasefire and the process of peace-talks started. The question of sustained peace in BTC was dependent on the prospects of development in the Bodo areas as well as amicable negotiations with the non-Bodos. But, by October 1993 the Bodo militants had started attacks on the immigrants from Bangladesh as well as all Bengali-speaking Muslims (believing them to be foreigners because of their language and religion). In 1994 about a thousand Bengali Muslim peasants were brutally massacred in Barpeta and this spread to contagious districts like Kokrajhar, Bongaigaon and Dhubri. The refugees in the government relief camps were once again attacked notwithstanding the presence of police. The communal mindset of the Army and the police is not uncommon in India; we have seen many such instances in various parts of India in times of inter-communal riots or inter-caste violence. We all know that the non-Bodos used to be and continue to be threatened by the Bodo militants even though their leadership insist that they never believed in ethnic cleansing. There are instances of Bengali Hindus also being attacked in 1994-95! In 1996 clashes broke out between the Bodos and the Santhals (who had been brought in by the British as tea garden labour). In 1998 a large section of the Santhals got internally displaced. There were several dimensions to this conflict; it was mainly on resource-sharing in an area which was increasingly getting over-populated and secondly, there were conflicts between the "sons of the soil" and "outsiders" even though demographic heterogeneity was a speciality of a State like Assam (which kept on getting divided and subdivided into various other States).

Since the colonial period Assamese nationalism has been largely defined by "immigration threats" and xenophobia about losing identity and culture to Bengali immigrants—both Hindus and Muslims. During the earlier periods of negotiations for BAC, it was made clear that the areas where the Bodos were less than 50 per cent cannot be included in BAC; that is how ethnic cleansing by the Bodos started so that the number of the non-Bodos decline to less than 50 per cent. Side by side with peace-talks the NDFB continued with violence against the non-Bodos. In 2010 the attack was mainly on the Hindi-speaking population; (they too, had been brought here by the British as tea-labour). The killing of the Bodo militants by the Indian security forces (which comprised of soldiers mainly from the Hindi region) was another ingredient to Bodo militancy/violence. Many struggles, in the process of establishing their own identity and political rights, have carried historical retribution to an extreme extent.

I.

Democratic politics in India is dependent on the logic of vote banks or the politics of numbers indicating many castes, tribes and religions. Territoriality and political power and control over resources (or economic power) for the ruling classes of the various communities have given rise to politics of exclusion and politics of fear. The Bodos, who claim to be the original-most inhabitants (from the days of Mahabharata) of Assam region, feel that their very existence is threatened by the influx of the non-Bodos. In July, 2012 the single MP Shri S. K. Bwismuthiary met the UPA Chairperson Smt. Sonia Gandhi as well as the Prime Minister of India demanding the implementation of Articles 2 and 3 of the Constitution, i.e. for granting Statehood to Bodoland. The Coalition government, led by Congress, had kept AIUDF (which represented the Bengali-speaking Muslims) out of power. The National Register of the Citizens Act had become important to keep the immigrant Bengali Muslims away and the Assam Accord of 1985 made the law binding to stop unwanted or illegal immigration.

Land and homeland are intertwined issues and homeland, as an imaginary space pervading a community, and land as a resource and source of livelihood, do not exist in opposition to each other. In the BTC space the imaginary space of "homeland," has been translated into a territory; this has been done in many other places of India with the help of the Fifth and Sixth Schedules of the Constitution. The Bodoland issue have experienced many land and resource-related conflicts all through. The claim to an exclusive homeland for the indigenous communities is closely connected with the issue of exclusive land rights. Colonial intervention in Assam and many other parts of North-east India transformed land relations, land-ownership pattern and demographic structure.

Colonisation had led to further marginalisation and impoverisation of the tribal people of the Brahmaputra valley. Since 1920s the tribal peasantry had been losing land to Hindu peasantry and later even to the East Pakistan immigrant peasantry. Various policies to protect tribal lands were practised even during the colonial period in an attempt to keep some land exclusively for the indigenous communities. It was not wise to alienate the tribes so badly; they could have taken to violent rebellion (as it had happened in present Jharkhand area under the leadership of Sidhu and Kanho). The genesis of the Inner Line system was to serve the purpose of stopping the transfer of land to the hands of the non-tribals. But, at the same time, immigration from other parts of colonial India too was encouraged for the purposes of achieving settled agriculture (which the tribes were not used to). The British or even the present governments (of independent India) badly needed revenue which could not have come from shifting cultivation or "jhumming" of the tribal people. In the BTC, unlike in the other Sixth Schedule areas, the non-Bodos were allowed land! Tarun Gogoi had said that in a shrinking land area, affected by floods and growing population density, the tussle for land and resources becomes a highly politicised issue especially if the land rights are defined as the rights of the "sons of the soil." It is in this context of simmering discontent amongst a whole section of population of various communities, varying from (i) citizenship or its loss, (ii) the empowerment of the marginalised tribal communities and the failure of the Sixth Schedule to deliver, (iii) the contest over land and resources, (iv) lack of development and (v) the fear of disempowered smaller groups are all tangled in the web of electoral politics of the ruling classes. The ruling and aspiring elites are playing narrow communitarian and communal politics and the present violence between the Bodos and the non-Bodos is a result of this type of politics.

J.

After a brief lull in July, 2012, violence returned to the Bodo Territorial Areas Districts (BTAD) of Assam. In August the number of non-Bodos killed in Kokrajhar and Chirag districts was as high as 78 and nearly 4,00,000 persons were displaced in Kokrajhar, Chirag, Baksa and Udalguri districts; more than 300 relief camps were set for them. Such a large-scale violence against the non-Bodos was the result of the killing of two student leaders belonging to All Assam Minority Students Union (AAMSU) and All Bodoland Minority Students Union (ABMSU). This had led to a retaliatory action by the Minority community thus killing 4 former members of Bodo Liberation Tigers (BLT). The lone Bodo MP had expressed the same view while interviewed. The above-mentioned students' unions demanded the dissolution of the Bodo-dominated BTC for its alleged role in the Bodo-Muslim tensions. Such political tensions have been further compounded by the perception in the Bodo areas that illegal migration from Bangladesh is relegating the Bodos to a minority status in their own land. The Bodos, at present, constitute only 29 per cent of the population in BTC! The Rajbongshis constitute 15 per cent and the Santhals only 6 per cent of the total population; the rest are the illegal Muslim immigrants from Bangladesh. The Bodos are thus worried about the lands they own or should have a right to own. The lack of any reliable statistics about the "illegal" immigrants makes the tension and violence worse. They are also terribly disturbed by the names of such "illegal" residents in the voters' list; they take it as a deliberate ploy on the part of the governments to disinherit the Bodos from their land and "indigenous" status. This has created a siege mentality among them and the NDFB (anti-peace talk group), along with the Birsa Commando Force of the Santhals further contribute to a situation of violence.

What was happening in the BTAD area was nothing new; similar incidents have taken place in the past. In 1993 large-scale massacre of the immigrants (about 50 of them) took place in Kokrajhar and Bongaigaon areas while the next year 100 immigrants were killed. In 1996 the Santhals (also treated as migrants even though they were brought in centuries back by the British colonialists) were attacked mercilessly; no non-Bodo was safe in the BTC districts. Thousands were displaced.

These areas are designated "Disturbed Area" where Armed Forces Special Powers Act (AFSPA) of 1958 and amended in 1972, has been imposed. While the Bodoland Accord of 1993 managed to persuade the BLT to give up violence, the NDFB did not believe in peace talks. The lack of the State government machinery to control illegal immigration cannot but keep violence in BTC alive. Immigration from Bangladesh, on the other hand, will continue because of the economic opportunities available in India. But, according to Bodoland Accord no Non-Bodo can settle in the declared Bodo lands though the provisions have not been implemented by the Assam government in letter and spirit. The land records are vague because those are not written down. Hence, a Bodo, whose land has been usurped by an "outsider," has no papers to claim ownership of the particular land. Violence by the Bodos against the non-Bodos, particularly the Bengali Muslims can be contained if proper land records are maintained and the Bodos are not deprived of their very precious resources.

K.

Ethnic conflicts in Assam have occurred often, but the Bodoland conflict of 1912 had polarised the local community and immigrant Muslims more sharply than ever before. The Bodos and the non-Bodo indigenous people, who had been fighting with each other for space and identity till 1998, have finally arrived at a tactical understanding; the crisis in Bodoland is a reflection of the abdication of duties by the Indian State is what the local leaders feel. They further feel that the State has failed to address the structural issues that confront the indigenous tribes like the Bodos and the Karbis. It has also failed to address the multi-cultural, multi-linguistic and multi-ethnic composite culture of the region.

The BTAD area is one of the most violence-prone and violence-ridden areas of independent India, though Bodo assertion had started during the British colonial period itself. The region has witnessed ethnic hostility, wanton killing, destruction and displacement of other tribes/indigenous population. In 2008, clashes in the northern regions of Darrang and Udalgiri districts had claimed 70 lives and displaced over two lakhs people; there was repetition of the same in July-August, 2012 also. This violence acquired new dimensions as the fear had spread to the North-eastern people living in Mumbai, Allahabad, Hyderabad and Bengaluru. Inflammatory websites spread hatred and violence against the Muslims of Assam and thus created a fear psychosis among the non-Muslim people of the North-east (because these were the cities where a large number of Muslims lived). Instead of appeasement policies towards both ethnic and religious minority groups, the State needs to promote an all-inclusive policy that ensures justice, fairness as well as representation to the various communities living within the BTAD area. The Assam government should implement the recommendations of the Bhupinder Singh Committee, which was appointed by the Centre in 1991. According to the Social Scientist Sanjeeb Baruah, "the colonial propensity of fixing tribes to their supposedly 'natural habitats' had actually triggered exclusive homeland consciousness among the minds of the tribal people." Post-colonial India has further intensified the ethnic exclusivity of the indigenous tribes by "legitimising exclusivist but false histories, memories and ground realities!" This is in spite of the fact that in the Constituent Assembly a separate sub-committee in charge of the minority rights was entrusted with the responsibility of looking into the issues of the Plains tribes (in which a prominent Bodo leader Shri Rupnath Brahma was a member). Some others believe that Shri Gopinath Bordoloi, Chairman of North-east Frontier Tribal Areas Sub-committee, failed to do justice to the plains tribes by treating them as an integral part of the Assamese, thereby depriving them of the special rights a tribal is entitled to.

Besides demanding special treatment in matters of education and appointments, the Bodo community of Goalpara district also wanted a second chamber in the Legislative

Council and urged the Committee not to transfer Goalpara district to Bengal. In 1993 All Assam Tribal league was formed by Shri Rupnath Brahma and others. The Saadullah Ministry had introduced a development scheme for the settlement of the wasteland among different communities including the immigrants. In the light of the wartime crisis the Ministry's "grow more food" campaign (in 1942) opened the forests and the grazing grounds for the resettlement of the immigrants from East Bengal; this had created too much of panic among the Bodos and the other communities.

L.

During 1947-51 the Assam government had constituted 31 belts and 31 blocks, covering an area of 15,000 sq. km. comprising 2,795 villages; the primary objective of such a protected zone was to safeguard the tribal areas from encroachments (from East Bengal) and thus protect the tribes from the onslaught of the non-tribals. The alienation of the Bodos and the demand for a separate Bodoland can be attributed to 3 factors, viz. (i) domination by the Assamese caste-Hindus, (ii) the unending influx from East Bengal and (iii) systematic encroachment of their lands and habitats by the non-Bodos (primarily the immigrants from East Bengal, a majority of whom were Muslims). A resurgent politically conscious Bodo movement is discernible from the beginning of 1960s. The imposition of Assamese language as the sole medium of instruction starting from 1972 created the demand for Udayachal by bifurcating Assam. The ABSU leadership had viewed this imposition as an effort to protect the interests of the Assamese Hindus; this, they felt, negated the composite and diverse socio-cultural milieu of Assam. In 1989 the Hindu Bodos attacked the minority Christian Bodos and as a result, the victims demanded a separate Christian Bodoland. The Christians, like in other tribal regions of India like Jharkhand, are better educated and more politically aware; we all know that this is because of the efforts of the Christian Missionaries (who paid proper attention to their health, education and general well-being). According to some scholars such organisation was to keep an eye on the borders with Bhutan and China (about which I have found no evidence). Unfortunately, there arose division among the Bodos only; in 1993 for example, the Bodos were divided into the "Brahmas" and the "Bwismuthiarys" camps. (The present MP is a Bwismuthiary).

The failed Bodo Accord of 1993 had sent three messages to the leaders of the Bodo Movement. First, they must prove a majority in the BTAD area; this was extremely important as in some areas they were in minority. While immigrants continued to flood the region, the government was accused of giving "illegal pattas" to these settlers. AASU became the reference point for the ABSU and ULFA too, became the reference point for extremism and secessionism that the various Bodo factions believed in. Secondly, the Bodo extremist groups believed that the political elite in Delhi and Dispur would not listen to the voice of non-violence. Thirdly, the extremist groups adopted violent means which affected not only the Muslims but also other indigenous and local groups living in those areas like the Rabhas, Koch-Rajbonshis, the Nepalis and even the Hindu Bengalis and Assamese. The Bodo violence against the Muslims that occurred in October, 1993, had displaced about 3,568 families consisting of 18,000 persons. There was violence by the Bodos inside the relief camps also in Bashbari and Barpeta districts in July next year! More than 100 Muslims were killed and about 70,000 displaced again thus proving the bias and/ or inefficiency of the government of Assam. More than 2,50,000 Santhals were also attacked by the Bodo militants in May, 1996 and even if they returned to their homes next year, they were forced to flee again in 1998. At the peak of Bodo agitation/ violence thus, Assam got the dubious fame of holding more than half of India's "internally displaced" persons.

Interestingly but, even though a majority of the secessionists want "nothing to do with Indian democracy," they put up their own candidates during the elections for the purpose of propagating their own agenda. A number of Bodo groups came together to form the Bodo State Movement Council (BSMC) with active support of BLT. The BJP government's persistent effort to arrive at a ceasefire with BLTF, mediated by an Assamese IB official, had paid dividends when the BLT had declared ceasefire in July, 1999. The objectives of the government were very clear—(i) to create an autonomous self-governing body to be known as Bodoland Territorial Country (BTC) within the State of Assam, (ii) to provide Constitutional protection under Sixth Schedule to the said autonomous body and to fulfil economic, educational and linguistic aspirations, (iii) the preservation of land rights, socio-cultural and ethnic identity of the Bodos and (iv) to speed up infrastructure development in the BTC area. But, this created unbridgeable gap between the Bodos and the non-Bodos (the Rabhas, the Koch-Rajbogshis and the Assamese themselves). As Harold Saunders wrote "politics is not just a linear series of government decisions, actions and programmes, it is a multi-level organic process of continuous interaction among people and groups."

The Bodos claim (as has been mentioned right in the beginning) that the Hindu Assamese too belong to the same ethnic stock as the Bodos (though the Anthropologists believe that the Bodos had come to Assam from the North-west of China). The other adivasis and the Muslims thus have enough reasons to be apprehensive of the political and economic consequences of a formal acknowledgement of the Bodo hegemony over the area which belong to the former too. Such apprehensions have to be removed and the true history needs to be established; otherwise, the functioning of the BTC will remain ever problematic. According to 1991 Census the total Bodo population—both within BTC and outside—is 12,67,015 or 11 per cent of the total population of Assam. Even the areas having minimum Bodo presence are reserved constituencies for the Bodos whereas the areas with a majority population of Bodos are open! The non-Bodos lose in both ways—they cannot contest where the Bodos are a minority and they do not have a chance of winning even in the unreserved constituencies because the Bodos are a majority there! That is why, the struggle of the non-Bodos also has intensified with the launching of an agitation by a non-Bodo conglomerate of 27 organisations of Lower Assam called Ana-Bodo Surakhya Samity (ABSS). It claims to have the support of the organisations like AASU, All Assam Minority Students' Union (AAMSU), the Bengali Youth Students' Federation (BYSF), the All Assam Gorkha Students' Union (AAGSU), All Assam Koch-Rajbongshi Students' Union (AAKRSU) and All Assam Tea-tribes Students' Union (AATTSU). The support by the powerful AASU to the non-Bodo forum has added a new twist to the situation. Nearly three million tea-garden workers or ex-workers makes up 50 per cent of the ST population of Assam. This is a fact of no mean significance.

The British colonial administration used to encourage the immigration of the Muslims and make them settle down hoping to create communal divide between the Hindus (remember that the Bodos consider themselves Hindus) and the Muslims and also to garner more land revenue from the fallow and wasteland areas of the Brahmaputra valley belonging originally to the indigenous tribes. Some scholars believe that the immigration of the Muslims from Bangladesh as "illegal" is a myth and there is no need to generate hysteria about "culture-in-crisis" in order to expel them. But, in August 1998 the Government of India (the Home Minister Shri Indrajit Gupta in particular) had declared that there were 40 lakhs "illegal" migrants in Assam. The same Minister could not have denied that there is a substantial number of "illegal" Hindu migrants from Nepal and Bangladesh itself; yet, only the Muslim migrants create a phobia! The growth rate amongst the Muslim population created and creates a panic; the undeniable fact that population (whatever its religion) grows and cannot stop growing (unless very stringent method like in China is adopted) is ignored (to create a communal divide like what the British had done to retain their power). In order to justify the attack against the Muslims, a "white paper" is quoted which talks of a 7 per cent decline in the Hindu population between 1951 and 2001. The white paper says, "a person born in India on or after January 26, 1950 but before July 1, 1987 is a citizen of India by birth irrespective of the nationality of his/her parents."

M.

The loss of land is a matter of grave source of concern to the tribal psyche as it means loss of "collective" resource to which they are attached since time immemorial. Land is not just a piece of commodity, but also a part of their culture and custom. This is what makes the tribal people so special and praiseworthy; to them all economic/Natural resources are collectively of the entire tribe living in a certain area and all social activities or rituals too, are totally collective, decided and organised collectively. This is exactly opposite of the non-tribal people and that is why the latter fail to understand the nature and the needs of the former and more often than not indulge in laws, planning and governance that are least suitable or helpful to the adivasis' economy and culture.

The present inflow of immigrants to the tribal areas and other parts of Assam is dictated by economic compulsions; the Bodos and the lower middle classes have withdrawn themselves from agriculture-centric operations and have moved to the organised or other private sectors not only in Assam but also in other globalised cities of India like Hyderabad, Chennai and Bengaluru. The agricultural lands are being leased out to the immigrants through some very informal contractual system. The gap is thus being filled by the immigrant Muslims to Assam. Besides, infrastructure projects like roads, bridges, hospitals and other institutions have brought cheap immigrant labour to the region. In terms of the proportion of Muslim population, Assam has the second largest Muslim population, the first being of Jammu & Kashmir.

Besides, the region under discussion has porous borders with China, Myanmar, Bhutan, Nepal and Bangladesh. The massive flow of arms has been a motivating factor for the aggrieved groups to fight with State of India. Till now the Muslim groups are not heavily armed like the Bodos, the Meitis, the Nagas and the Hindu Assamese. The ground has now become fertile for free flow of arms, radicalised ideologies and jihadis, especially through the porous borders of Bangladesh, Myanmar and China.

The Government of India had appointed a three-member expert committee to determine the areas for the Bodos and other plains tribes in the north of Brahmaputra as also to make recommendations regarding autonomy or the legislative, administrative and financial powers that may be given to them. Contrary to the half-hearted attempts of many such government reports, the Bhupinder Singh Committee report can be said to be the best researched and comprehensive and thus relevant to the multi-cultural set-up of Assam. It is a different matter that the proposal has been rejected by the Bodos for failing to fulfil their exclusive homeland demand. After all, the crisis in Bodoland is a reflection of the abdication of responsibility by the Indian State.

N.

Here is a sample of the type of questions I had asked the leaders of the movement for Bodoland; it used to be informal chit-chat without any set questionnaire in front of them. (All my earlier books are field-study based and my experience is that set questionnaires make them feel inhibited. So, I first engage them in small talks and try to bring out the required information from their casual answers.) But, I do prepare a kind of questionnaire in my mind so that I do not go too off-track. Those are like the following and the questions are followed by a gist of their answers.

1. *Why the Bodoland movement? How old it is and how much of popular support does it get?*

Answer: The Bodoland movement is for the self-assertion and identity of the Bodos with a specific territory. The movement will help in attending to the rights and privileges, which are not enjoyed by the Bodos because of the discriminatory behaviour of the so-called original inhabitants of Assam. The movement is going on since last 40 years and it is very popular as Bodos from all walks of life participate in the movement with the spirit of "Do or die, but Bodoland must for the Bodos."

The Bodos had claimed a separate State for the plains-tribes of Assam in 1967 itself when a national policy for the re-organisation of Assam on federal lines was adopted. Language and historical background were taken as the basis for the formation of a separate State and the Central government had agreed to the Bodos having a specific language and history (at that time). So, a democratic movement demanding the implementation of these principles had started, viz. Plains Tribal Council of Assam (PTCA). They also demanded that the new State shall be called "Udayachal." The movement had suffered a setback during the period of internal Emergency in 1975-76. All Bodo Students Union (ABSU) had revived the movement in 1987 and decided to name the demanded State as "Bodoland." This 47 years –old movement has now got attention of the world even.

The movement, which had started for the land rights and cultural-cum-linguistic identity of the tribe, has now turned into a movement against exploitation, suppression and oppression by the Assamese ruling clique. Assamese language was imposed as the only language for sundry other communities; Bangla and even English were also removed! But, that was impractical and English had to be brought back; (how else could have Assam survived in the globalised India?) One of the chief reasons why Nagaland, Mizoram and Meghalaya had torn themselves away from Assam was this faulty language policy. (But, could anybody or any of the

Constitution-makers think that there will be two States of the same language, viz. Telengana and Andhra Pradesh?)

2. *Do you feel cultural and/or financial discrimination? If yes, is it from the State of Assam or from the government of India?*

Answer: Yes, there is cultural discrimination with us since in the cultural life of Assam there is no reflection of the life of the Bodos; we are looked down upon in the educational institutions also as we are considered culturally backward/ under-developed. There is financial discrimination also; we come to know of these through the media. We get step-motherly behaviour from the State and the Centre both, though the State of Assam is the worse culprit.

Hegemony of the high-caste Assamese ruling clique had adopted the policy of rooting out Bodo and other non-tribal languages like Bangla and English around 1960s. Secondary Education Board of Assam (SEBA) attempted to make Assamese language compulsory in all schools and tried to assimilate the cultures of other ethnic groups into that of the Assamese. Even traditional dresses of the Bodos were mocked at till about 1980 and Assamese dresses were made compulsory in the schools and the colleges.

Yes, there is financial discrimination also; some semblance of developmental work had started as late as in 1993 i.e. after the Bodo Accord was signed and Bodoland Autonomous Council (BAC) was created. In 2003 but, BAC was dissolved and the second Bodo Accord, viz. Bodoland Territorial Area District (BTAD), was created and special development packages were gifted by the Centre. But, all such money had to flow through the State government, which consciously delayed the execution of the developmental works! There were thus (i) hold-up process, (ii) siphoning, (iii) diversion and (iv) misuse of funds—in one word "conscious neglect of the area" and, of course, corruption (rampant all over India in large or small quantities).

Unemployment problem remains the same, educational achievement and basic health care are still at the lowest and roads, electricity and internet are miserably undeveloped. Just as "illegal immigrants" are flooding the land of the Bodos, outward emigration of the unemployed Bodos is at a continuous flow.

3. *Do you support other regional movements like for Gorkhaland and for Telengana? (The question was asked a year before the Centre granted Telengana).*

Answer: Yes, we vehemently support these movements as these regional movements are the inspiration/harbinger of our movement. The demands of all our movements are for the betterment of the people of these regions; there will be proper/better development of these areas if/when Statehood is granted/achieved. We support all movements of the people for autonomy, Constitutional safeguards, and of course, Statehood. Of course, the issues can be resolved according to ground realities and the local conditions. There is a powerful history behind the Telengana movement; it cannot be compared to the Gorkhaland movement. Time has come for redesigning the nations (within India) by re-organising the States in order to ensure good governance, social security, faster growth, development and peace. (Development has no meaning and good governance is impossible unless there is peace in the particular region as well as the entire India).

4. *Do you think your problems can be solved to a certain extent at least, if a non-Congress government comes to power both at the State and the Centre? Did you get a better deal when NDA or Vajpayee was in power and do you expect the same with Modi as the Prime Minister?*

Answer: The earlier NDA government at the Centre helped the Bodos to some extent to get their rights and so we need a non-Congress government. But, there is the fear of communalism taking over with Modi as the Prime Minister; Hindutva may take over and the citizens of India will no longer be treated equally irrespective of their caste, creed or religion! We do not want Hindu fanaticism or Hindu fascism because our country (we must note here that the secessionist Bodos are considering India "their country!") is a nation of various Minorities; so Modi needs to win the hearts of these varieties of Indians before he can become a successful Prime Minister. We hope that the present government at the Centre will address the problems of the Bodos and consider their demands sympathetically. Besides, the present BTAD was created during the NDA regime at the Centre but, with Congress in power at Dispur. NDA or BJP had made similar promises in their election manifesto; so, who is the Prime Minister is not so important; what is important are the governments' policies. The NDA at the Centre and the Congress in the State have to work together; then only any solution can come.

5. *What are the solutions you suggest?*

Answer: The very first solution may be to grant Union Territory status in the beginning; the political parties can be and should be trained in the art of democratic governance; then only Bodoland can become a successful State. NDA needs to fulfil its commitments for smaller States though evolving consensus within all variant groups will be hardest to achieve particularly when the Government of Assam, with its unsympathetic attitude towards non-Assamese communities will never agree as it was vehemently opposed to the formation of Nagaland and other tribal States. A new political map must be redrawn.

6. *Why was there a backlash against the Muslims in Kokrajhar? Are the Muslims affecting your economy adversely and/or taking the jobs that are due to you? Are the Assamese also denying you of your economic and cultural rights/dues?*

Answer: It is the media which distorted the actual news and reported the protest by the Bodos (against illegal immigrants) as a backlash against the Muslims. The dishonest media reporting lighted the fire and the State government took very lethargic action on this matter; or else, the situation would have been under control. The State government did not try to understand or introspect into the real cause of the problem. So, the situation took the worst shape. The Muslims are taking away the lands that originally belonged to the Bodos and are thus destroying the economy of the Bodos. Yes, the other Assamese are also denying economic and cultural rights to the Bodos. They do not regard the Bodos as at par, and consider them as under-developed and inferior; therefore, we believe that reservation in education, the jobs and politics is necessary for us.

Yes, there is extremism and backlash in our land since 1979 and the immigrant Muslims become the soft target; the attacks are also designed to divert the attention of the security forces. Political conspiracies also work and give bad name to the Bodos, who only want their original, centuries-old land back. Bodos against the outsiders (who happen to be Bangla-speaking Muslims mostly) cannot be considered "communal" backlash, it is the nexuses between the political parties and the insurgents; some insurgents attack one community just to get the support of another community. Unfortunately, now the insurgents are split into different groups with the support of some political party or the other (national or regional). These are opportunistic political exercises. When there was clash between the Bodos and the "illegal immigrants" in 2012, a majority of the political parties (even national) had justified the clash and termed it as between "the natives and the foreigners." In 2014 the situation was completely different—the Muslims in the BTAD area were attacked because they had not listened to the boycott of the poll. This time all parties univocally condemned it—what a volte face! It is immoral to blame the Bodos or the Muslims; rather, there should be a powerful movement for peace instead of inciting them wrongly (by all political parties).

7. *Is there any Maoist influence on your movement? If yes, then do you think that the Maoists in the other parts of India should get humanitarian treatment and the people they are fighting for should get their economic and cultural dues?*

Answer: No, there is no Maoist influence on our movement. Yes, they should get humane treatment because the Maoist movements in the other parts of India are because of the discriminatory attitude of the States towards the common people, who do not enjoy the fruits of development, whether it is economic, cultural, educational, health, transport and communication-wise. There are many other fields in which people need development. The governments, both at the Centre and the States, should try seriously to solve the problems of the people raised by the Maoists. Their demands, raised on behalf of the oppressed tribes and other people should be sincerely paid heed to just as the demands of the Bodos should be heard and paid attention to.

Another view is that the Maoists are born out of India's defective system that divides the society on the basis of religion, community and caste. India's economic powers are wielded by certain castes and communities, who exploit our common people. Rich-poor divide, poor governance and lack of proper education are the chief factors that have created Maoists. It is so unfortunate that 67 years of independence till now is a grand failure. Long-term social agenda with humane approach in politics and paying proper heed to the dissatisfaction of the poor and the illiterate and listening to the demands for fresh organisations of the States are the only answer to the Maoist problem.

8. *Do you think that the tribes in India, in general, get a raw deal and particularly the tribes of North-east India?*

Answer: Yes, the tribes of India do not get justice and development and the tribes of North-east India definitely suffer more. That is why, the tribes are still in the same economic state as they were under the British colonialism.

There is an attempt from the Majority communities to swallow or absorb the Minority tribes. There is no scope to develop their languages and cultures and the tribes in the North-east and particularly Assam are yet to attain due status in the so-called mainstream society.

9. *Do you believe in a pan-Indian movement of the tribes? To what extent it will solve your problem if that happens?*

Answer: A pan-Indian movement of the tribes may not be possible since the different tribes face different types of problems/issues; but, if it happens, it will greatly benefit all the tribes of India and the efficient leadership of one tribe will inspire leaders from other tribes. Besides, the pan-Indian movement can force more effectively the governments both at the Centre and the States to pay attention to the tribal-dominated areas and thus develop the way they need and demand.

Some other view is that a pan-Indian movement will help since each tribe is terribly marginalised—may be a little more or less. Such a movement can ascertain Constitutional, civil and human rights and the movements for political and economic rights can get emboldened. But the different tribes, united under such a movement, need to be sensitive enough for a greater cause and not bicker among themselves; well thought-out common interests and rights should be internalised. Pan-Indian movement, if organised under wise, honest and able leadership, can be successful by brightening their future and ensuring security.

O.

In the general election just concluded, a truly surprising thing happened; a non-Bodo ULFA militant, Aba Kumar Sarania, got elected from Kokrajhar (the hub of Bodo agitation)! He is not only a non-Bodo to be elected from Bodoland, but won by a margin of as high as 3.55 lakh votes! According to some reports and analyses, it was the overwhelming support for Sarania that triggered the attacks on the Muslims in Baksa and Kokrajhar in the beginning of May 2014—one of the many that have continuously happened against the Muslims (who are hated because they are successful cultivators when the Bodos are not). Sarania had been expelled from ULFA's pro-talk faction in the beginning of April 2014 and the most significant factor about him is that he won due to the votes from the non-Bodos (in the Bodoland). According to him, the Sarania and the Kachari communities share the same root with the Bodos. He, as a commander, had played a crucial role in setting up the base for ULFA in Bhutan even (since he belonged to a village absolutely adjacent to Bhutan). But, this base was busted by Royal Bhutan Army (with the help of the Indian Army). Sarania was not totally sure of his action plan as an MP. He felt that Assam has remained as undeveloped as it was six decades back and that is the chief reason why he was in ULFA. But, as an MP from Kokrajhar, he must dedicate himself to the development of this region. He further felt that even if 70 per cent of the non-Bodos supported him, he believes that he is everybody's MP and there needs to be peaceful co-existence of both the Bodos and the non-Bodos. Kokrajhar constituency is composed of the Bodo areas of Kokrajhar, Baksa and Chirang; but, there are non-Bodo areas of Barpets, Bongaigaon, Goalpara and Nalbari districts also. He therefore, is not a champion of Bodoland State and believes in the politics of adjustment. He further believes that the Government of India should solve the problem of illegal immigration of the Bangladeshis and it should not be made into an election issue. He assures that he is not a supporter of Modi or BJP but, if the new government can solve the problem of Kokrajhar successfully, he will appreciate that and support that act of the government. "I am fighting for the security and development of Bodoland and so shall support whichever government does that."

P.

It is believed that he won with such a big margin because of the anti-Muslim attacks in Baksa and Kokrajhar by the

Bodoland People's Front. He chose to become a member of the Parliament in spite of having little faith in the Parliament or the Parliamentary methods. He said that in more than 6 decades the Parliament or democracy has too little for the people of Assam and he was going to the Parliament with an ULFA agenda which will be for the benefit of the people of Kokrajhar. This sounds a little paradoxical since the Bodos are anti-Ahoms. He won with the support of 70 per cent non-Bodos inside the most powerful constituency of the Bodos! So, he has to talk of "peaceful co-existence of all tribes and non-tribes within the demanded Bodoland." Interestingly, Kokrajhar Lok sabha constituency has only three Bodo districts, viz. Kokrajhar, Baksa and Chirang; the rest of the districts, viz. Barpeta, Bongaigaon, Goalpara and Nalbari, comprise of a majority of the non-Bodo people. So, he does not believe in a separate land for the Bodos only; he appeals for a politics of adjustment and not in driving away the Bangladeshis just because they are Muslims. Lastly, he believes in supporting Modi and his NDA if he takes positive steps towards the welfare and development of the Bodos and the Assamese in general. But strangely, all the non-Bodos had rallied behind him! We know that the Bodos are staunch Hindus in spite of claiming to be a tribe! According to some scholars and political observers the Saranias and the Kacharis share common root with the Bodos.

CHAPTER VII

Karbis in Assam

The demand of the hill-people of Karbi-Anglong and North Cachar hill districts for an autonomous State within Assam is rooted in the long history of similar movements in the North-east, which led first to the formation of a separate State of Nagaland, then Mizoram and finally the Constitutional experiment with the tribal State of Meghalaya; (the region used to be in Assam with its present capital Shillong as Assam's capital). The demand for Karbi-Anglong and Bodoland became powerful due to the decline of the Congress Party (in this region), the erosion of the Left forces and the success of the youth-dominated Asom Gana Parishad (in Assam). Ever since India's independence, Assam is experiencing several movements—both violent and peaceful—and there has been drastic reduction in its size due to State re-organisations several times.

In the period preceding 1987, both Government of India and the Assam government have been opposed to further bifurcation of the State; but, they could not stop the process or the numerous movements for more and more dismemberment of this reasonably big State. The various tribes feel exploited and oppressed, but did not and do not unite in protest; each want a separate territory and administration of its own. It will not be too out of context to point out that the innumerable tribal communities of India are in a worse state than the SCs or the Dalits because the latter are more or less organised in a united manner while the former or the STs are not; they are too particular about their variant cultures, languages and traditions to develop a sense of united struggle against the economic and political hegemony of the non-tribal leaders deciding their fate either from the State capitals or the national capital. The fate of the tribal communities, who want separate homeland, lies in the strength of their political mobilisation for the fulfilment of their 'democratic' aspirations within the present limitations of their political and economic structures. We are already aware of the demands of the Bodo tribe on the North bank of the Brahmaputra; now we shall try to understand the demands of the inhabitants of Karbi-Anglong (on the southern bank of the river). It will be worth mentioning here that North-east Frontier agency (NEFA) was created by the Government of India on the border of China for strategic reasons (by taking away a big chunk of land from original Assam) even though there was no such demand from the people of this area! (We all know this region later became the State of Arunachal Pradesh within sovereign India however much China claims this region as its part).

Historically speaking, the hill-tribes of North-eastern India were neither a part of Assam nor of India; British colonialism played the trick. The tribes had trade relations with the neighbouring nations like China and Burma (and they continue to have notwithstanding heavy military presence). Such activities of these tribes are ignored by the governments fearing violent movements and demands for secession. They maintained and continue to maintain their own distinct tribal culture, tradition, taboos, social systems, which are totally different from that of the people of the valley. The major hill tribes of undivided Assam were Nagas, Mizos, Khasis, Garos, Jaintias, Karbis and Dimasa Kacharis. They had their own small States free from much trouble from the outsiders. On the other hand the Bodo-Kachari plains tribes had created their first civilisation in upper Brahmaputra, and thus regard themselves the first natives of the valley.

The Christian missionaries had substantial influence in educating them and exposing them to the enlightenment from the West. These educated tribes became the motivators for social and political changes. They started feeling and propagating that the 'autonomy' granted by the Constitution of India is not enough for their developments in the right path. They were very conscious of their distinct identity and therefore, apprehensive about the motives of the immigrant plainsmen. The language policy of the government of Assam led to the hardening of tribal attitudes; the creation of Nagaland inspired them to fight more determinately for a separate hill-State for the tribal people. These two factors gave both a new basis and vitality required for the success of the movement. But, in contrast to Nagaland and Mizoram, the people of the Garo Hills and the United Khasi & Jaintia districts had carried on their movements within the Constitutional framework for another separate hill-State without violating peace, law and order.

The strategic location and united tribal movement had forced the Government of India to reformulate its internal policy towards the North-east. Accordingly, in January, 1967 it came out with a federal scheme to reorganise Assam to satisfy the agitating tribal communities. But, both the hills and the plains people opposed this scheme! Various political parties like All Assam Students' Union (AASU) were very much opposed to the reorganisation of Assam and the creation of the hill-States out of it. They indulged in powerful protest activities throughout the Brahmaputra valley; they had neither the organisational network nor popularity in the hill areas. As a contrast the All Party Hill Leaders Conference (APHLC) reached its height without indulging in a threat to the law and order situation. But, a section of the Khasi leaders had threatened to go to East Pakistan to get training in guerrilla warfare if their demands for a separate Hill-State were not heeded to. Finally, they got their autonomous State under Article 244A of the Indian Constitution; the new State was thus given powers over 61 out of 66 subjects enumerated in the State list under the Seventh Schedule.

The new autonomous State became smaller in size than originally conceived i.e. include all the hill districts of Garo Hills, Khasi & Jaintia Hills, United Mikir (Karbi), North Cachhar and Mizo Hills. This had added up to an area of 22,732 sq. miles out of Assam's total area of 47,257 sq. miles. However, that time United Mikir and North Cachhar districts decided to continue to stay within Assam. After the formation of Bangladesh, the Government of India declared its plan of further re-organisation of Assam and granted full Statehood to Manipur, Tripura and Meghalaya. Arunachal Pradesh was also born and each of these States was granted Legislative Assemblies of their own. The Reorganisation Act of 1972 provided for the setting up the "North-eastern Council" for the purposes of co-ordinated development processes among the States newly born. The provision for autonomous States was not taken away and thus the movements for Bodoland and Karbi-Anglong started and took concrete shapes. Therefore, there is definitely a Constitutional-legal basis for such demands though within the State of Assam. The leaders of the movements believe that the higher-caste dominated bourgeois press does not deliberately provide adequate information about the movements launched by the tribal people of the Karbi-Anglong and North Cachhar hill districts for the creation of autonomous States (even though within the State of Assam). After a visit to Karbi-Anglong headquarter Diphu, and talking to the leaders and the people from all walks of life, it has clearly occurred to me that the goals and the ideal of the movement has percolated down to the common masses and they cannot be made happy without a full Statehood. Definitely, there are a few deep-rooted causes which had manifested in the form of a mass movement for Statehood.

Unlike the tribes of Nagaland, Mizoram and Meghalaya, the tribes of the above-mentioned areas are Hinduised (though not believing in the pernicious caste division and discrimination). The Bodos too, declare themselves as Hindus. A very important reason why they refused to join Meghalaya (in spite of geographical proximity) was this religious identity (which they did not want to lose).

A. The root of these movements for autonomous States lies in the severe economic backwardness of the tribal areas in an economically backward Indian State. The tribes of Assam are the most economically backward (compared to the other States of the North-east, particularly Sikkim). The movements thus reflect the political frustration of the tribes (which is again very much unlike Sikkim, where the voters are so happy with the concern and performance of the ruling party that they repeatedly brought the same party back to power with not a single seat to any other party or independents; 2014 broke the tradition with 12 seats going to the newly-formed Sikkim Krantikari Morcha). The dissatisfied lot start with the movement for autonomous State; but, they do not stop till they get a full-fledged State because the former does not have the financial powers and there can be no other power more important than financial power.

B. The AGP government, by its inherently intransigent ideology and the resultant narrow political outlook and behaviour, has contributed decisively towards the emergence of this movement in a relatively short span of time. What was most disturbing to the tribes was their language policy (which had made the Bengalis and the Cacharis of the Barrack valley also unhappy). Added to this was the large-scale eviction of the tribes from their land that was taken over by the governments (at both the Centre and the State of Assam) in the name of "reserved" forests; they were thus deprived of their means of livelihood. (We know this process of disempowering the tribes had started in British India and got accentuated in independent India in the name of stopping the jungles getting depleted.) No provision for alternative employment or source of income for the original inhabitants of these forests was thought of or planned. This continuous discriminatory policy and practice have deeply sharpened the process of alienation. AGP did not understand this problem of the tribes as it was composed mainly of the high-caste persons both in the Cabinet and the Assembly. Though these new States have given a distinct political identity to certain groups of tribals, at the same time it has made them almost entirely dependent on central grants in the absence of internal resources.

C. The restoration of the autonomous council of the hill district of Karbi-Anglong has accorded renewed recognition to the autonomy movement in the region, led by the Autonomous State Demand Committee—the only tribal autonomy movement in the country spearheaded by the Communists and waged with a consistent revolutionary-democratic orientation. The Gauhati High Court gave a verdict quashing the Assam government's order dissolving the autonomous hill council of this district. The Supreme Court also gave a verdict validating the High Court's order. The Autonomous State Demand Committee (ASDC) had an overwhelming majority in the dissolved council. The ASDC stood firm against the Saikia government. According to a few scholars and political activists the ASDC victory became more visible when viewed in the context of the more well-known Jharkhand movement. It was a significant defeat of the Saikia government vis-a-vis the 8 years old movement for independent Karbi-Anglong (in 1993). The Congress had tried to retain power by expanding the jurisdiction of the district council and upgrading the autonomous district council to the status of autonomous territory. In return, it expected that ASDC gives up its demand for an "autonomous State within the State" as promised in Art. 244A of the Constitution of India. ASDC rightly emphasised that Art. 244A is a battle for upholding the limited federalising effect of the Indian Constitution and for stretching the federal space in our polity in the face of the Indian ruling classes' relentless drive towards increasing centralisation of economic and political powers. The Karbi Students' Association (KSA) had also sparked off a new phase of militant popular activism. It started with a massive march to Diphu (district headquarters) and a powerful siege of the district administration; a series of bandhs rocked not only the district but also entire Assam. The Congress was called a "party of goons." The KSA had won a decisive victory in the college union elections followed by the biggest ever mass rally. The ASDC-KSA combine emerged as a key factor in Assam politics instilling a sense of unity, purpose and direction among diverse streams of democratic forces in the State. A powerful ASDC-KSA was of importance to the Left movement also leading to an impressive CPI (ML) May Day rally in Guwahati. It was this combination of factors—the growing popular appeal of a nationality movement and the pressure of broad democratic opinion with a principled leadership—that had forced the Assam government to withdraw its appeal (against the Karbi-Anglong movement) in the Supreme Court. Some scholars and activists believe that the ASDC movement is the only nationality movement led by the communists with a revolutionary-democratic appeal. The ASDC MP and the Chief of the district council Shri Jayanta Rongpi was a Central Committee member of the CPI (ML) and the leader of the Four-member ASDC presence in the Assam Legislative Assembly

Shri Holiram Terang also is a member of the same party. These are striking facts considering the decline of the Communist movement not only in India, but in the entire world. It should not be ignored that influence of revolutionary communists in the above-mentioned movement has saved the movement from narrow ethnicity, which happen to turn separatist, reactionary and thus, anti-national. On the contrary, the movement has grown as a "bridge of unity," bringing different tribes into the common battle for regional autonomy under India's basic federal structure. Thus, the dissolution of Karbi-Anglong Council had been the second clear instance of dismissal of communists-led governments, the first being the toppling of the Nambudiripad's government in Kerala as early as in 1959. The 1989-92 ASDC government of Karbi-Anglong had to suffer continuous friction with both the State and the Union governments; it faced dissolution in 1992 notwithstanding the fact that it had paid the right kind of attention to agrarian reforms and the specific problems that the peasants face. It had tried to free the peasants from the clutches of the money-lenders and helped them get their mortgaged lands back. It had also tried to develop co-operative movements with mutual aid centres and similar agencies to facilitate high-productivity farming. The ASDC had also tried to organise trade union movements with clear class connotations. It is also worth noting that while 33 years Left Front rule in West Bengal had failed to catch popular imagination and to spread to the neighbouring States of Assam, Bihar and Odisha, the ASDC's short stint with power had endeared the movement to the people of North Cachar Hills. The ASDC had shown the potential of moving towards a broader unity not only of the other democratic forces (in Assam), but also of different tribes, nationalities and ethnic identities in the entire North-east.

D. Karbi-Anglong is situated in the central part of Assam, said to be the most desolate hill-district, lacking almost every basic amenity/necessity, which its neighbours get to enjoy the flow of socio-economic, political, educational and civil attainments. (This does not mean that the rest of Assam is highly developed; the State, in general, is backward compared to many other States of India. What is written above is the feeling/notion of the people living in this area). They further feel that social changes are deliberately slothful and therefore, economic development is lethargic. Frivolity towards people's wills to get civic amenities is the deliberate negligence of the policy-makers. Concept of liberty and freedom should be genuine and must reiterate the process of educating young people towards religious tolerance as the keyword for enlightenment.

Karbis are found in other parts of Assam as well like in Dima Hasao, Kamrup, Moregaon, Nagaon, Golaghat, Karimganj, Udalguri and Sonitpur districts. A good number of them are found in the Papumpare district of Arunachal Pradesh apart from the Jaintia Hills, East Khasi Hills and a few areas of Nagaland. A few are settled even in Bangladesh in a small village named Umjalong (adjacent to Meghalaya) and the Karbis are recognised as Scheduled Tribes in Meghalaya. A very important reason for the backwardness of the Karbis is their coy nature; they prefer to live aloof far away from the disturbances of industries/factories, busy roads and direct contact with the people of other communities. They, like the Bodos, belong to the Tibeto-Burman linguistic group of the Mongoloid race; they had originated in Western China close to the sources of the rivers Hwang Ho and Yang-tse Kiang. They had lived there for centuries till the mega-exodus down the flow of the rivers; such things happened all over the world when people migrated to far and near in search of food, water and shelter. China used to be known as the "celestial kingdom" because of the origin/presence of many ethnic groups in various parts; a majority of them had migrated to India and other parts of South and South-east Asia. The chief reasons behind such migrations are understood to be Natural calamities and grave diseases. The Karbi tribe had moved south along the course of the rivers Chindwin and Irrawady; thus they first entered Burma and moved later to different parts of North-east India and mainly undivided Assam which had embraced various communities, but prior to the invasion by the Ahoms.

The Karbis started living in present Karbi-Anglong area ever since they got driven away by the Jaintias. The Jaintias, on the other hand, claimed that they were driven out of their ancestral land by the Karbis. (Even now there are about 56 racial groups enjoying freedom to practise their own cultural and linguistic traditions). Karbi-Anglong Autonomous District Council was formed within Assam on October 14, 1976. Diphu became the District headquarters administering three sub-divisions and 11 developmental blocks. The density of population was only 93 per sq. km. with a sex ratio of 956/1000. There were 2928 villages with 29,520 SC populations and ST population was composed of 9,65,280. It is worth noting that even in the apparent gender-equal tribal societies of the North-east (where there is no son-preference and no female foeticide/infanticide) the number of females is less (even though better than the national average).

Inadequacy of medical services, particularly in the village areas, hinders the normal life of the people who suffer due to the absence of good roads, hospitals, etc. (there are not even small dispensaries) to attend to the patients in times of emergencies. Educationally also they suffer with no good schools or colleges. There is abysmal absence of the knowledge about the Fundamental Rights of all citizens apart from the duty of the States under the Directive Principles of State Policy. Unfortunately, thus there is absence of knowledge about the Constitution of India and the rights that the citizens are entitled to and the governments are bound to fulfil. The hypocrisy on the part of the administration and even the politicians gave rise to the self-styled militants like Karbi National Volunteers (KNV) and Karbi People's Force (KPF). We have noticed riots/violence between the different communities living in this area. (It is very prominent in the region of the Bodos, we all know). This is due to affiliations to different ideological and political dogmas imposed on the simple, innocent citizens of these areas. We saw ostracism and eviction of the newly converted Christians by even their own relatives. Sectarian fanaticism became and is ever becoming more and more powerful. In 2003 the Kuki-Karbi conflict on account of ban on jhum cultivation was instigated by the proscribed UPDS, caused bloodshed between these two indigenous tribes. There were bloody clashes between the Karbis and the Dimasas also. There was fanatic anger against the Biharis also and which movement in Assam (by whichever tribe) is and has not been against the Biharis and the Santhals, etc. or the tea-tribes brought to this region centuries back by the British colonialists? It is believed by the scholars or the social activists that chauvinism among the tribes and nepotism and corruption on the part of the political activists are mainly due to the lack of proper education and conscientisation. Undue biases and prejudices needed to be wiped out.

A majority of the Karbis are agriculturists engaging primarily in jhum or shifting cultivation; those living in the lowlands practise permanent cultivation (by means of ploughs drawn by oxen along with hoes and daos). But, with passage of time and exposure (however little) to the modern methods, many Karbi farmers are rejecting jhum cultivation; they have realised that this method leads to deforestation and degradation of the soil. It appears suicidal to them. Cattle-rearing is next in importance. Other sources of income like business or jobs in government offices, schools, hospitals are very few due to the negligence by all the governments of Assam and very poor general development. Poverty is acute and so is the absence of the opportunities for economic activities and a decent income in the regions which are agitating for Statehood in whichever part of India. Neither the Central governments nor the State governments realise this and thus they try to kill the agitations by means of violence by the police or the Army. Mental and physical retardation are found among the residents of these regions due to the absence of nutritional food and the absence medical amenities and knowledge.

The tribal areas of India are usually rich in Natural and mineral resources; Karbi-Anglong too, is rich and is plundered by the contractors with the support of the political power. Limestone is found in Dillai and Sailinangso, china-clay in upper Deopani and Silonijan, Feldspar and white coal in Koilajan and Silbheta. A few small-scale industries are there but they operate without machines and manually. There are Bokajan cement plant, Karbi Chemical mini-cement plant, rubber plantation, citronella plantation and of course as many as 12 tea gardens. But, the gross domestic product from these manufacturing centres is extremely meagre and the labour is poor and untrained. The Karbis are even denied jobs in the N.F. railways passing through this region touching stations like Diphu (the district headquarters) and other 10 stations.

As mentioned above, the number of schools is inadequate and the standard of teaching very poor; the overwhelmingly poor population cannot send their children to the better town or city schools. The students intending to study engineering, medicine or IT are rarely able to do so; there is no provision for scholarships or financial aid to such Karbis. Yet, the rate of literacy is encouraging, viz. 73.52 per cent; but, like in the rest of India, less number of females is literate, viz. 82 per cent males and 65 per cent females. This achievement is in spite of the fact that teachers are untrained and are paid a salary as low as Rs. 2,500 per month! There is most unscrupulous and inhuman level of human exploitation. According to 2011 Census, the total population of the district is 9, 65,280, out of which 8, 51,158 live in the rural areas, deprived of all the benefits of development.

The surrendered UPDS is now taking active part along with the civil society, in the political arena; they are reaching out to all four Assembly segments named Bokajan Baithalangso, Diphu and Horaghat (all reserved for the STs). There is only one MP from this area.

Let me now put down in gist my conversations and interactions with the important political figures among the Karbis like

1. Shri Biren Sing Engti, present MP from Karbi Anglong,
2. Dr Jayanta Rongpi, ex-MP from the same political entity,
3. Ms Kuntila Ronghangpi, ex-CEM (Chief Executive Member—the highest executive authority) of Karbi-Anglong Autonomous Council,
4. Shri Jayram Engleng, present CEM, KAAC,
5. Shri Holiram Teron, ex-MLA (of Assam Legislative Assembly),
6. Dr Mansing Rongpi, MLA,
7. Shri Dhorom Sing Teron,
8. Shri Bidya Sing Teron, President, Karbi Students Association,
9. Shri Elvin Teron, another ex-CEM,
10. Shri Pankaj Teron, students' leader,
11. Shri Mirjeng Kro and Shri Kangjang Teron, student leaders believing in Maoist path and
12. Shri Atul Kalita, a teacher in the college at the District headquarters, Diphu and though an upper-caste Assamese by birth, extremely empathetic with the struggle of the Karbis. (I could not name the Bodos I had interviewed because they demanded anonymity.)

The following are the main points of importance and interest that came out from the interactions; I am not quoting the opinions and beliefs of the above-mentioned persons separately, and am instead clubbing the views under certain major categories.

a. The student leaders talked of Sanmilita Ganashakti Party agenda and expressed disgust at the way the Assam government is handling the acute problems of the Karbi people. They say flooding is an acute problem of the area since it rains almost incessantly from mid-March to mid-October and the money granted by Central government for relief is thoroughly mishandled; most of the money is looted by the Assam government officials who are sent to this region to apparently perform relief work! They mentioned the problem of the river island Majuli particularly and blamed both the Congress and AGP governments. Dhamaji and Lakhimpur were also mentioned. Money for development is earmarked in April and gets finished by October due to mismanagement and random corruption; people seldom get the aimed at development. Some of them, that is how, joined the so-called terrorist outfit ULFA and demanded a special budget session in October (in the middle of the financial year) so that investigations can be made on why the allotted money for development get finished so early! But, for obvious reasons the contractors and their beneficiaries (viz. the bureaucracy) oppose the idea. The Karbis believe that about one thousand crores of rupees were looted in the Karbi area alone!
b. This disgust and disappointment get expressed as severely as their anti-Bengali feelings (whom they regard as "foreigners"). They think that the "illegal immigrants" are taking away their jobs and other financial benefits, which they would have got otherwise! And it is a fact that the immigrants from Bangladesh are better skilled agriculturists and so they earn better. The tribes also think that the number of the tribal

people is much less than that of the "illegal immigrants" (only 10 to 15 per cent), which, of course, is not true. They even believe that the number of non-indigenous Assamese is higher! And, that is why, the politicians try to woo the "illegal" citizens for votes; for them it is their victory (by hook or by crook) which is more important than the good and development of the Assamese! Let me remind my readers that this "anti-foreigner" feeling is very pronounced among the Bodos also—may be in a greater intensity. Both the Karbis and the Bodos strongly believe that the ST population has declined remarkably from 80 per cent to only 60 per cent because of the massive rise in the population of the illegal immigrants mostly from Bangladesh, who are earning a lot, as skilled agriculturists, from the fertile land of these two tribal areas; they are good in handling precious teakwood, rubber and even oil thus depriving the tribes of their own resources.

c. According to both these tribes the government at Delhi is pro-Muslim, appeasing and pampering them at every step! In fact, they hate all "immigrants;" so, they hate the tea-garden workers also even though, they had been brought in Assam centuries back by the British colonialists and the present Assam government, in no way, is responsible for that. The tea-garden workers have adapted themselves so well that they regard the tea gardens of Assam as their homeland. In the Karbis' estimation, 35 per cent of the Assamese population consists of immigrant Muslims (meaning from Bangladesh) whereas 18 per cent consist of the tea-garden workers who had been "imported" by the British from Bihar, Uttar Pradesh and even Tamil Nadu. So, they strongly believe and demand that these foreigners should be sent back to their own homeland and this should be the main agenda of the governments both at the Centre and the State of Assam. There are 126 members in the Assam Assembly and 16 members of Parliament from Assam. So, there are huge demonstrations (of 30 to 40 thousand people) demanding mainly two things—one, there should be "Inner Line Permits" (like in Arunachal Pradesh) and two, the foreigners should be barred from big business ventures. Meghalaya too, has started demanding Inner Line Permits to stop the outsiders from marrying Khasi girls because they believe that the outsiders thus get control of the family property which is owned by the woman (in a matrilineal society).

d. The Muslims (including the Assamese Muslims), the tea-workers and the various tribes vote on ethnic issues; besides, they are too poor and over-worked to think politically and to assess the virtues of the candidates; they mostly vote for those (of whichever political party) who offer them money and other incentives. During the election campaign they are offered blankets and other items of dire necessity, apart from rice at Rs. 8 a kg. One thing they have realised too well that no vote-seeker is welfare or development-minded and the voters' fate will not improve after the election; so, they grab at whatever little they get before the election. Even the rich voters are greedy and politically illiterate! The caste-Hindu votes get divided among the Congress, the AGP and the BJP. The last two are anti-Muslims also. Yet, they fail to get the support of the tribes like the Bodos and the Karbis because they cater to the needs and beliefs of the caste-Hindus, whom the tribes consider as harmful as the Muslims!

   a. According to a caste-Hindu Assamese, teaching in a government college at Diphu (district headquarters of Karbi-Anglong), the Bangladeshis are demanding and thus are prominent in the job market (where about 40,000 positions are lying vacant). They are both dominated and domineering. This is because the Assam government supports the Bangladeshis for their votes, however much the Karbis and the Bodos demand their expulsion.

e. Karbi-Anglong is the largest districts in Assam, but with scarce population and utter backwardness, which has not changed since 1901; this is the belief of the leaders who are fighting for complete Statehood. My impression, while visiting the area, was not too different; even Diphu, its district headquarters or the capital of the KAAC, looks more like a village than a town! The water connection is 24 km. away and the very long rainy season creates havoc with no proper roads to travel to the villages for relief and routine administrative work. The engineers and the bureaucrats are most disinterested in the walfare of the people and are corrupt; this is a strong feeling of the leaders who are fighting for Statehood.

f. The Karbi-Anglong Autonomous Council (KAAC) has been constituted since last 18 years and Shri Bhuvan Pegu's party got 70 per cent of the votes in the Panchayat elections. About 80,000 votes were secured in the last election. The members of KAAC are elected from as many as 26 constituencies for a period of five years. There are 4 MLAs in the Assam Legislative Assembly, elected from Diphu, Bokazan, Hauraghat and Baithalangso and only one Member of Parliament, elected from both Karbi-Anglong, and Dima Hasan. KAAC has been granted for 50 years and the elections are fought on party basis (like in a parliamentary democracy). The most powerful party was the United Peoples' Front (UPF). There are no Panchayat elections since the Councils are like the Panchayats both in the Karbi and the Bodo areas. But the people of North Cachar Hills and Mikir Hills want separate States for themselves; their argument is if the inhabitants of the hills in Nagaland and Meghalaya could get separate Statehood, why not they? The Karbis, with seven lakhs population, is the biggest tribal group and the leaders feared that they may turn Christians like the people of Meghalaya and Nagaland; so, they were vehemently against joining geographically contiguous Meghalaya.

g. This region, like all other backward tribal regions of India (e.g. Jharkhand and Chhatisgarh), is rich in minerals like coal, petroleum, china clay, granite and stone quarries. Its forest resources, like medicinal and aromatic plants, are worth exploiting for the good of the people and the nation; local health centres should take advantage of the tribal knowledge about these and use those for the cure of so many diseases because, as expected, there is shortage of modern medicines and qualified doctors in the so-called health centres. But, like again in the other tribal regions of India, the adivasis or the original inhabitants are debarred from the forests and the mineral-rich areas and thus deprived of what are their birth-rights! But the government does not take any initiative in developing these rich resources—not even for the good of the State and the nation, forget doing anything for the benefit of the Karbis! A welfare state would have exploited the Natural resources properly so that the local people, as well as the nation, would benefit. The only occupation of the Karbis is agriculture (in which they are not as competent as the immigrant Bangladeshis are). No storage facilities are there and the government of Assam does not fix any minimum support price. Besides, agriculture is badly affected due to shortage of water/irrigation canals and electricity. Water level is very low in Dimhasa, south of Karbi-Anglong where too, Karbis live.

h. Karbi language uses Roman script and the Karbis are vehemently against the imposition of Ahomiya and Bangla languages and the cultural programmes in these languages apart from in English and Hindi, though over-all development is the chief issue in their list of demands which are mainly for good roads, convenient transport, efficient communication systems, comprehensive irrigation system for better agriculture and of course, proper education facilities so that they can compete equally with the rest of Assam and India. At present there are schools even without buildings, not to speak of the absence of blackboards, libraries, laboratories and well-qualified teachers! The only college and ITI are in terribly bad state thus forcing the locals to migrate to other parts of India for proper education or to remain half-educated and untrained. The polytechnic building has been handed over to the CRPF thus indicating that the integrity of the Indian landmass is more important to the government of India than the development of the people of the backward areas! The governments, both at the State and the Centre, do not realise that full-fledged development can automatically cut the roots of discontent and the tendency towards secession. The Indian government has accused these neglected communities by remarking "insurgency is the biggest industry" in this area and that is how, it justifies the rampant extortion by the Army and the police.

i. The State government is doing little to address the root causes with the excuse of too little funding from the Centre. Every election time promises are there for 100 per cent electricity and drinking water but, there is only 100 per cent corruption running into Rs. 1,000 crores, allege most of the Karbi leaders. Besides, there is struggle for identity also and not mere development. Such a demand is found in all the tribal belts of India and particularly of the North-east. Some of the youth and student leaders allege that corruption has spread even amongst those in KAAC and also amongst those leading the struggle for full Statehood! It may not be too irrelevant to refer to the newly formed party against the "corruption and the VIP culture," the Aam Admi Party; so many allegations of corruption have come from the opponent parties against a few of its important leaders! Politics in India has become equivalent to corruption and non-fulfilment of the promises made to the voters during the election campaigns; India's democracy is thus severely hampered as it has become and is increasingly becoming the nation of the billionaires along with the increasing number of people 'below the poverty line'. The Prime Minister and the ruling UPA continuously tried to mislead the common (not so educated) people by talking of high growth rate and remaining silent on true development in the fields of education, health, employment to all. China, on the other hand, does not have to face incessant secessionist demands (in spite of adopting the capitalist mode of production) because it is already developed in the fields mentioned above. Besides, China gives special attention to the comprehensive development of the Minorities, including their very different and distinctive languages, religions and the other aspects of culture. That is why; there has been no secessionist movements there.

a. In 1969 there had been demand for Statehood under Article 244A (of the Constitution) for the first time because as an Autonomous State, Karbi-Anglong could not have powers over finance and police and law & order. It is needless to point out that these are the most vital powers for a group of people demanding self-rule. As mentioned earlier, the region is rich in mineral resources, especially petroleum (the source of high income) and yet, it is remaining under-developed due to the absence of financial power. PWD, Health and Education are under KAAC, which is not able to develope the opportunities for the people due to under-funding and the absence of financial power; this is the reason why the common people are anti-bureaucracy, blaming them eternally for the absence of the required developments. Like with the Bodos, the anti-immigrant feeling among the Karbis is quite strong though they have accommodated the Bengalis (Hindus only), the Nepalis (who too, are Hindus) and even the Garos in their KAAC. Clashes between the Kukis and the Karbis are noticed sometimes. They have a tribal court of justice of their own which are known as "Customary Courts." Like all tribal people, the Karbis too, have greater faith in their traditional system of law and justice than in the courts of democratic India because, they rightly feel, that non-tribal system of governance and justice cannot possibly understand the specific needs and beliefs of the tribal people. They further, believe that if the non-tribal so-called mainstream wields all the economic and political power the tribal regions can never be developed and if at all developed, those cannot be developed the way the tribes require. Similarly, Indian judiciary is mainly composed of the mainstream Indians; how can they therefore, deliver justice? They are totally ignorant of the tribal laws and system of justice. The governments try to create positive or pro-government political awareness through these cultural festivals, which are held mostly in Hindi and English languages. The justification behind such steps seems noble i.e. to bring the alienated tribes into the "mainstream." The upper-caste Hindu governments do not realise that the choice of the word "mainstream" (meaning the politically and economically powerful Indians living in the areas outside the tribal belts) is insulting for the tribal communities. They ask why are the non-tribal people or cultural groups "main" in India, a country with endless varieties of ethnic and cultural entities?

j. Karbis are five clans and numerous sub-clans; three clans live in Hanjang area and the rest in Mukreng area. But, language and the customs are same with every clan and sub-clan and (like with the caste Hindus) marriages cannot take place within the same clan or sub-clan (we all know that in case of the Hindus marriages within the same gotra are prohibited even if it is within the same caste). The chief grudge of the Karbis, like most other tribes of India, is not so much about the absence of development or economic and educational advancements (in fact, a majority of them are quite proud of their culture, which is so very different from that of the mainstream Indians) but, about the absence of the opportunities to practise and develope their culture, customs and tradition; they are more bothered about their own typical identity which make them so distinct from those who wield economic and political powers in independent India. They have as much dissatisfaction and anger against the government of independent India as they had against the colonial power, which had started destroying their forests, habitats and means of livelihood. To them corruption is not merely in money terms but, in terms of destroying their very typical culture and imposing the culture of the non-tribals and even of the West and international capitalism. They feel that economic and other developments will automatically come if they are granted Statehood and their very own culture/identity is allowed to develope When I brought in the examples of Jharkhand, Chhattisgarh and Uttarakhand to point out that Statehood did not lead to better development and the political and economic power have continued to remain in the hands of the outsiders and the national political parties, they evaded the answer. They get angry if referred to as Hindus; but, they hate to be Christians like the Khasis, the Garos and the Nagas! Why then (unlike the Bodos) there is no assertion by the Karbis as a distinct people with a powerful identity? The chief reason is the mass-scale absence of the knowledge about Article 244A of the Constitution. The Government of India allots more power to the KAAC whenever the movement is escalated; but, carefully avoids alloting financial powers and the control over police. We all know from the recent demand of the AAP government in the National Capital State of Delhi for control over the police; the dharna by the ruling party made us conscious of the fact that no government can act meaningfully and fulfil its promises made to its voters unless and until it has law and order under its control; how can a party or a ministry implement its promises and people-centric desires without an enforcing authority in its hands? (We also know that Shiela Dikshit, the outgoing Congress Chief Minister, had also made many requests to the Centre for these powers). After all, in a multi-party democracy with a capitalist economy, where corruption is rampant, there have to be various opposing views and demands, which have to be anti-common people's developments and rights. Secondly, implementation of the pro-people plans become impossible if the government does not wield financial powers. And these two were never granted either to the Bodos or to the Karbis, however much autonomy was granted in other matters like health, education, agriculture and the enjoyment of their tribal culture and traditions.

a. The Bodos are in a better situation because they have more MLAs and are not peaceful unlike the Karbis; their continuous insurgency and violence on and often have attracted much more of national attention. Another serious problem faced by the Karbis is that those living outside the STH (Scheduled Tribe of the Hills) as well as the STP (Scheduled Tribes of the Plains) receive no benefit as an ST if they happen to live outside Karbi-Anglong! This kind of unreasonable discrimination naturally incites them towards insurgency. So they start demanding a separate State under Article 3 of the Constitution and also demand the implementation of the tribal customary laws and not of the Indian Constitution or of the Indian Judiciary. What else can they do when they are denied the benefits of statutory job reservation? After all, they need employment and they need to survive. All insurgencies and violence take place due to the making of a Constitution by the upper-class-cum-upper-caste Hindus (Dr. Ambedkar was an exception because he had managed to become highly learned in spite of suffering untouchability) and the rule of the same containation both at the Centre and in the States ever since independence. Even the Communist parties have always been led by the upper-caste-cum-upper-class Hindus and Muzaffar Ahmed was an exception. The job reservations granted to the SCs and the STs were eyewash; how can a traditionally poor and educationally backward person compete with the smart and confident job-seeker from a traditionally advanced class? Job reservation cannot possibly pull the backward and the poor up unless there is reservation in education also and the first generation learners can go to a good public school and get the right kind of technological training. Right to education should have been made a Fundamental Right in the Constitution or a right from the beginning.

k. One important leader and an ex-MLA (when I visited in 2012) was a member of the CPI(ML) in 1986 and had to stay underground for a certain period; later he formed the Autonomous State Demand Committee (ASDC). Earlier he had contested from AASU and PDF and had signed an Accord on behalf of the Karbis in 1985; he had later, in 1991, contested for the Assembly again. He believed that political behaviour of a certain "nationality" depended largely on how it is mobilised. The Assam Movement of 1977 was anti-"foreigner" and it had faced too many political uncertainties. The Karbis, under this leader, had participated in this movement, though indirectly. At a point, they had even voted for AGP, which had taken the anti-foreigner movement forward. The People's Radical Students Politics had started calling the various communities wanting freedom "nationalities," thus completely ignoring the fact that they were actually residing within the nation called India. They also demanded a total transformation of the Congress government both within the State of Assam and at Delhi.

   There were other Karbi leaders who also contested as CPI(ML) but, could never win. Left students' movements appeared quite powerful but, could not be successful. Later AASU took over the political scene by opposing the Left movement.

   The "foreigners" or the Bangladeshi immigrants were found to be hard-working and good agriculturists. Originally, they had settled down in the "char" (river-island) areas but, had to leave those due to heavy floods. Antagonism and violence against them had started ever since because the original inhabitants of these areas found them as intruders and grabbers of their lands even though the former were not so developed in agricultural methods. They grow only paddy, corn and sugarcane. But, there is terrible shortage of water since the irrigation system is not developed; they can grow paddy only once a year. Yet, there was peace march in Karbi area when Bodoland, particularly Kokrajhar, was burning with anti-Muslim violence. But there was quite a large-scale violence in the Karbi region during the election campaign of 2014. Maybe the Karbis too, have started believing that violence is the only way left when the governments do not pay any heed to peaceful agitations!

l. Ms. Kuntila Ronghanpi was not only ex-CEM (i.e. Chief of the Autonomous Council), but also the President of Karbi-Anglong Mahila Congress. Karbi women enjoy all social benefits and freedoms (like all other tribal women of the North-east), but like the Khasis and the Garos (of Meghalaya), are least interested in politics or political power. Ms. Ronghanpi joined politics after marrying a politician. (This reminds us of the pre-independence freedom movements where women took part as wives, daughters, sisters of the important male political leaders. Even now the women Panchayat members seldom exercise their rights without the advice and support of the male members of their families.)

m. As mentioned earlier, the area does not have Panchayats because the Council is regarded as a local body and the mandatory 33 per cent reservation for women cannot be fulfilled since women are so terribly disinterested in politics or power. They remain contended with the social equality and freedom that they enjoy under their customary laws. Ms. Ronghanpi had also organised the women under Self-help Groups (like it is found in the non-tribal States).

Farmers' Societies too, were formed through which the farmers used to get and continue to get benefits like seeds, fertilisers and tractors at highly subsidised rates or even free. She herself was a farmer's daughter and uneducated. Yet, she had the required strong will and courage to force the Assam government to distribute free books and uniforms in the schools. So many doctors, engineers and lawyers have come out of this backward society because it is a perfectly equal society and there is equal distribution of benefits. Domestic violence too, was tactfully handled by inspiring and encouraging women into protest and not lying low (the way it does not happen in case of even highly educated and highly earning women of the non-tribal communities in the rest of India). Ms. Ronghanpi, the Chairperson of Community Development Society (which was meant for women's economic development), preached that the women have to be enlightened, even if not highly educated and doing a fruitful job; she also insisted that such women should not be counter-violent." Town Committees" were organised where women were given training in computer, tailoring, etc. and loans were also given at easy interestrates. There are 10 wards in her constituency.

Ms. Proneeta Ronghanpi is another spirited woman who fights for women's rights and formed All Women Neighbourhood Committee for women's advancement and enlightenment; the ward meetings are held to discuss the needs and the priorities. The number of women in jobs is very low in spite of reservation; the reason mainly is the absence of women's interests in politics or life outside the domestic boundary. This is notwithstanding the fact that the customary laws do not prohibit women from anything that the men are allowed to do or enjoy!

One significant point to note is that women politicians like Ampreen Lyngdoh (of Meghalaya) and Kuntila Ronghanpi (of Karbi-Anglong) are invariably admirers of Sonia Gandhi and therefore, supporters of Congress Party, while both the regions, in general, are anti-Congress and against any national party! It is the regional parties which always won in Meghalaya thus leading to coalition governments and coalition Oppositions always (as noted in the chapters on Meghalaya). For elections after elections such was the political scene in Meghalaya (totally opposed to single party rule found in Sikkim for decades). But 2013 Assembly election in Meghalaya and the 2014 Assembly election in Sikkim have drastically changed the political scenario. The national party Congress (ruling over India) secured as many as 29 seats in an Assembly of 60 seats and the regional parties together got only 18 seats! And Sikkim Assembly got an Opposition (viz. 12 seats of Sikkim Krantikari Morcha) after 13 long years of not a single MLA in the Opposition!

Karbi-Anglong movement too, is against Congress and Asom Gana Parishad for decades. Kuntila was Mahila Congress President for nine years, but turned anti-Congress in 1986 when she was suddenly stripped of Lok Sabha ticket 10 days after being allotted. The contribution of Ms. Ronghanpi (Karbi) and Ms. Lyngdoh (Meghalaya) is worth noting because women (of these communities), in general, are disinterested in politics even though there is no bar or discouragement from the society; these societies, in any case, are not patriarchal or oppressive of women. The typical excuse given by the women interviewed is "there is too much work at home to find time for politics or any outdoor activities" (as if women from the so-called mainstream communities do not have to perform these chores!) The men, like in most tribal societies of the hills and the Himalayas (including of Tibet on the other side of the Himalayas), are lazy and the women are hard-working and enterprising.

Though the CEM of KAAC complain about absence of funds for development, a few leaders (particularly the teachers) believe that the absence of development is not so much due to absence of funds as it is due to the absence of the right kind of vision. They also complain about too many students' unions and too may bandh calls; the latter definitely is against development which cannot happen unless there is right vision, plan and execution; the less number of days' of work (i.e. due to bandhs) means fewer opportunities for developmental work. Besides, there is a large-scale complaint by a few radical student leaders that the politicians or the vote-seekers forget about their voters once elected. This is a complaint that comes from all parts of India except Sikkim.

Some of the student leaders have been initiated into politics or Statehood demands from their schooldays onwards because they were thoroughly dissatisfied with the infra-structure of the schools (which were not too few in number). They also demand engineering and technology colleges and high level teachers' training. There is only one Government College in Karbi and the locals are discriminated against while trying for jobs here. The real reason may not be discrimination; it is the absence of opportunities; how can a Karbi compete equally with an Assamese for a job unless well educated and well trained? Those opportunities are missing; so they do not succeed in spite of job-reservation. (The Sikkim government, on the other hand, puts the meritorious students from the government schools to renowned public schools so that the students develop the required aptitude and confidence, necessary for succeeding in the job screening.) Job reservation has no meaning and cannot serve the desired purpose until and unless there is reservation at the education level and the government schools in Sikkim, both in the villages and the towns, have the required infra-structure and well-trained teachers. The Karbis get only 20 to 30 per cent of the jobs and the rest goes to the non-Karbis.

A dangerous trend in politics had started; people are dissatisfied with the Congress because they felt that the Congress party did not pay heed to the local issues whereas the BJP does UPA hardly ever paid attention to their needs and problems because the corrupt intermediaries were not punished. To the disadvantaged people the CBI is also corrupt and that is why, the corrupt officials are never put in jails. They further believe that such undemocratic, anti-people acts take place because the awareness level is low amongst the common people and the leaders too, get into the widespread corruption tangle! (Similar feeling must have been in the minds of the voters from other parts of India and that is how BJP won with thundering majority in 2014 general election and before that in so many States.) Only 60 to 70 per cent of the population are literate (but, not properly educated) in Karli-Anglong. Drop-out rates in the schools and child labour are high because of the poorly trained teachers and poor infrastructure in the schools and the only college. The disinterest on the part of the students is also because neither their literature, nor their history is taught. Sometimes adivasi literature is taught only at the primary level; otherwise all-India syllabus is followed. This is a serious complaint of most of the adivasis of India and yet, no steps have been taken in 67 long years to eradicate it.

People of this region are taking to Hindu idols like Shiva, Parvati and Ganesha, but are not copying any of the Hindu superstitions like son preference, dowry, and, like with the Muslims, it is the groom's mother who seeks the bride's hand and the property is owned by both man and woman. And the married women do not have to take their husband's surname. As an example, Ms. Kuntila Ronghanpi's husband's name is Bidya Sing Engleng and he is an MLA.

According to the radical group of student leaders and the leaders of the Karbi Youth Council, Article 244A of the Sixth Schedule of the Constitution is not followed by the Government of India. The demand is that Autonomous Statehood must be granted to the land of the Karbis. These insurgents attack government properties having formed Karbi People's Liberation Tigers though there have been several peace accords between them and the Government of India. With each accord the power and the jurisdiction of the KAAC have gone up; it started with power in 30 departments and now the power has gone up to as many as 52 departments. But, as mentioned earlier, the Karbis are forced to learn Assamese language in the schools.

The Centre pretends that it has no power to grant full-fledged Statehood to Karbi-Anglong and only the government of Assam can. The mostly uneducated Karbis, educated in the poorly equipped schools and hardly ever in the single college that exists, are thus, hardly aware of Article 244A of the Constitution; the leaders have to take great pains in making the common people understand what the fight is about and how full Statehood will help them to develop better both economically and educationally.

But, some other leaders believe that the Karbis are not separatists or exclusivists; they like mixing up with the people of other communities and even adjust. Similar is the nature of the tribes of geographically contaguous Meghalaya (even though lately they are demanding Inner Line Permits for their State). Why then the movement for separate Statehood? It is because the tribes or the original inhabitants of India or of a particular region were not consulted while forming the language-based States in independent India and no special effort has been made to give due recognition to their language, culture and history. Their anger is more against the State of Assam because the Assam Re-organisation Association leaders played counter-offensive in 1969. The Karbis demanded election (separated from Assam); but, no election was held since 1961. There was no election in KAAC even; so, they started demanding full Statehood (like Assam and Meghalaya) since, as mentioned earlier, Assamese language and history were imposed on them. Thus, the movement is more for identity than for development (as mentioned earlier). The tribes all over India are extremely particular about their distinct cultural identity. Same is the situation with the Dalits; their fight and struggle are more for Dalit identity and recognition. Both the adivasis and the Dalits feel that development and economic opportunities will automatically follow once their special identity gets recognition.

There are 4 Karbi MLAs in the Assam Assembly of 136 members and in 1969-70 all of them were allotted ministry. The first Prime Minister of India Pt. Nehru had given 99 per cent autonomy and a special commission was set up for looking into the problems and demands of the hill areas. Article 371B was suggested by Nehru, and as a result, Ashok Mehta Committee was formed to look into the special and specific problems that disturb the tribes because the non-tribals in power fail to understand why the tribal cultures should be respected and promoted so that they can live with their very special identity and dignity. The Committee went to the extent of suggesting that both economic and political powers should be transferred to the tribes and Assam should be a federation of the various tribal States. Yet, in 1973 a memorandum was sent to the Government of India containing many grievances and the demand for their remedies because the plains people could not agree to such a suggestion by what their powers would get reduced drastically.

Article 244A stressed mainly on

1. Starting with the administrative powers and then
2. Legislative powers, but the
3. Financial powers in the hands of the Government of India. But, ultimately,
4. The Autonomous State will become a full-fledged State with even law and order and finance in its hands.

As mentioned several times earlier (in different contexts), the chief reason why the tribes, discussed in this chapter, wanted full-fledged States with law and order and financial powers in their hands was the presence of the Bengali Muslims (whom they call "foreigners") and their fast increasing numbers so much so that the Karbis used to be 71 per cent of the population in 1951 Census and got reduced to 51 per cent in 1971! The 4 MLAs in the Assam Assembly and one MP in the

Lok Sabha also kept on demanding the expulsion of the "foreigners" from their land, which they claim is from the days of Mahabharata. Conveniently, they forget or ignore the fact they too are intruders and foreigners having migrated centuries back from the arid lands of North-west China. Even though BJP did not get any significant number of seats in Assam, Hinduisation of the Karbis and the Bodos had slowly taken place (as mentioned in a paragraph above). In 1981 a powerful agitation against the "foreigners" was witnessed in this region. In spite of poor status of schools and colleges the level of education kept on increasing from mere 30 per cent (when KAAC was formed) to 60 per cent and more and the more educated the tribes became, the stronger was their anti-foreigner feelings; the demand for a separate State also became powerful. The illiterates, like in most States of India, usually voted for Congress; they failed to comprehend the neglect of the tribal areas by the government at the Centre and in Assam and the benefits of a sovereign State of their own. The leaders feel or rather, strongly believe, that rampant corruption in Karbi-Anglong is because of the Assamese ruling bureaucrats, police, etc. The Assamese elites do not even allow the mandatory 5 per cent job reservation for the Karbi people and they, in reality, get about 1.6 per cent reservations approximately. Thus, thousands of posts remain unfilled.

CHAPTER VIII

Meghalaya: People and Natural Resources

Meghalaya was created as an autonomous State within the State of Assam in April, 1970 and it became a full-fledged State in January, 1972. It is bound on the North & East by Assam and on the South and West by Bangladesh. This hilly State is now divided into seven administrative districts; they are Jaintia Hills, East Garo Hills, West Garo Hills, East Khasi Hills, West Khasi Hills, South Garo Hills and Ri Bhoi. These are predominantly inhabited by the Khasis, the Jaintias and the Garos. The Khasi and the Jaintia Hills are primarily plateaus with rolling grasslands, hills and river valleys. There are deep gorges in the extreme South ending with a narrow strip of plains bordering Bangladesh.

Long before the advent of the British, the indigenous people in the hills of North-east India had organised themselves under the political systems of their own, which had been the natural outcome of their social evolution. Two distinctly different types of governance have been evolved viz. (i) democratic system in the clan-based village societies, controlled by the village councils and headmen and (ii) autocratic system of chieftainship, controlled by the clan or the village chiefs.

The extent of power and authority of these traditional political institutions in relation to their people used to vary from tribe to tribe. While in certain communities these traditional institutions were well-organised and well-structured (in some cases they even led to the formation of miniature States), in some other communities these institutions were loosely organised without any central authority. The Garo system of governance of clan-based village community however seemed to be much immature compared to those of the Khasis and the Jaintias.

This relative backwardness continues to this day. The rural system and economy remain as backward as before and this is due to the absence of equal access to the basic resources like land and forest—the prime assets of any society. The Sixth Schedule has totally failed as an instrument of land management and the social and economic changes in the rural sectors of Meghalaya. The Eleventh Schedule under the 73rd Amendment Act promised more democratic way of land and community asset management for a better rural society of economic viability.

Meghalaya is basically an agricultural State with 83 per cent of the population depending primarily on agriculture and horticulture though the prevailing land conditions provide limited scope for extensive cultivation. Rice and maize are the major food crops; wheat has been introduced recently and its production is proving encouraging. Besides, there are potato, jute, cotton, mustard, ginger, turmeric, areca nut, black pepper, etc. and fruits like orange, pineapple, banana, guava, litchi, jackfruit, plum, pear, peach; production of tomato, mushroom and tea also has started. See, how the State of Assam as well as the Government of India were exploiting such rich agricultural and horticultural resources of this part of North-east by not granting it Statehood and this is the practice of our governments all over India. Jharkhand and Chhttisgarh are the latest examples; these are very rich in mineral resources, but were not allowed to benefit from those.

Meghalaya is also a power-surplus State and is able to supply 36 per cent of the electricity generated to the neighbouring States. Yet, only 47 per cent of its villages have been electrified! Does it speak of the inefficiency of its administration or of the coalition parties forming the government? It is difficult to deny that the coalition form of government for a very long time is not the best way to governance or the welfare of the common people. There is the strong possibility of too much of difference of opinions and the absence of the right vision and universally accepted policies.

There is a cement factory at Cherapunjee and a number of small-scale industrial units covering service industries like bakeries, furniture-making, iron and steel fabrication, tyre retreading, spice-pounding, etc. The subsequent governments have been giving encouragement to entrepreneurship and Meghalaya Industrial Development Corporation is offering term loans and also participation in equity capital. The forest coverage of the State is 8,510 sq. km. Thus the State is rich in timber, medicinal herbs and plants and a variety of beautiful orchids. The mineral wealth of Meghalaya includes coal, silimanite, limestone, dolomite, fire-clay, quartz and grass-sand.

B. Colonial Period

After colonial annexation the present State of Meghalaya used to consist of the Jaintia and the Garo Hills with a semi-independent status of the Khasi areas as per a treaty with the British Crown. Shillong became the District Headquarters of the Khasi & Jaintia Hills in 1964; it had become the headquarters of Assam also in 1874 and in 1905 the present Meghalaya had become part of the province of Assam. Curzon had wanted to divide Bengal and annex this hill region to East Bengal. Shillong, being the provincial headquarters, had seen the gradual evolution of parliamentary democracy; the Council of the Chief Commissioner, set up under the Indian Councils Act, and the first independent Council for Assam was set up in 1912. The Council met for the first time after four long years in 1916 and again in 1919 under the Government of India Act. Along with the parliamentary institutions, Meghalaya still retains, through the Sixth Schedule of the Constitution, the age-old, grassroots system of tribal democracy as practised through the traditional rulers, viz. the Syiems, the Nokmas and the Dolois; this continues to exist side by side with modern parliamentary institutions.

Now Meghalaya has a Legislative Assembly of 36 members and a Council of five Ministers. It had a common Governor and a common High Court with Assam. The overall responsibility of law & order in Meghalaya had remained with the Assam government though the State had its own village and town police and it had powers over 61 out of 65 subjects. Meghalaya had higher percentage in education (31.5 per cent) than Assam (27.4 per cent) and now too, it is ahead of Assam in this respect. The tribal people, in general, are much more eager for learning and vocational training than the other communities like the dalits, kept deliberately backward by the governments (both at the Centre and the States) conducted mainly by the elite upper-castes. This tactics is followed to subvert the benefits of "reservation" endowed by the Constitution of India. The tribes, in general, used to be more or less satisfactorily educated than any other non-mainstream community because wisely, a good number of them took to Christianity and thus reaped the benefit of the welfare activities of the Christian missionaries (who had unwittingly helped British colonialists by winning the confidence of the common people by taking care of their health and education.)

C

Ethno-culturally, Meghalaya can be divided into two distinct categories, viz. the Khasis and the Jaintias of the eastern side and the Garos on the Western side. They are regarded as two branches of the similar society by some scholars. There are conflicting views about the origin of the

Khasis, the most advanced tribe demographically and politically. The capital of Meghalaya, Shillong, is in the region dominated by the Khasis and the Jaintias. The Khasis are divided, in general, into 4 sub-tribes, viz. the Bhoi in North, the lyngngam in West, the Wars in South and the Khynrium in the central plateau. With the Khasis the village boundaries were co-terminous with clan boundaries and they being strictly exogamous, marriage within the same clan was strictly prohibited. So, slowly and slowly various clans had to be accommodated within the same village. A different type of village administration had to come up in order to accommodate the interests of the so many different clans.

The Khasis, like the Garos, is a matrilineal society—the youngest daughter inheriting the property from her mother and by continuing to live in her mother's home even after marriage; her husband has to come and live in his in-laws' home. But the decision-taking powers are with the brother of the girl's mother; thus, it is not a matriarchal society. I have not heard of any society in the present age which is matriarchal; matriliny is found with a few communities in Kerala also.

D.

The Garos are believed to be of Bodo group ethnically, having Tibeto-Burman lineage and they trace their origin to a place named Tarua in Tibet. There are Hills Garos and Plains Garos and the major groups are Marak, Sangma, Momin and Machong. Unlike the Khasis and like many tribes of Arunachal Pradesh, they are polygamous and the number of wives is a sign of power and prosperity. Like the Muslims and a few tribes of Arunachal Pradesh, the Garo man has to take the permission of his first wife, which he quite easily gets because the first wife continues to hold all the power of the household and she likes to have many "servants" i.e. the latter wives of her husband. Polyandry is never, never allowed. The Garos intermarry with any other Garo community except the Jugis or the sweepers. Do they believe in untouchability like the caste Hindus?

The highest political institution among the Garos was the office of the Nokma, i.e. the village headman and there were as many Nokmas as there were the number of the villages and no uniform pattern of relationship was found between the Nokmas and the other villagers. These differences were due to the variations in the clan traditions and the local customs, apart from the personality and the competence of the different Nokmas.

The Garos, like the Khasis, are matrilineal, i.e. lineage is through the mother and the daughter (unlike the Khasis, not necessarily the youngest daughter) owns the deceased mother's property. But, the husband is given patriarchal authority and if he is a Nokkrom, i.e. the husband of the heiress, his position is next only to his father-in-law (whose position and power he gets after the latter's death). The husband can beat his wife but, the wife is condemned thoroughly if she beats her husband—quite like in the mainstream society whether Hindu, Muslim or Sikh or of any other religious group. Each clan in the villages have bachelor's dormitories where they sleep at night and also learn singing, dancing, playing musical instruments and art and craft. No females are allowed. This practice is prevalent with some of the hill-tribes of Arunachal Pradesh also.

The Garo marriage is regulated by two important laws, viz. exogamy and a'kim. People have to marry outside his or her clan like, a Sangma cannot marry a Sangma and a Marak cannot marry a Marak. Those, breaking this law, are looked down upon, but unlike in the caste society the couple is not punished or tortured. According to A'kim law a man and a woman once married, will never be free to marry somebody from the other clan—not even after the death of the spouse; a man usually has to marry the sister of the deceased and the woman the brother or nephew of her deceased husband. In case such a match cannot be found then the widow or the widower is free to marry anybody of his/her choice. This custom again is same as with a few tribes of Arunachal

Pradesh. A man can even marry his mother-in-law when his father-in-law dies though this is very rare. A man can marry two sisters; but, he must marry the elder one first. He can marry anybody from his father's clan, but never from his mother's clan. I could not find from the many books that I read if there is the custom of bride-price; it was not clear from the conversations either. Like in the Hindu society, the proposal for marriage must come from the girl's side and never from the boy's side; this is unlike what happens with the most tribes of Arunachal Pradesh. Child marriage is totally absent; the boys and the girls are allowed to marry when they are able to manage their lives themselves. Hindu Garos are very orthodox and marriage with Christian Garos is totally prohibited; they are not allowed to marry a non-Garo even. Most of the Hindu Garo families have migrated to Nowgong district of Assam to find a place among the Assamese Vaishnavites.

Divorce is very rare and only on mutual consent; the other causes may be adultery or sterility. Daughter can be adopted if the couple has no daughter; this is so much unlike the Hindu society where daughters are killed immediately after birth or as foetus only. The reason is the same—ownership or inheritance of property, in this case, by the daughter. Caste Hindus do not want daughters because the son inherits the property and dowry has to be given by the girl's father at the time of her marriage.

E.

Folktales tell us that there were female rulers, thus proving that the females were not debarred from politics and administration. We know of female rulers from the Tibetan folktales also and the Tibetan women are assertive to this day, particularly economically. Accounts of Hieun Tsang say that the king of as far a kingdom as Kashmir had attacked the Jaintia kingdom which was known as "Stri-rajya" or the kingdom of women. There was a female ruler of the Bhoi area and the story of Ka Latympang is well-known; she was a wise and powerful ruler of a small State of Manar in the Jaintia Hills. Yet, the women of today or the colonial period are/were least interested in politics (in spite of no socio-economic barrier)! Most of the women's organisations of this region start by declaring that their goal is social and economic empowerment and not political; they strangely do not realise that all powers emanate from political power only. (That is the reason why the women's movement in India is demanding reservation of seats in the legislative bodies since decades.) With this kind of attitude of the women and with men not being anti-women, reservation of seats is meaningless. Women themselves feel that their first priority is towards their family, children and household work; they have no time or energy left for politics, they insist.

CHAPTER IX

Traditional Political Systems and Birth of Meghalaya

A.

In 1914 the Garo National Conference was formed with a view to have integrated policy for Garo education for all the Garos. In 1924, the Garos started having a share in their own administration. Some of them got involved in the national movement also. Phukan Sangma had taken part in the Quit India movement in 1942 and was also jailed. In 1946, Garo National Council, the first political party was formed with Mody Marak and Emonsing Sangma as the President and the Vice-President. When the Eastern India Tribal Union was formed in 1954, the Garo National Council got affiliated to it. Side by side, Indian National Congress was also organised in the Garo Hills and Shri Phukan Sangma became its first President. Congress contested the District Council elections hand in hand with Garo National Council and kept winning, thus being in complete charge of the local administration.

B.

Every Khasi village has its local Assembly known as "Durbar Shnong," which used to be presided by Rangbah Shnong or village headman; he used to be elected by adult male franchise, irrespective of clan affiliation. This perhaps is the reason why, till this day, women are not interested in politics or any administrative position (in spite of the society being matrilineal with no social discrimination against women). The Rangbah used to run the village according to traditional laws, apart from the rules and regulations made by the Durbar or the Assembly. Health, water supply, sanitation, roads, education, etc. used to be in the agenda of the Durbar and the Rangbah used to be particularly responsible for the setting up of those amenities for the village people. The Durbar used to have the power of making laws and the village headman used to perform the dual function of a magistrate and a police officer. He was allowed to perform religious rituals in case of the absence of the village priest. He had to supervise the payment of tribute to the Syiem by the village community. He had to be obedient to the Syiem because his election had to be endorsed by the latter. He had to refer the unsolved cases to the higher political authorities. It is not mentioned clearly who exactly was the "higher political authority" when the Syiem is the "supreme political authority."

Issues of inter-village interests or conflicts naturally could not be solved by the Durbar or the village Syiem; those had to be referred to the "Raid," which was a political unit comprising a number of Khasi villages for the purposes of social control and harmonious civil and judicial administration. The head of a Raid was elected and known as "Basan," "Lyngdoh" or "Sirdar" in various Raids. The disputes that could not be settled at the Raid level, particularly the cases involving life imprisonment or death, used to go back to the Syiem! And, interestingly, all the Raid officials were appointed by the Syiem and were subordinate to him. The Syiem, along with his officials, used to rule the Khasi States under the overall supervision of "Durbar Hima" or the State Assembly—the supreme authority in the Khasi political system. The elders of the villages used to be usually present in the Durbar Hima. The "Bakhraws" or the noblemen used to choose the Syiem;

the post generally used to be hereditary—though not necessarily. As mentioned earlier, the Syiem performed all the duties, viz. administrative, military, religious, ceremonial and judicial functions in consultation with the members of the Durbar, Durbar Myntri or Durbar Hima. There was no land revenue and even the Syiem had no power to confiscate public or clan property since it was not he who owned the land, but the clans, the villages and the individuals owned. The main source of income of the State were the crown or raj lands, "pynsuk" or state subscription, market toll or "khrong," judicial fines and registration fees, etc. The three-tier hierarchy of the Khasi political system was thus, interdependent & interlinked with each other in such a way that the relative autonomy was granted at every sphere; as a result, the legitimacy of the system was not questioned. Since at every level, the Durbar was much more powerful than the institutional head, the will of the people was always upheld over the individual interests.

Unlike the Jaintia and Garo Hills the Khasi States were not annexed to British India. In December 1947 the Khasi States joined the Indian Union and got judicial, administrative and legislative powers. Prior to the commencement of the Constitution of India in 1950, the administration in Khasi, Jaintia and Garo Hills remained, as before, under the charge of the Deputy Commissioners as Political Officers under the government of Assam. The area was brought under the Sixth Schedule under the Bordoloi Committee Report; this resulted in the formation of Autonomous District Council in 1952. As a result, the offices of the Syiem, Doloi & Nokma in Khasi, Jaintia and Garo Hills respectively turned into subordinate officials of the respective district councils. The District Councils used to set up (i) the village courts, (ii) the subordinate and additional subordinate district council courts and (iii) the District Council Court. At the village level, Doli, Nokma, Basan, Lyngdoh, Lyngskor, Laskar or the village headman holds the post of the Chairman of the village courts. The offices in the traditional political systems are integrated with the new judicial arrangements under District Councils. These have, as mentioned earlier, wide-ranging legislative powers covering all aspects of material and cultural life of the people; in the socio-political field the role and functions of the traditional political institutions are well-defined. But, now those have been made accountable to the Constitutional bodies. But, the laws, in no way, affect the traditional tribal political ethos & the village level powers though, have been greatly reduced. Panchayati Raj, on the other hand, proposes to give wide-ranging roles to the village level institutions and that has proved greatly beneficial.

C

When the North-eastern Re-organisation Act of 1971 came into effect in 1972, a full-fledged State of Meghalaya came into existence. The Act had effect on a certain paragraph of the Sixth Schedule; Para 12A clearly states that the State government and the District Councils make laws on the same subject though that made by the State prevails. This paragraph has been agitating the minds and the thoughts of the people of Meghalaya as well as of the political leaders; Hill State People's Democratic Party has been demanding the deletion of this Para. The other regional political parties like Hill People's Union and Public Demands Implementation Convention have gone on pressing for years with this demand. They call this Para "discriminatory" as the laws of the State government over-ride the laws made by the Autonomous District Councils even in matters allotted to the latter by the Constitution; the District Councils and the State government are supposed to be having powers of equal weight. The State government feels that if Para 12A is allowed in its true spirit then its powers get diluted. In 1988-89 a Commission of Inquiry was formed under the Chairmanship of Justice S. K. Dutta of Gauhati High Court; it recommended the deletion of this highly controversial Para. It pointed out the difficulties that the Autonomous District Councils were facing.

D

Women in Meghalaya enjoy social and economic freedoms but, politics and administration are considered men's domain; traditionally women are not allowed to attend Darbar and they themselves are not interested in politics in most of the States of the North-east. But, women are allowed to give views and suggestions on various issues that affect them and their society and they do that quite often.

A number of women's organisations were formed since ages before the creation of Meghalaya; one of the oldest was Mothers' Union formed in 1941 at Tura in the Garo Hills. This organisation has played an important role in bringing about radical changes in the socio-economic lives of the Garos. The oldest voluntary welfare organisation in the Khasi and the Jaintia Hills, formed in 1947, continues to work effectively for the uplift of the women and the society in general. Another premier women's organisation, formed in 1979, is concerned with the protection of the tribal lands, trade, foreigners' issues, etc.

The first general election of independent India was held in 1952 and there were 6 women of this region who had filed their nominations; of these 4 were from the plains of Assam and 2 from the hills of the Khasis and the Jaintias. There was no reservation of seats for women and no woman could win; as mentioned earlier, neither women were encouraged to politics (not even the village level politics), nor were they themselves interested. Ms. Bonniley Khongmen was selected by the Congress Party to contest for Lok Sabha and she was the first woman elected from Assam. (That time there was no separate Meghalaya.) She had been an MLA of Assam from 1946 to 1952 and had been elected Deputy Speaker in 1952.

After the creation of Meghalaya in 1972, a number of women came forward to contest in the first election of the Meghalaya Legislative Assembly. Four women contested from the Khasi & Jaintia Hills and two from the Garo Hills and none of them won except Ms. Percylina Marak from the Garo Hills. In the next election of 1978 again no woman won from the Khasi Hills and only Ms. Mirium D. Shira came out successful again from the Garo Hills. In 1983, as many as 8 women contested from the Khasi Hills and nobody could win. Even Ms. Shira from the Garo Hills got defeated and the Meghalaya Assembly was totally a male affair. Such political behaviour on the part of the voters is surprising because socially women are not discriminated against and they enjoy a lot of socio-economic freedoms, the society being matrilineal. In 1988, only Ms. Maysalin War got elected and she was inducted into the Ministry. In 1993, Ms. Roshan Warjri got elected to the Assembly. I found a single woman MLA (who became a Minister also) when I was interviewing the MLAs and a few Ministers in November, 2012—just a few months before the next Assembly election.

In the autonomous District Councils there were a number of women representatives, who were either elected or nominated; Ms. Larium Shullai was nominated to the first Autonomous Khasi District Council in 1952-57. Dr (Mrs) K. Rymbai was nominated to the Jaintia Hills Autonomous District Council. Ms. L. B. Lamin & Ms. E. Syiem won the elections in 1972 and Ms. M. War won a seat in the Khasi Autonomous District Council on Congress (I) ticket in the same year. In the first election to the Garo Hills Autonomous District Council in 1952 there were two women members in a House of 24. In 1957 Ms. S. W. Momin contested against two male candidates and yet won and Ms. R. Marak was nominated by the Governor. In 1964 Ms. E. Marak contested, but lost; so Ms. B. Sangma was nominated by the Governor. In 1972 also the same thing happened—two women contested and lost in spite of the fact that women voters turn out in large numbers—sometimes, higher in number than men! So, two women were nominated because of the belief that if there is no woman in the policy-making level, women's interests cannot be taken care of. On the other side, we know that traditionally women are not allowed to attend the Durbar because of the tribal belief "it will be the doomsday if the hen crows."

Interestingly, but there used to be female rulers in the folklores and thus one tends to believe that women were not debarred from taking part in political matters! The story of Ka Latympang is well-known—she was a wise and powerful ruler of a small State of Manar in Jaintia Hills. Yet, in spite of rapid changes towards modernisation going on in these societies, politics is considered a male prerogative and most of the women's organisations begin their Constitution by saying that these are solely social organisations and therefore, do not get involved in politics of any kind. In Meghalaya a strong women's movement is needed for asserting their rights which should be equality with men in every field.

E

Meghalaya has only two Lok Sabha seats, viz. Shillong and Tura. As we know Shillong is inhabited by the Khasis and the Jaintias and has a larger population than Tura, which is inhabited mostly by the Garos. The Khasis like to speak in their own language while the Garos are mostly English-speaking. The Khasis and the Jaintias seem to understand each other's languages well and it is not easy to differentiate between the two. A great many cultural and ritualistic differences exist between the Khasis and the Garos even though both the communities are matrilineal. Geographically also they are quite distant; one has to travel through Assam for going from Shillong to Tura (the headquarters of the Garo Hills). Besides, their traditional political systems differ a lot.

Meghalaya has favoured neither the Right (Sangh Parivar) nor the Left politics. The NCP had some support due to the personal charisma of the former Speaker of Lok Sabha, Shri P. A. Sangma. The party, though was in coalition with Congress at the Centre, formed the Opposition in this State; but after the 2013 Assembly election it has joined Congress, which performed extremely well in this election and fell short of absolute majority only by two seats! Mr. Sangma's political journey was interesting—from Congress to NCP, to BJP, to Trinamul Congress and finally back to NCP. He had won this seat nine times. He had resigned from Tura Lok Sabha seat in 2008 in order to contest for a seat in the Assembly; the Lok Sabha seat came to his daughter Agatha Sangma. Congress tried its best to bring in Debora Marak, but to no avail. The campaigns were marked by vitriolic personal attacks apart from appeals to sectarian interests.

The 15th Lok Sabha election was conducted in Meghalaya while President's rule was in force. Congress, obviously, supported it while other parties, led by NCP, vehemently condemned it and dubbed it as the Central government's ploy to bring Congress back to power. There was a proposal for a single candidate from all non-Congress political parties to defeat Congress; but, ultimately, the pathos for Coalition took over all other considerations; nothing perhaps, can upset the love for coalition politics in Meghalaya—exactly opposite of the continuous one-party rule in Sikkim! But, the pattern has changed drastically after this Lok Sabha election; there is one-party rule in Meghalaya now and an Opposition party in Sikkim!

Altogether there were seven candidates from the Shillong constituency and 4 from the Tura constituency. The State has four unreserved seats–three from Shillong and one from Tura. In Tura NCP scored more in 16 Assembly segments and Congress in 8 out of a total 24 constituencies. Only 47 per cent voters had turned up in 2004 elections; over 62 per cent voters came out to vote in the next election in Shillong while in Tura the percentage of voters were 61 and 68 percent respectively. The collapse of the MPA ministry, change of political allegiance of some MLAs, imposition of President's rule and subsequent claims and counter-claims of the political parties for numerical majority in the Assembly sparked up keen political interests among people/voters and may have helped increase in the turnout. Since election took place during the President's rule, the voters' opinions on the righteousness of the President's rule were taken during the election rallies. More than 40 per cent of the voters expressed strong resentment against the President's rule and found it most unjustified. But, more than 36 per cent expressed no opinion at all. Opinion polls were taken on the possibility of the bifurcation of the State since the Garos felt that their interests were not getting adequate attention the capital of the State being Khasi-dominated Shillong. That time only a small minority wanted a ban on the residence of the outsiders in the States of the three major tribes. Now, it is a strong movement and the political parties are demanding the law of "inner-line permit" (the way it is in Arunachal Pradesh) to stop the non-tribal outsiders from marrying the tribal girls/women and getting land in the region (since under matrilineal system the lands belong to the women only).

F

In 2003, the major players were two all-India parties—the Congress with 22 seats and the Nationalist Congress Party with 14. The largest regional Party was UDP with only nine seats and all other regional parties put together won only seven seats; this was the first time that the regional parties were reduced to such a minority though none of the national parties could win absolute majority in an Assembly of 60 members. Though highest vote-catcher, the INC, got three seats less than what it had got in 1998. The BJP got one seat less; it had got three seats in 1998 and was hoping to increase its tally. UDP, one of the formidable parties in the last Assembly, won only nine seats—a loss of 11! This happened because Meghalaya Democratic Party got formed by the dissidents from UDP though MDP could win only four seats. Hill State People's Democratic Party, a regionalist party with strong pro-Khasi sentiments, managed only two seats—one seat less than in the earlier election. It is difficult to understand why a regionalist party should perform so badly in a State where regional sentiments are very high! It appears that the voters care more for the person and the personality of the vote-seeking candidate than for the manifesto or ideology of the Party he belongs to. KH National Awakening Movement, a party of the students' unions (like the AGP formed out of All Assam Students' Union of Assam) could not tickle the tribal sentiments much and won only two seats only.

Ever since the State of Meghalaya was carved out of the composite State of Assam in 1972, unstable coalition and governmental instability have been the rule rather than exception. Barring the very first election, the electorate has never given a clear verdict. (It did again in 2013 election with Congress getting only two seats short of absolute majority.) In the very first election, All Party Hill Leaders' Conference (APHLC) had won as many as 39 seats in an Assembly of 60. The Congress and the HSPDP had won 12 and eight seats respectively. One seat had gone to an Independent. But, in 1976 the APHLC split under the pressure of national politics following Emergency in 1975. Politics of defection, unstable coalitions and repeated fractured verdicts started in Meghalaya and except in 2003, national parties could never win a substantial number of seats here and Meghalaya politics remained dominated by regional forces. The regional movements were led by newly emerging educated elites; formidable social forces like feudal lords or bourgeoisie were absent and the power of the working class had not yet evolved. Class relations have not been able to displace clan relations and in the absence of industrialisation, proletariat also had not emerged. The British had not much interfered with their social life except for introducing Christianity and Western education. As a result, kinship ties and tribal loyalties often over-ride ideological or party loyalties and at times, even individual interests.

Clan divisions within each of these small tribes do not affect electoral politics because most of the clans are too small in size and the relatively bigger ones are no longer living together. Other factors that erode the influence of the clans are the larger identity of the tribes, now often called "nationality" by the tribal leaders. The influence of the Christian organisations cannot be ignored. The tribal or nationality identity and religious identity claim supra-clan loyalties. Of the seven national elections only two—in 1972 and 1988—their regional parties could win 50 per cent or more seats. The performance of the regional parties seems to have suffered a sharp decline in these areas from 1990s. In the 1993, 1998 and 2003 elections the regional parties could win only two, three and two seats respectively out of the contested 24 seats. This is a sharp contrast to the performance of the regional forces in 1972. That time APHLC had won 17 out of 24 seats and INC had won only five. W. A. Sangma, a Garo leader, had become the Chief Minister in 1972 and surprisingly, it was he who split the Party in 1976 in order to merge with Congress. The move was bitterly opposed by most of the senior Khasi leaders of the APHLC. The North-eastern experience of democratic mobilisation clearly suggests that when the educated elite or the educated middle class of a less developed community begins to emerge, it tries to benefit by remaining close to more powerful and hegemonic forces. But, when it gains strength, it uses regional or ethnic politics as a bargaining strategy. The Khasi Hills has the largest concentration of higher level educational institutions and in 2001 the Khasi-Jaintia Hills had a literacy rate of 66.6 per cent while the Garo Hills had 55.85 per cent only. Yet, the Garos speak mostly in English and the Khasis prefer talking in their own language.

The elite understands that one of the ways of capturing the resources of the State is by mobilising people on ethnic lines to influence the number games of democratic politics. The Khasi-Jaintia ethnic politics seems to have become more and more strident over the years particularly from the mid-1980s. This is clearly reflected in the aggressive ethnic politics of the students and the youth

The Garo educated elite is still in its formative stage and is yet to find it necessary or opportune to come out of the shadow of national political forces and to vigorously pursue regional politics based on Garo identity. That is why the elections in the Garo Hills, as distinct from those in the Khasi Hills, remain dominated by national parties. In the 2003 election, 19 out of 24 seats were occupied by national parties. Because of such diametrically opposite political behaviours of the Garo and the Khasi voters, the regional-national divide in Meghalaya politics is increasingly becoming a tribal divide. During the dark days of Emergency, the leadership in power could not survive without merging with the Congress.

In 1998 BJP also had contested but, not in the next election; but the INC did not score as much as it had scored along with BJP in 1998 viz. 3778 votes. The BJP votes, apart from a big chunk from the Congress, had gone to the regional parties. INC scored only 519 in 2003! The electorate seemed to vote for the person and not for the Party—exactly opposite of what happened in Sikkim for more than one decade. The only thing that matters in election is political power. Pursuit of power as ideology weighs heavily in Meghalaya politics particularly amongst the educated elite and their organisations. The results of 2003 Assembly elections confirm that national issues or ideological considerations are of little importance in Meghalaya politics; election manifestoes are of little significance here.

CHAPTER X

Meghalaya: Pattern of Coalition Governments

The present Meghalaya, consisting of the Khasi-Jaintia Hills and the Garo Hills of Assam State had its first taste of coalition politics as a part of Assam State only. The process had started during the colonial rule in India when Rev. Nicholas Roy participated in the various coalitions of that period (1920-46), and during the composite period of Assam when EITU members joined the Chaliha ministry. Captain W. A. Sangma and EITU leaders joined the Congress-led coalition on May 27, 1958 as Cabinet Ministers; but, this coalition lasted for only two and a half years.

The ministry of the Meghalaya Provisional Legislative Assembly was a grand coalition where there was no opposition party at all. Meanwhile, the Autonomous State of Meghalaya was upgraded to a full-fledged State of Meghalaya separately from Assam with a Legislative Assembly of its own under the North-eastern Areas (Reorganisation) Act of 1971. The first general election to the 60-member Meghalaya Legislative Assembly was held on March 9, 1972 and there were pre-poll alliances between APHLC and the Congress Party in the Garo Hills—18 APHLC and 6 Congress. And, in the Khasi Hills there were 25 APHLC and four Congress MLAs.

Strangely, there was no pre-poll alliance in Jaintia Hills and the 6 seats were free for all. The Congress here fought against APHLC. The results of the election were against Congress—APHLC got 39 seats and Congress got only 11. The other 10 seats went to the independents; eight of them belonged to Hill State People's Democratic Party or HSPDP.

When APHLC, led by Capt. Sangma, merged with Congress and formed the single-party ministry of the Congress in Meghalaya for the first time in Nov. 22, 1976, the other APHLC group, led by B. B. Lyngdoh, had to sit in Opposition like HSPDP. Some HSPDP members had defected to the APHLC of Sangma. This coincidentally, happened when Congress Party had split at the Centre.

On March 10, 1978, Meghalaya United Legislative Party coalition ministry was sworn in with D. D. Pugh (APHLC) as Chief Minister. The other coalition partner was PDIC. As it was a three-Party coalition, it was popularly known as "Three-Flag government." The Opposition under the Congress-led coalition vizi the Meghalaya United Legislature Front (MULF) came to be known as the "Lottery Government."

The third general election to the Meghalaya Legislative Assembly was held on February 17, 1983. This time again, no party could attain majority; the following are the number of seats the various parties got—Congress 26, APHLC 15, HSPDP 16, PDIC two and three independents. They formed the Meghalaya United Parliamentary Party. But, the leadership issue was the main bone of contention. Ultimately, the Chief Minister was Lyngdoh from APHLC and the Deputy Chief Minister from HSPDP. Congress got no say in spite of becoming the single largest party. There were too many differences and defections; so the ministry lasted for only 29 days!

After the fall of the MUPP coalition ministry, another coalition ministry, called Meghalaya Democratic Front, got formed. This time the Chief Minister was Capt. Sangma from Congress. This coalition was successful and lasted till 1988. If the regional parties could merge together thinking of the greater interest of the people and the State, they could have formed a successful non-Congress ministry. So once again Congress headed the coalition, named United Meghalaya Parliamentary Forum, with P. A. Sangma of the Congress as the Chief Minister. The Deputy Chief Minister Lapang was also from Congress. The UMPF was a three-party coalition of Congress, HPU and APHLC where Congress had the highest number of seats. This ruling coalition had 35 seats in a House of 59 seats. The Opposition coalition, led by Khongyir, was known as United Democratic Front. A no-confidence motion was moved quite right in the beginning but, was defeated.

The MUPP was in a precarious position when during the trial of strength in the House, the Speaker had disqualified 5 members thereby turning MUPP into Minority. The President's Rule thus got imposed in Meghalaya in October, 1991. The MUPP challenged the action of the Speaker in the Court of Law. Its contention was that it had not become a Minority even after five members left the coalition. In the meanwhile Congress (I) proved its majority of 32 members and was called upon to assume power on the revocation of the President's rule. This Congress (I)–led UMPF coalition government was led by Shri D. D. Lapang as the Chief Minister. Mr. P. A. Sangma had by then got elected to the Lok Sabha during the 1991 general election. During 1993 elections Meghalaya once again could not elect any majority party and a coalition ministry, led by Shri S. C. Marak, formed the government. There was a split in APHLC and HSPDP. A few independents supported the ruling coalition. Despite a small margin of majority, this government, called Meghalaya United Front, could complete its term of office. This was the only coalition which could complete its full term in 25 long years of Meghalaya's coalition history.

The next coalition ministry in the 6th Assembly called the United Democratic Front under the leadership of Shri B. B.

Lyngdoh of UDP, assumed office in March, 1998; there were 20 UDP, 3 BJP, 3 HSPDP, 1 GNC and 4 independents.

The 1998 General Election in Meghalaya had produced the following special features—

1. The Congress (I)-led coalition ministry of Marak lasted only 12 days—the shortest possible for any government in the State or at the Centre. (The first Vajpayee ministry at the Centre was for 13 days only.)
2. Formation of three coalitions within a period of exactly five months—the highest number in the history of coalition history.
3. An oversized coalition ministry of 35 Ministers, including the Chief Minister, in a House of 60 members; this was biggest ever in 25 years.

Meghalaya, perhaps, is the only State in the world—not merely in India—which has the unique distinction of having coalition governments continuously. The other distinction is that all MLAs become Ministers some time or the other. The multifarious parties have the only goal of coming to power unlike some of the stable national or regional parties, which have some ideology or the other. The recently concluded Assembly elections gave as many as 29 seats to Congress—only two short of absolute majority. The next highest number was of the independents and the present government is of Congress with the support of a few independents.

CHAPTER XI

Meghalaya: Political Behaviour of the People

A

I spoke to various strata of people—the students, the teachers, shopkeepers, cab drivers, restaurant and bookshop owners, staff of the North-eastern Hill University library and the ICSSR library (situated in NEHU campus) and so on and so forth to get an idea of the political consciousness and electoral behaviour of the people of Meghalaya. Yes, I talked to quite a few MLAs also to get the other side of the picture. What struck me most was the absence of a powerful political consciousness among the electorate or an ideology with the parties. They voted for the candidate (judging him/her as a human being with the required leadership capabilities) thus, ignoring the political party he or she belongs to. The various political parties—mostly regional—do not have an ideology or a national agenda; their only motto or aim is to come to power. I don't mean by this that the national political parties are not keen for power; they, of course, are. Otherwise, what is the purpose of an election? But, they have an ideology or at least a manifesto by which the voters more or less understand what kind of government with what kind of goal they will get if the party they have voted for comes to power. The voters can clearly differentiate between the BJP and the Left Parties or these from the Congress. At the national level the regional parties like TDP, AIDMK, RJD, TMC or BSP (to take a few examples) have an agenda and a goal. For example, when a voter votes for BSP, he/she definitely wants power to and welfare of the Dalits and the other under-privileged; or when he/she votes for TDP, he/she wants power for the Telugu people of Seemandhra. As we know, the Telugus now have two States and they are, in all matters, at loggerheads.

In Meghalaya, on the contrary, the voter votes without realising what benefit he/she will get from electing the candidate of his/her choice; the various parties, forming the coalition, decide on the policies for the people or for development only after they come to power after an election. Such a coalition is quite different from the coalition government at the Centre; there the major party, i.e. the party with single highest votes, chalks out the policies and has an overwhelming say. The UPA I & II was a coalition of many national and a few regional parties, led by Congress; the Left Front government in West Bengal also was a coalition of radical-minded parties, led by CPI(M) (the party with the highest number of votes) and there is the coalition government of NDA now at the Centre even though BJP scored not just absolute majority, but two-thirds majority all by itself.

B

Long before the advent of the British, the indigenous people in the hills of North-east India had organised themselves under the political systems of their own which had been the natural outcome of their social evolution. Two distinctly different types of systems of governance had been evolved in the hills viz. (1) democratic system in the clan-based village societies controlled by the village councils and village headmen and (2) autocratic system of chieftainship controlled by the clan or village chiefs. The extent of power and authority of these traditional political institutions in relation to their people used to vary from tribe to tribe. While in certain communities these traditional institutions were well-organised and well-structured, in some cases they led to the formation of miniature States; in some communities these institutions were loosely organised without any central authority. Unlike the Khasis and the Jaintias, the Garo system of governance of clan-based village community seemed to be much immature. Every Khasi village had its local assembly known as Durbar Shnong presided by the village headman, who used to be elected by the male members of the village irrespective of their clan affiliation. The headman used to follow the traditional customs and traditions apart from the rules, legislated by the Durbar. The women in Meghalaya enjoy social and economic freedom, but politics and administration are considered men's domain; women were not allowed to attend Durbar. But, after India's independence there were a good number of women representatives in the Durbar (which is like the Panchayat), who were either elected or nominated. Dr. (Mrs) K. Lymbai was nominated to the Jaintia Hills Autonomous District Council. Ms. L. B. Lamin and Ms. E. Syeim contested and won election in 1972 after Meghalaya State was formed. In 1984, Ms. M. War contested and won a seat in Khasi Autonomous District Council on a Congress (I) ticket.

Unlike the Jaintia and Garo Hills, the Khasi Hills were not annexed to British India; yet these were brought under the Garo and Jaintia areas for administrative purposes. Prior to the commencement of the Constitution of India in 1950, the administration in the Khasi, the Garo and the Jaintia Hills were under the charge of the Deputy Commissioners (as political officers) under the Governor of Assam.

The Meghalaya experience is exactly opposite of Sikkim's where a single party kept winning all the seats and there was no Opposition in the Assembly and this was happening in election after election, for decades! The other parties, not even the nationally important party Congress, had no influence in the hearts of the voters; the Sikkim Democratic Front ruled supreme after every election because the people used to be fully satisfied with the pro-people performance of the Chief Minister Dr Pawan Chamling. It appears, on the contrary, that in Meghalaya the voters are always experimenting with their elected representatives. In the absence of a clear manifesto or an ideology or programme from the political parties, the voters are in the most indecisive position; they fail to understand what are the substantial differences among Congress, APHLC or HSPDP, for example. In the national scene, on the contrary, the voter knows very clearly the path the Indian politics or economy will take under the NDA coalition, which has now got power in place of the UPA coalition.

C

We all know that Meghalaya is an overwhelmingly Christian country, though tribal tradition and rituals are very powerful and observed with fervour. Animism is also practised. The role of the Church therefore, is very important. They, that is why, do not usually accept the marriage of a tribal girl with a non-tribal, particularly if the groom is a non-Catholic. Recently, there was an agitation, lasting over weeks for the introduction of "inner-line permit" (like in Arunachal Pradesh) for Meghalaya. The complaint is that the outsiders are not only marrying away the tribal girls, but are also buying/ occupying lands. (We know that in a matrilineal society the land and other property belong to the women and particularly to the youngest daughter.) But the highly educated or those working in other parts of India or the world are generally broadminded and secular and do not mind marrying outside the tribe. The opposition, if any, from the community is not that rigid, unlike that from the caste Hindus or the Muslims or the Tibetans of Arunachal Pradesh.

Women, like in most tribal societies—whether of the plains or the Himalayan regions—are more active than men; they manage both property and household though the ultimate decision with regard to property rests with the maternal uncle of the owner.

D

People in general are not much politically conscious; the reason can be either of the two. First, the sundry regional parties do not have any ideology or firm agenda; secondly, it may be that the parties are not much bothered about well-defined agenda because it does not much matter to the electorate. Curiously, a voter may vote for one party in one election and for some other in the next election. Not only that; a voter need not necessarily vote for the same party in the Assembly and the Parliament elections. Such behaviour cannot be explained by anti-incumbency factor, which happens without exception in Himachal Pradesh and very often in the States of the Hindi-Hindu belt of India. The reason is nothing-else except the fact that no party has permanent and strong ideology or agenda— unlike the BJP, or the Communist Parties.

My most disappointing experience was with the students and the most satisfactory with the teachers. The latter gave very thought out explanations of the political behaviours of the people in general. They felt that the tribal and Catholic sentiments and rituals of the people were overpowering. Besides, the tribes are geographically too distant from mainland India; so, the influences of the national parties are minimal. Neither communalism, nor secularism, nor socialism or Marxism matters to them very much unlike the tribes of the central India or southern India. All that mattered to them were their tribal identity, language, religion, rituals and customs. There is a feeling among the residents of West Khasi region that they are being neglected; so, they vote for the local parties only. The other categories of people I interviewed were most indifferent and were avoiding questions.

The other reason why the people of Meghalaya are apolitical is that there is no leader with mass appeal and there is a Khasi-Garo divide and the Garos feel neglected. The reason may be that the Garo region is difficult to reach from the State capital Shillong; one has to travel through Assam to reach Tura, the headquarters of the Garo Hills. Besides, all developmental activities take place in and around Shillong. It has a huge income from tourism also. That is why, we hear of Garo upsurge every now and then.

The voters are interested in programme of action though it is very difficult to satisfy so many varied ethnic groups (there are sub-tribes within the three major tribes and each one of them has its own dialect even though the major dialects are Khasi and Garo; the Jaintias too, speak Khasi).

According to some MLAs of the Meghalaya Assembly, the voters are not interested in Party manifestos; they are interested in those candidates who appear to be willing to or capable of tackling local and minute issues—the issues may be only of water and the availability of medicines in the hospitals or Health Centres or the inclusion of the history of the Khasis in the school text books. Therefore, a Party has to take up different issues in different localities or constituencies (many localities or villages may constitute a constituency); there is no scope for a common Manifesto for the entire State whereas the national parties have the same manifesto for all States of India, the local issues may be taken up though in a particular/ regional election meeting. They may even give a twist to a few sections of the common manifesto; for example, the Congress Party may attack Modi and the BJP in Gujarat and Madhya Pradesh but Akhilesh Yadav in Uttar Pradesh; the Communist parties too, will change their targets in different States of India. The local issues, which vary immensely from State to State, will get different levels of importance depending on the State; in UP it may be eradication of poverty and illiteracy whereas in West Bengal it may be annihilation of the CPI (M) because of what it did in Nandigram and Singur. In the current election, of course, the issues are more or less the same in every State, viz. pro-Modi or anti-Modi though large-scale corruption at all levels of the society and the administration is perhaps, the most eye-opening issue.

Another curious aspect of the voters of Meghalaya is that they may care for the wealth and education of the candidate and not bother about his commitment or service to the people! They perhaps, know too well that all vote-seekers try to show off their commitment for the people before the election and forget once they win! This is quite unlike in Sikkim where the MLAs spend most of their time in their constituencies and very little in the capital Gangtok. Even the Ministers are found going to their constituencies every now and then. In both the States, therefore, the voters care more for the Assembly election than the elections to the Parliament since the MPs have to spend most of their time in the national capital New Delhi and cannot possibly pay much attention to specific local problems.

There are too many regional political parties with issue-based agenda like disputes on the boundaries with Assam, exploitation of the environment, coal-mining and secret export to Bangladesh with whom Meghalaya shares a long border; many Bangladeshis live incognito in this State like in Assam and Tripura. Referendum, that is why, would have been a better election option for Meghalaya it seems.

The electorate does not pay much heed to the election campaigns because the voters choose a particular person, to whichever party he may belong to! P. A. Sangma, for example, gets votes even after forming a new party and the vote-seekers change parties or form new parties at the drop of a hat; they know too well that the voters do not vote for the party, but for the candidate they like. Anti-incumbency is not too common because no party gets majority. But, participation in election, i.e. casting of votes is very high. There is no family pressure for a particular party or a particular candidate, very much unlike in the States where the Party matters and the candidate matters rarely. The women and the first time voters are usually tutored and pressurised by the male elders of a family who may get influenced by the manifesto and the campaigning of a particular party or—more often than not—may have been bribed by money, things of necessity and/or liquor.

E

The educated, highly qualified people of Meghalaya, who work outside Meghalaya in major cities of India, vote for a Congress candidate even if he is very corrupt because they find the candidates from the regional parties very narrow-minded, self-centred and not less corrupt. They did not even support Mr. P. A. Sangma for the post of the President of India because they found him corrupt! They found Shri Pranab Mukherjee competent as a Minister in the Centre. They believe that money granted from the Centre is not less and is enough to develop the infra-structure like roads (which are always in bad condition due to excessive rainfall); it is the State government which does not use the money honestly and most of it goes into the pockets of the ministers and the government officers. Their general knowledge and knowledge about the developmental activities in the other parts of India and the world are good and they are smart enough to discuss any and everything in the world. Such people are modern-minded like the youth from other parts of India and they are even gender-sensitive and believe in equal rights of the women. The election/political scenario in Meghalaya and Sikkim (both tribal States) are very disappointing because women are not encouraged in politics—not even in Panchayat politics! It is sad that in a matrilineal society women have neither social, nor economic nor political power; the property is owned by women but, the decision-taker is a man—the brother of the mother (even though the youngest daughter inherits from her mother).

I had tried to confine my questions to the MLAs and the MPs by preparing a questionnaire; but, the interview or discussion did not remain limited to the answer of those questions. The following is the questionnaire though the answers did not follow strictly.

F

1. What is your constituency and which Party you belong to?
2. Since when are you an MLA/MP? Did you always contest from the same Party and how many times you lost in between?
3. What are the important issues that you address while campaigning and after getting elected?
4. What is your opinion about coalition government? Is it good and necessary for the kind of politics that prevails in the State?
5. Which coalition you belong to—the ruling or the Opposition? Does your affiliation change with every election? Any insight into why the State has coalition government as well as coalition Opposition always? Why are the voters so undecided about the merit of a particular party? Is it because the tribal and the sub-tribal interests always clash?
6. Are you happy the way the present government (I had interviewed them a little before the Assembly election there) is working? Were you happy with the earlier governments or not?
7. What is your prediction about the coming election? What will be your agenda or stress during your campaigning? Will you like a radical change and want single-party rule or a national party rule?

As I mentioned above, women are not politically conscious and the voters or the parties too, do not much care for women politicians; thus, there is only one woman MLA, Ms. Ampareen Lyngdoh and no woman MP at all. I had asked the following questions, in addition to the questions above, to this lady MLA—

1. Do you face any problem because you are a woman, and
2. Why political awareness is low amongst women in an otherwise egalitarian society?

G

The following is a summary of the answers I received from various Ministers and MLAs.

1. Political awareness is high and that is why the voters are not satisfied with any particular party; their expectations are very high. Besides, the voters fear autocracy if only one party comes to power.
2. Literacy and level of education too, is very high; that is why, no single manifesto or agenda can satisfy the voters. The illiterates have a high level of common sense.
3. Less than 30 lakhs is the population of the State and each constituency has about 20 to 25 thousands of voters. There can be coalition of Congress with NCP and BJP even! The most non-communal tribal people even vote for BJP! This party has a very different face in the North-east; their communal, anti-Minority face is covered behind the mask of promise of economic progress and development. (Let me point out that the present BJP-led government in the Centre till now is following policy.)
4. Garos are found in West Khasi Hills and even in Bangladesh, though we find Garos returning from Bangladesh also. They are a restive community compared to the Khasis and the Jaintias; there are sometimes, demands for separate Garo State, but the movement is not powerful enough.
5. There are District Councils like the Panchayats in the rest of India; only the tribes are allowed to vote—not the outsiders. We all know that recently there was a political agitation seeking the ban on the buying of

land by the non-tribals (outsiders or immigrants) and marrying tribal girls because lands belong to the youngest daughters in the clans and the communities; an individual tribal also can buy land but not an outsider. There is a "Durbar" system for the members of a particular tribe in a particular area. There is also demand that 95 per cent of the government jobs should be for the tribes and only 5 per cent can go to the outsiders.

6. Agriculture is quite developed in the Khasi Hills. Men and women work together though I am not sure if the women are allowed to plough the lands. Women prefer being full-time housewives and work in the agricultural and horticultural sectors as helpers. But, in Shillong and Tura I found many women in offices and in teaching though much less in proportion to their population. Unlike most of the tribal people both in the Himalayan and the plains regions, Khasi men are as hard-working and smart as women.
7. According to some MLAs, there is no difference between APHLC and UDP or any other regional party. Congress, to them, is cosmopolitan and has money and muscle-power like in the mainland. Its style of functioning is generally criticised by the simple-hearted hill people. Congress presence is felt a bit in the Jaintia Hills areas.
8. Money from the Centre is much less than needed for the building of the infrastructure; yet, all the money is not spent for people's good; some go to the pockets of the powerful and the rest goes back as unspent. The Centre sends 90 per cent of the total budget-money; the State has to bear only 10 per cent of the expenses.
9. There are 20 odd rivers flowing into Bangladesh from Meghalaya; as a result, the former gets flooded while the latter suffers lack of enough water for agriculture.
10. There is general grudge amongst the educated voters the teachers, the doctors, the nurses, etc. that hardly

anything is done for them—Only the very poor get some benefit from the governmental schemes. There are working Public Health Centres, but hardly any government hospitals worth its name. There are many missionary schools also, but giving education only up to class VIII! This kind of grudge of the middle class is found in so many other States also. There are schools for the mentally retarded also but, nothing of high standard for the children of the educated middle class!

11. Like in almost all the States of mainland India, the poor and the illiterates are offered cash and kind before the election; corruption is no less.
12. According to some, the present Chief Minister (let me remind my readers that the interviews were conducted just a little before the February, 2013 election) is better than the earlier ones. The condition of roads, especially road connectivity to all the villages even in the remote areas, is an important demand of the people and the Chief Minister is paying attention to that and especially to the Guwahati-Shillong road. They believe that this bye-pass will cover 4 more districts.
13. Women, in general—both urban and rural—are not interested in politics though they sit in the Durbar and are, in general, more educated. There are discussions within the family about who to vote for; yet, political interest could not be created amongst the women! Ms. Ampareen Lyngdoh is the only woman MLA in the Assembly and it is next to impossible to implement 33 per cent reservation for women in the Panchayats. I could not get any answer to why so much of political disinterest among women in a society where women have almost equal socio-economic rights! Perhaps, oppression and ill-treatment by the males and the powerful make one politically aware and active so that he/she gets a platform for fighting for his/her rights. The same is the case with Sikkim and Arunachal

Pradesh even though there is patriarchy in the latter where land and property are owned by men only and they can have more than one wife; but, unlike in the patriarchal societies of the 'mainland' caste societies, men are not repressive or oppressive, there is no long list of "Don'ts" for women whereas even the Dalits and the non-Hindus are oppressive of their women in the non-tribal areas.

14. In most cases, the laws of Assam are followed in Meghalaya even after the latter got separated from Assam as a result of a powerful movement for autonomy by the tribes of the hills. To add fuel to the fire, the IPS and the IAS officers of Moghalaya are also mostly from the Assam cadre.
15. There is a demand from a few regional parties that the Assembly should sit for a much longer period and thus make separate laws for the people of Meghalaya and that the IPS and the IAS too, should be from Meghalaya cadre only. They also believe that only the graduates and the educated should become members of the Legislative Assembly and the Parliament. This kind of thinking is usually not found in the States outside the North-east; here a lot of importance is attached to education and the need for egalitarian societies.
16. Durbar elections are usually held through consensus; this shows the mental make-up of the tribes who have great faith in unity and peace and not in competition or fighting against each other. MLAs are found, more often than not, executing the decisions of the Durbars (which, let me repeat, are through consensus).
17. Unfortunately, like in the mainland, so many competent and committed persons do not get elected because they do not have the required amount of money or they do not get tickets from a party.
18. Ever since the Right to Information Act has come into existence, corruption has got a bit controlled and only

those candidates can win who do something for the people or their constituency.

19. There were 36 Khasi-Jaintia MLAs and 24 Garo MLAs before the election of February, 2013. The Khasis and the Jaintias are geographically contiguous and are regarded as very similar to each other culturally, linguistically, religiously and even politically. The Garos, every now and then, talk of separate land and political power, but the Jaintias never demand separation from the Khasis. They are the weakest tribe socio-politically; but, economically they are the richest as they own the coalfields in the Jawai area.
20. Garos feel neglected because of the physical distance from the capital Shillong and because they are less educated (62 per cent) than the Khasis (70 per cent); they do not even have satisfactory representation in the top administrative positions. The Tura campus of North-east Hill University is also neglected; a majority of the competent teachers do not like to leave Shillong and therefore, the serious and aspiring students have to come to the main campus in Shillong.
21. But, the Garos are politically more aware than the Khasis or the Jaintias; they choose their representatives carefully. They, for example, go on choosing P. A. Sangma whichever party he may contest from. They believe that Sangma gives the best leadership. But, they are not able to explain what exactly they mean by "best leadership!" They are not even sure about what all this most popular leader has done for them! They feel that he has represented Meghalaya and particularly the Garo community well by holding the very important post of the Speaker of the Lok Sabha and by contesting for the post of the President of India. This is the view of the Garos only and I could not get any objective view about the political awareness of the three major tribes of Meghalaya; all the tribes praise their own tribe and

blame the others for the economic backwardness of their State.

22. But, the grudge against the non-tribals/outsiders is found amongst all the three major tribes; they feel that their economic condition cannot improve because the major small-scale industries and the commercial avenues of income are in the hands of the outsiders. I have already mentioned above that there is a strong movement against the outsiders buying lands and marrying tribal girls; in a matrilineal society the land and property automatically go to the girl even if she marries an outsider. The tribes do not get too disturbed if a tribal man marries an "outsider" woman (that is why).
23. The tribes, in general, are exempted from paying tax; a sense of belonging is missing because the people of the mainland India, including the national leaders, do not regard them as part of India. The tribes, particularly of the North-east, are regarded as "they" and not as "we"; such a feeling exists with regard to the Kashmiri Muslims also. But, we get very upset when these "set-aside" people talk as "we Nagas and you Indians" or "we Khasis and you Indians" or "we Kashmiris and you Indians" etc., etc. The latest glaring example is the elections in 4 Hindi-speaking States and Mizoram last year. All discussions on the media and the worries of the politically conscious people and scholars were about Delhi, Rajastan, Madhya Pradesh and Chhatisgarh; seldom we heard of Mizoram! This obviously, is because the local politics of any of the North-eastern States do not affect the political scene of the 4 mainland States! Yet, the government of India gets terribly disturbed when the Chinese forces cross over to Arunachal Pradesh or when the Myanmarese refugees try to take shelter in the border-States of India!

24. In the Meghalaya Assembly before the 2013 election, the Khasis and the Jaintias had 36 seats while the Garos had 24. The Jaintias are politically the weakest, but are advanced economically because of the vast Jowai coal-fields. The Garos are less educated mainly because of their geographical location and distance from the capital Shillong. Sixty-two percent of the Garos are educated while the percentage is 70 amongst the Khasis (we do not have data about the Jaintias). The Garos do not even occupy top administrative positions even though they are politically more aware than the Khasis. The politics of geographical location plays a very significant role in Indian politics; that is why, the entire North-east, barring Sikkim, is underdeveloped economically and this gives rise to a strong sense of alienation from the mainland India. (Let me explain that I do not like to refer to the eco-politically advanced part of India as "mainland;" but, how else do I describe the negligent attitude of Delhi towards the North-east? This obviously, is the chief cause of the insurgencies found in almost all the States of North-east, barring Sikkim again, which had pro-poor government of a friendly, understanding single Party election after election with no Opposition in the Assembly. The picture has changed after the 2014 election; now there is an Opposition of 12 MLAs.)
25. The tribes in general, are anti-industries since that involves destruction of Nature and extortion from them by the unscrupulous industrialists and contractors and the monetary benefits go to the non-tribals; their age-old customs and traditions are very dear to them and they totally lack business acumen and mentality; we find even the shops and eateries are owned by the Marwaris and the other non-tribals, who have migrated from the so-called mainland of India.
26. The tribes, on the other hand, like to remain cocooned—may be because they are too conscious and proud of

their tribal identity, tribal laws and rituals. They are exempted from paying taxes—one of the many bribes for drawing them near the Centre and the party in power there; but, they rather want development—particularly roads, electricity and water; they care a lot for education and higher education also. They, in general, are not very enterprising; the men particularly, are lazy; the Reservation policy has made them lazier and less enterprising and non-competitive. They do not much care for change either. The leaders feel that true change in these regions can come only with education. The level of education or urge for higher education is not low; yet, the region remains backward because political awareness is not developed enough—not even with their leaders. As explained above, people are anti-change though they want development; for example, people want good roads, electricity and water but all that from what their Nature has given them and not by destroying Nature. Like all the tribes of India and perhaps, of the world, the tribes of Meghalaya too, believe that "they should leave for their children and grandchildren what their fore-fathers had left for them." They are very much anti-change when it comes to the destruction of Nature (though they do not realise that the method of 'slash and burn' agriculture is also destructive), but they are not anti-modern. They are very fond of their cultures, dialects, history, oral literature and tradition, but are far from being orthodox and obscurantist. They are not at all like the Hindu or Muslim chauvinists. They do not like their girls marrying outsiders, but do not get violent if one does; there is no notion of honour-killing at all.

27. They understand the value of education and there is a general urge for higher education particularly amongst the girls. The central university at Shillong (with its extension at Tura, the Garo headquarters) is rather rich

with a list of dedicated teachers and a wonderful library—both physical and digital. The highly educated ones are anti-reservation; they find such an advantage below their dignity. The highly educated and competent ones have been able to get good jobs, like that of the Principal of a medical college, even outside Meghalaya though rarely outside the North-east. What do we call this attitude of the non-tribals towards the tribals? Why a tribal cannot get a good job in any other part of India if he or she so desires?

28. Some think that the tribes do not have a sense of belonging because they are exempted from paying taxes and the spirit of competition is missing in their nature and lifestyle and also because of the "reservation" in jobs that the Indian Constitution has given them; in a capitalist economy and polity how can any person or a group survive without a spirit of competition? P. A. Sangma, one of the very popular leaders, feel Reservation has made the tribes lazy; same is felt by the uncrowned king of Sikkim Dr. Pawan Chamling. Both of them want justice and non-discrimination but not Reservation. My observation is that the policy of reservation for the SCs and the STs do not serve much purpose in reality; the privileged communities and castes do not allow the seats reserved to be filled in by the right candidates by giving the excuse of "none found suitable;" later, those posts get filled up by the non-SCs and the non-STs. Can we then blame the tribes if they suffer from a sense of 'unfair segregation'?

29. Ninety per cent of the financial grants come from the Centre; they blame the State governments for not utilising the money properly and allowing that to go back to the source while the roads remain in terrible condition and very few villages get proper electricity, water, education, school buildings, etc. The voters feel

that the money gets squandered, goes into the pockets of the politicians and the government officers while they remain ever denied. However popular an MLA or an MP may become, the inefficiency shown in solving the local issues affect the voting too. No Party gets a majority because the voters are ever dissatisfied with their elected representatives; they have noticed that the vote-seekers, to whichever Party they belong, are as corrupt, incompetent and insincere; the voters thus are at a complete loss and thus go on gambling with their votes. I wonder if the voters would have opted for NOTA in the EVM if that facility was introduced before the last Meghalaya election in February 2013! In Sikkim the story is totally opposite; the electorate there is so satisfied with the performance of the Chief Minister and all his Ministers that election after election they vote for the totally pro-people Sikkim Demcratic Front. But, the scenes have totally changed in these States as a result of the 2014 general election—Sikkim Assembly got an Opposition and Meghalaya got single party rule with Congress securing near absolute majority. The rest of India has thrown Congress out of power in a major way. We have seen drastic changes in political power all over India! Have the Hindus become powerfully chauvinistic or the people desperately wanted a change even if it came with the supreme power of a fascist party?

H.

With India's independence, the Constitution of India provided for the protection of interests of the tribal people both in the hills and the plains and their interests lay mainly in the ownership and protection of land and forests and their resources and allowed autonomy in their social and political developments. The Sixth Schedule of the Constitution was meant to protect these rights and autonomous District Councils were set up. All the headmen and the tribal chiefs were placed under these Councils. The traditional arrangements of the local self governments became complex with the introduction of the Autonomous District Councils. There was a Chairperson and a Deputy Chairperson in each District Council and their political positions were like those of the Speaker and the Deputy Speaker of the Legislative Assembly. The District Councils also had terms like the Assembly—five years; but the elections were not held regularly and were miserably devoid of female members.

The Shillong Municipality had its first woman representative in 1966, while in 1971 the first elected female Chairperson was appointed. In 1977-78 a female Executive Member of the Khasi Autonomous District Council was appointed; but, her term lasted for five months only. The Autonomous District Councils have the powers to assess and collect land revenue, impose taxes on professions, trades, employment, animals, boats, ferries, entry of goods in the market for sale, extraction of minerals under leases granted by the government. They could establish primary schools, dispensaries, markets, cattle pounds, fisheries, build roads, and provide road transport—all these subject to the jurisdiction of the Gauhati High Court even though they could exercise certain judicial powers—both civil and criminal. The Councils got grants both from the Central and the State governments apart from the incomes they had from the above-mentioned sources. They had special grants for the protection of forests and special hill development schemes.

Yet, the developments in this area are not as expected because there is always a clash of interests of the various parties in the coalition; the criticisms do not also get constructive because the Opposition too, is weak due to coalition. The case here is exactly opposite of what happens in Sikkim, which is the other extreme being under the same party elections after elections! Strangely, the absence of Opposition has not yet made the ruling party conceited! The absence of any opposition has made it easier for the government to carry on pro-people tasks; they know that they can continue in power if they continue to have people's trust.

The Sixth Schedule provided a compact mechanism for self-government in the tribal State of Meghalaya safeguarding the traditional rights, practices and customs of the tribal people and preserving their distinct culture and identity. In 1969, the Sixth Schedule was amended to empower the State government to entrust the Autonomous District Council with functions related to agriculture, animal husbandry, community development projects, co-operative societies, social welfare, village planning or any other matter. Even though the District Councils had the powers to make laws for land reforms and land development, they unfortunately, had not taken any steps in this field. They failed to inject dynamism for social change. The State Legislature too, had these powers and the actions, if taken in these areas, over-rode the powers of the District Councils.

Inadequacy of financial resources and administrative experiences and expertise were the major constraints in the proper functioning of the District Councils. The District Councils are like the Panchayats in many respects and the former are found only in the North-east and the international border areas. Paragraph 12A of the Sixth Schedule states very clearly that if the State government and a District Council make laws on the same subject, the law made by the former will prevail. This Paragraph thus lays down the over-riding authority of the law made by the State Legislature of Meghalaya though this Paragraph also insists that both the State and the District Councils would exercise their powers independently of each other!

We cannot help but mention here that the design and the content of the Sixth Schedule have failed to inspire the process of democratisation of the society; there was an initial promise but later failed miserably in bringing about social changes in Meghalaya. The scholars and even the politicians believe that this failure is due to the presence of a very weak middle class;

somehow, the educated middle class has always been the one which transforms in almost all societies and polities. The Eleventh Schedule under the 73rd Amendment Act promises more democratic way of land and community asset management for a rural society of better economic viability.

India of the 80s has witnessed a significant shift in women's development strategy; the National Perspective Plan for Women (1988) was meant to give women empowerment and development. The 73rd. Constitutional Amendment Act is an enabling mechanism for bringing women in the national development process, in democratising rural society by bringing women on par with men. Even matriliny of the Khasi and Garo societies could not empower women like the Panchayati Raj did because women do not have the decision-taking power in spite of owning land. Unfortunately, Panchayati Raj could not give the required power to women of this region because women themselves are too satisfied with the existing system and do not like to take part in politics or any protest movement.

I.

Meghalaya was carved out of the composite State of Assam by the 22nd Amendment Act of the Indian Constitution in 1969. Full Statehood was granted in November next year under the pressure of the elite tribals. But, there were conflicting expectations of the three major tribes, viz. the Khasis, the Garos and the Jaintias and this led to terrible governmental instability. The Indian National Congress (INC) and the Nationalistic Congress Party (NCP) were the two main contenders for power in the beginning. In the first Assembly INC had won 22 seats whereas NCP had won only 15 seats; BJP, which was wiped away in the latter elections, had won three seats. The rest of the seats were divided amongst the local parties.

Williamson A. Sangma, a Garo leader, became the first Chief Minister of the State; but, it was he who later, took the initiative to break the APHLC to merge with the Congress in 1976. This was seriously opposed by the Khasi leaders of APHLC and from then on till 2003, the differences between the Garo and the Khasi-Jaintia areas took the national-regional breaking line—the former preferring the national and the latter, more often than not, supporting the regional forces. Thus the North-eastern experience of democratic mobilisation clearly suggested that when the educated elite or the educated middle class of a developed community begins to emerge, it tries to benefit by remaining close to the more powerful and hegemonic forces. But, when it gains strength, it uses regional and/or ethnic politics as a bargaining strategy. Garo educated elite is still in its formative stage and is yet to find it necessary and opportune to come out of the umbrella of national political forces and to vigorously pursue a regional politics-based Garo identity. The Garo elites also make it a point to distance itself from the politics, dominated by the Khasi parties, which were close to the national parties. Thus, it became evident that the splits in regional/tribal parties strengthen the national parties during the elections.

During the British period itself Shillong (in the East Khasi Hills districts) became a centre of quality schools and colleges and with the establishment of North-eastern Hill University in Shillong, the number of educated amongst the Khasis and the Jaintias grew impressively. According to 2001 Census, the literacy rate in this region was 66.6 per cent, while in the Garo areas it was less than 56 per cent. The Tura campus (in the Garo Hills) of NEHU too, was visibly neglected. Thus, it was obvious that the Garo regional parties will be inclined towards the national parties.

J.

The just concluded election of India has thrown up many unexpected political developments; whatever the media hype, no voter could imagine or calculate that there will be single party rule once again! Coalition had become the pattern in the

Centre for many elections, as it was in Meghalaya; the electorate appeared too confused and undecided. This time (in April, 2014) it appeared determined to get rid of the uncertainties and confusions that arise out of an unwilling combination of many big and small parties, both national and regional; it wanted to experiment with a totally new political situation by voting for BJP and its Prime Ministerial candidate Narendra Modi. The electorate, thus, was undecided about what was greater evil—communalism or large-scale and deep-seated corruption and cheating of the common people!

The same thing happened in Meghalaya Assembly election last year; Indian National Congress won as many as 29 out of a total of 60 seats whereas Meghalaya was famous for coalition governments elections after elections! This trend was the opposite of what used to happen in Sikkim; all the Assembly seats used to go to a single party elections after elections—democracy without Opposition! But, in the just concluded Assembly election this trend got broken and a totally new party named Sikkim Krantikari Morcha got as many as 12 seats out of a total of 42 in the Assembly. The ruling SDF will be ruling once again no doubt, but this new situation with an Opposition shows clearly that there are some ethnic groups which are not too happy with SDF and want to experiment with a new alternative. When I was in Sikkim in 2003 the new party had just emerged as a single-member party and a majority of the people was making fun of this rebel from SDF. But, I did meet a few Lepchas (who claim to be the most original and indigenous ethnic group), who believed that single party rule elections after elections and without a single member in the Opposition is not indicative of true democracy; they wanted a change even though they had no clear-cut grudges against the ruling party.

Chapter XII

Sikkim: Ethnic Groups & Their Politics

A.

Sikkim is an ethnically diverse State. It has its own share of language and identity-related constituencies with different groups jostling for representation and clamouring to be re-classified. It has an interesting language and class politics as well. But, the most remarkable achievement is that it has refused to remain hostage to these issues; it has found a way for the politics of development. In a democracy which way one is going matters more than where one comes from. The ruling party of Sikkim under the leadership of Dr. Pawan Chamling, has shown that with some imagination, artful political mobilisation and honest sincerity, any other State can also achieve as wonderfully as this newest democracy and a very small State has achieved.

The Lepchas, the Bhutias and the Nepalis are the major population groups of Sikkim, the aggregate of whom being five lakhs and 40 thousands. The Lepchas were the very first inhabitants and the Gurkhas or the Nepalis are the last; yet, the Nepalis (particularly the Hindus) are now the dominant community numerically (75 per cent) and politically with their language as the lingua franca. (This is true not only with Sikkim, but also with the Darjeeling district of West Bengal.) A few Lepcha families are to be found in the lower valleys of western Bhutan and eastern Nepal, where they may have settled down while coming to Sikkim. They could not have bothered so much about the international borders. (Don't we every now and then hear of Indian fishermen unknowingly sailing into the Pakistani parts of the Arabian ocean and the Burmese into the Indian part of the Bay of Bengal?)

The Lepchas are believed to have originated in the legendary kingdom of Mayel in the vicinity of Mt. Kangchendzonga, which they worship; and they worship a few other mountain peaks also as their deities. There are scholars who believe that the Lepchas had originated in Arunachal Pradesh, whereas some others have found some similarity with the Khasis of Meghalaya however much they had spilled into parts of eastern Nepal and southern Bhutan though. Their language is one of the eleven official languages of Sikkim.

The next group to have entered Sikkim was the Bhutias from Tibet, some of whom had migrated to Bhutan also. Their primary occupation now is agriculture and horticulture though they had come as traders and herdsmen. They are big and sturdy with similar to Mongolian facial features and are neither aloof, nor fond of keeping themselves secluded, unlike the Lepchas. They prefer living in a joint family system with patriarchal pattern. They speak a dialect of the Tibetan language group and follow Lamaism or Tibetan Buddhism. In 1641, a Lama from Lhasa converted a great majority of the Sikkimese and the Bhutanese population into Lamaist Buddhism or the Vajrayana/Mahayana Buddhism. They had also performed the very significant act of appointing Penchoo Namgyal as the first Gyalpo (King) of Sikkim.

Therefore, for every help/aid the Namgyals had to turn to Tibet. It used to be their ultimate shelter too; they fled to Tibet and not to India whenever unable to resist hostile encounters. Nathu La and Jelep La are the early trade routes between Lhasa and Kalimpong (India). Lepchas are in economically disadvantageous position due to, and ever since, the entry of the Bhutias and the Nepalis, though it was not true about the Christian Lepchas. The Bhutias, like the Tibetans, are extremely conservative about their religion and the great perseverance of the Christian missionaries has proved almost unsuccessful. Christian Bhutias can be counted in one's fingers.

B. The Bhutias

The name "Bhutia," sometimes pronounced as "Bhotia," is derived from their original habitat "Bhot" meaning Tibet. The "Drukpas" are people from Drukul or Bhutan meaning thunder or dragon. Chumbipas from eastern Tibet, Dhopthapas from southern Tibet are all clubbed as Bhutias; besides, Lachenpa and Lachungpa from northern Sikkim also constitute the Bhutias culturally. Bhutia migration seems to have started in the 16th Century through the northern and western parts of Sikkim and their chief concentration is in North Sikkim which is characterised by hilly terrain with dense forests, high altitude, cold climate with heavy rainfall and medium snowfall. Bhutia language is different from Tibetan, but the script is same. But all the Bhutias, like everybodyelse in Sikkim, can speak Nepali (the language of the 80 per cent of the residents of the State).

The Bhutias are non-vegetarian and prefer beef and pork to mutton—quite like the residents of Meghalaya; their staple diet is rice. They, like the Khasis again, are fond of the Tibetan favourite momos. They are addicted to milk, tea and home-brewed alcohol (like almost all the tribes along the Himalayas); but, they are mainly non-smokers (except the urban ones). According to some smoking is against their religion (like with the Sikhs).

Before their migration from Tibet the Bhutias were endogamous; in fact, in Sikkim all communities are endogamous except the Lepchas, the Sherpas and the Tamangs.

Wives are, like in almost all other parts of India, younger than the husbands though the other way round is not all that uncommon. Monogamy is the general practice amongst all communities except with certain communities (like the Lachung and the Lachen) of North Sikkim where fraternal polyandry (like in the Kinnaur district of Himachal Pradesh) is noticed. Like the Tibetans, the married Bhutia women tie a striped apron waist downwards. There is bride-price like with most of the tribes of Arunachal Pradesh. But, unlike in AP, it is nominal and not a financial strain on the groom's father/ family. They are both patrilocal and matrilocal according to the needs of the old parents. The custom is quite like in present China and Tibet. And, like in Arunachal Pradesh and most other tribal societies property is owned & inherited by men only; sons have the first claim. The system is exactly opposite of the Khasis of Meghalaya; the youngest son is given the responsibility of taking care of his aged parents (like the youngest daughter in a Khasi family) and that is why, he is given a bigger share in the father's property. He has to take care of his younger sisters also. Like with the Tibetans and the Monpas of Arunachal Pradesh (who are influenced by the Tibetan religio-culture a lot), one son becomes a monk. (It used to be a custom with the Hindu Punjabis that the eldest daughter got married to a Sikh and sometimes the eldest son became a Sikh.)

Women have no right to inheritance; yet, they are almost equal socially and are seldom dominated over or oppressed. They, like women in all other societies—tribal or non-tribal—manage the household, take care of the old, sick and the children, work in the agricultural fields and also bring water, fodder & fuel from a distance. Bhutias are basically agricultural and pastoral. They are semi-nomadic; they come down with their cattle and sheep to a lower altitude in winter like the pastoral tribes of Himachal Pradesh. Women are equally educated and work in government services also; sometimes, a woman may be more educated than her husband, brother or father! Men, surprisingly, do not suffer from inferiority complex unlike in the societies of mainland India or China. Marriages are usually arranged and the maternal uncle has the final say and the boy's side goes to the girl's house seeking her hand in marriage; the custom is once again, like in Arunachal Pradesh. The marriage is solemnised by a Lama like with the Tibetans and the other Buddhists of Arunachal Pradesh and other areas of India. (it may not be too out-of-place to mention that the maternal uncle enjoys a very important position in the Khasi and Tamil societies also.) The Bhutias cremate their dead bodies, but the body is preserved non-cremated for as long as 49 days, depending on the social status of the person! Is it something like the caste system? The Lama conducts the last rites and nobody is allowed to touch the body unless and until the Lama blesses it. After the cremation some religious function is performed in order to drive away the demon which has taken away the soul of the dead. Various rituals are performed by the Lama till the body is cremated. The Bhutias have always been Buddhists like the Tibetans and their chief god was the Himalayan peak Kanchendzonga apart from Buddha of course. They have many other deities represented by the lakes, forests and the other mountain peaks. In the gumpas of each village the idol of Buddha is surrounded by various idols of other deities. Some monasteries have their own estates. The monks or the Lamas are not vegetarians, but they do not drink or smoke. (They could not have been vegetarians since they originally belonged to the barren lands of Tibet where before the post-1959 developments and modernisations the poor ate meat only and the lamas or the feudal lords ate a little bit of fruits and vegetables the latter being so rare in a barred land like Tibet-a cold desert.) There are dances and songs accompanying all social and religious festivals.

There are 8 auspicious signs in Sikkim on the paintings, carvings and sculptures. The symbols of Mahayana Buddhism are wheel for dharma, umbrella for protection, conch for fame, a pair of goldfishes for unity, pitcher for fulfilment, banner for victory, eternal knot for eternity and the lotus for purity. These symbols or one of these are found almost all over Sikkim—on the hotels, government offices, residential buildings, etc.

Zumsha was like a village Panchayat before the system of Panchayat-raj came to India and Sikkim; but, women had no right to become a member of that Panchayat, where all male members of the village took part in the necessary discussions (like it was in India before independenc). The community has its own scholars, artists, teachers, administrators, etc. Political leadership has emerged more recently at village, regional and national levels. Dissemination of information takes place through the propaganda activities of the political parties. Though there are banking facilities available now, there is not much interest among them about saving. They strangely depend a lot on the money-lenders and the shopkeepers.

In spite of their low status in the social hierarchy, the Bhutias show signs of progress in educational, economic and political terms alike; there are MLAs and administrators in the ranks of Secretaries and District Magistrates from the community. They retain their cultural practices irrespective of whichever position they are in.

C. The Lepchas

The principal tribal people of Sikkim, the Lepchas, are supposed to be the original inhabitants of Sikkim and they call themselves Rong-Kup. Rong means both to "wait" and "peak." They are called Monpas by the Tibetans; it means "Kirat tribe of the lowland." And the Bhutias call the Lepchas "Maris" (meaning same as above). The Lepchas are supposed to have come from upper Assam and upper Burma. But, they believe that their original residence was around their deity Kanchendzonga. Some others believe that the Lepchas came from Kailasha (in Tibet); this appears to be the result of later Hindu influence on them. They, like the Bhutias, live in the regions of extreme cold, medium snowfall and heavy rainfall, though they live at a lower altitude than the Bhutias. Lepchas are found all over Sikkim though the concentration is in the North (like with the Bhutias).

The Lepchas have their own language Rong though their script is different from that of the Tibetans; yet, it is considered a branch of the Tibetan language. According to the famous linguist Shri Suniti Kumar Chattopadhyay, Rong language has the influence of the Burmese language also. Like the Bhutias and all other communities of Sikkim, the Lepchas can speak fluent Nepali and also Hindi once they are educated in schools. Their food habit is like that of the Bhutias—eats beef, pork, mutton and even monkeys sometimes; their staple food is rice, followed by barley, maize, wheat, various types of pulses, etc. They eat wild plants including bamboo shoots (like the Nagas), in the lean season. They, like all tribes, brew their own alcoholic drinks and women too drink equally. But, they avoid smoking. They drink tea with salt and butter like the Tibetans though the modern Lepchas and Bhutias drink tea like people from the rest of India.

The Constitutional status of the Lepchas and the Bhutias is that of the Scheduled Tribes. They are patrilineal, patrilocal and exogamous. They are divided into various groups and clans though there is no caste system; they usually use their clan names as surnames (like those believing in caste system). They observe community endogamy and clan exogamy and have now started accepting marriage with the Bhutias. In Sikkim and the Darjeeling district of West Bengal there are marriages between different communities, but no Buddhist will or is allowed to marry a non-Buddhist though love marriages are accepted; the Nepalis (of Sikkim) are not so orthodox in spite of being Hindus though the Nepalis of Nepal are very orthodox. Like with the Punjabis the widow of elder brother has to marry the younger brother of her deceased husband and cannot marry an elder brother. The widow can be claimed by all the younger brothers of her dead husband and even by the paternal and maternal uncles; In the event of the wife's death, a girl from the deceased family has to be married by the widower. Any relationship between the daughter-in-law and father-in-law and between the mother-in-law and the son-in-law is strictly prohibited and highly condemned. How I wish Imrana of Uttar Pradesh was from Sikkim; then she could not have been ordained to live with her rapist father-in-law and regard her husband as her son!

Bride price is common like in Arunachal Pradesh and unlike with the other Sikkimese. Divorce or separation is very rare; but, the bride or the bride's family has to pay back the bride-price if the proposal for divorce comes from her side or she elopes with another man. This system is found with some of the communities of the Kullu district of Himachal Pradesh also. In case the husband divorces then he must arrange for another man to marry his wife.

The Lepchas are slow but steady workers. They, like the Bhutias and most of the Arunachalis, are patriarchal; the property like the land and the animals are owned equally by the sons and unlike with the Bhutias, the eldest son gets the maximum; he owns the house. The unmarried daughters and the widows live with the eldest son. In the absence of a biological son, an adopted son is allowed to inherit. The brothers look after each other in times of any calamity or need. And, like with all other communities of India (or, may be of the world), the women have to work on the agricultural field, take care of the domestic animals, bring fodder, fuel and water, etc. in spite of having zero right over property. This is quite unlike with the Tibetans where the house and the property are owned by the family as a whole; the decisions are also taken collectively. Like with a majority of the tribes of Arunachal Pradesh, a would-be Lepcha groom visits his would-be bride many times before marriage.

The dead body is either cremated or buried or thrown into a river unlike with the Bhutias. The process is decided on the Lama's advice who takes the decision depending on the condition of the dead body traditionally, though the Lepchas used to bury the dead bodies. The custom of cremation has come along with the adoption of Buddhism. Throwing into the river—particularly the dead bodies of the monks and the nuns—is done during the rainy season when the river is in full spate. Lepchas converted to Christianity have ceased to follow the elaborate life-cycle rituals and go to the Church for the necessary rituals. They adhere to two religious systems simultaneously—Lamaism and Shamanism. The second type is based on supernatural beliefs and superstitions; Lamaism is the Tibetan form of Mahayana Buddhism, not totally devoid of superstitions though. The services of the "mun" (of Shaminism) are necessary for all socio-religious ceremonies. The Lepchas had got converted to Buddhism in the 17th. century. Yet a strong element of their ancient animistic tradition persists. They have deities for the family, the clan, the village and the region and they are named after the mountain peaks and/or rivers. Music and folk-dances are an integral part of their religio-cultural life. Their folklores and folktales are also powerful having deep influence on their daily lives. They take part in Nepali Hindu festivals also. Marriages with the Hindu Nepalis are no longer that uncommon or discouraged.

The Christian Lepchas do better in life, profession and politics (as it is true with all other tribes converted to Christianity) and the Lepchas in general are inclined to higher studies. Education and love for education have spread a lot in Sikkim under the Pawan Chamling government. The poor meritorious students are admitted in good private schools so that they can perform as well as the well-off ones in interviews for jobs. The expenses are borne by the government. The poor Nepalis are employed in the agricultural fields of the Lepchas and the Bhutias.

Land and forests are the main footholds of their economy, though the forests are owned and taken care of by the government. Traditionally, like with all communities in the various periods of human civilisation, they had been hunters and food-gatherers and preferred animal husbandry before they became shifting cultivators like almost all tribes of the hills and the mountains. Now there are permanent cultivable lands also. Rice and cardamom are their chief produce. Urban Lepchas are mostly in government services or in politics; a few are in business.

D.

Flanked by Nepal on the west, Bhutan on the east and Tibet on the north, Sikkim is like a lively painting framed with care. It merged with India in 1975 and some of the Sikkimese, particularly the Bhutias and the Lepchas, think that Congress Party is not popular there because of the "forceful" accession to the Indian Union. It covers 7,300 sq. km. with a population of about 3, 50,000. The population was 60,000 in 1901and rose to 1,00,000 in 1931; it was 3,16,000 in 1981. The Nepalese, the largest component of Sikkim population, had alleged that a large section of them was left out during Census counting.

The others believe that the Sikkimese people's struggle for the demolition of monarchy and establishment of democracy had been going on since India attained independence. Phuntsong Namgyal became the first ruler of the Namgyal dynasty which ruled Sikkim till it became a part of India. But, the history of Legislature in Sikkim can be traced to 1890s when an effort to introduce a rudimentary system of government on modern lines was made. An Advisory Council with nominated members was constituted to aid and advice the Maharaja; the members were nominated from the Kazi and land-holding classes even from the Bhutia and the Lepcha groups. From 1930s the Council started representing the interests of all the classes and creeds of Sikkim. But, the ruler enjoyed the privilege of taking any decision without consulting the Council though a special session of the Council could be convened any time of the year if the Maharaja so wanted. It was stated that subject to the assent of the Maharaja, the Council could have powers to enact laws for the peace, order and good governance of Sikkim. Any reserved subject could not be taken up without the permission of the King.

In 1950 there was a serious law and order problem in the State and India had to rush contingents of police from the neighbouring Darjeeling district. As a result this Himalayan State became a protectorate of the Government of India which became responsible for the defence, external affairs, communications and territorial integrity of Sikkim. Bhutan now enjoys similar privileges. Otherwise, the State enjoyed autonomy. The Lok Sabha voted on September 4, 1974 the 35th Amendment Bill to include Sikkim within the Indian Union, thus ending the "protectorate" status. Sikkim Pradesh Congress Committee with 106 members got constituted with Kazi Lehndhup Dorji as its President and later it got fully integrated with the Indian National Congress. On April 10, 1975 the Sikkim Assembly unanimously adopted a Resolution abolishing the institution of Chogyal and declaring Sikkim as a constituent State of the Indian Union. At a Referendum, held on April 14, 1975 14, 59,637 Sikkimese voted in favour of accession and only 1,496 voted against. Some say that a few from the Minority groups constituted this number. On April 26 Rajya Sabha passed the 36th Amendment Bill.

When Janata Party came to power in the Centre in March 1977, three Janata units emerged in Sikkim. However, Kazi Dorjee decided to merge with Janata Party the latter thus getting recognition. In a House of 32 there were 16 Nepalis and 8 each of the Bhutias and the Lepchas—the last two thus getting more seats than the percentage of population could have given them. Prime Minister Morarji Desai was against the accession of Sikkim, but he could not undo what was done by the Prime Minister Indira Gandhi. He had rightly felt that it was wrong for a big country to devour small countries around it; the other small nations had started feeling insecure. The anti-merger slogans helped Nar Bahadur Bhandari (a former school teacher, who as a student used to carry fodder on his back) to become the Chief Minister; his Party, Sikkim Parishad, got 17 out of 32 seats in the Assembly. He got invitation from Indira Gandhi to join her Congress Party and Mr. Bhandari agreed. But, in 1984 Bhandari was dismissed on charges of corruption. Within 10 months he regained his popularity on a massive scale winning 30 out of 32 seats! During his election campaign he had succeeded to impress upon his electorate that Sikkim should not be surviving on New Delhi's mercy. He openly told people, "if we cannot get rice from India, we can get from China and Nepal!" Could any other State of the North-east been spared for such "anti-national" propaganda? The people would have been accused of terrorism and the Armed Forces Special Powers Act would have been enforced.

The Sikkim Parishad had passed a resolution in January 1981 demanding the continuation of the "sons-of-the-soil" policy indicating that Sikkim's doors were not open for employment to the citizens of the other States of India. The Representation of the People's Act was amended giving full protection to the three ethnic groups of Sikkim even though the Nepalis were and are by far the largest group. The Act had further said that "no single section of the population acquires a dominating position." Section Seven of the Citizenship Act of 1955 gave equal rights to all—big or small group—residing within India—whatever or whichever is the territory. The Chief Minister Bhandari even believed that the "outsiders" should be thrown out of the State though in present Sikkim there are many Bengalis, Biharis and Marwaris like in almost all hill areas of the North-east. He had even asked 7,000 Nepalis working for Border Roads Organisation to leave the State. The Sikkimese Nepalis were afraid that without some kind of Constitutional guarantee, as has been granted to the Lepchas and the Bhutias, they would soon be completely swamped. This fear was in spite of the fact that the Nepali population comprised of three-fourths of the total population of the State. The Lepchas and the Bhutias enjoyed the security of being declared as Scheduled Tribes which the Nepalis did not. During Chogyal's regime there was reservation of seats for the three major communities proportionate to their population. Chogyal had recognised that this was necessary for the maintenance of peace, harmony and brotherhood among the various ethnic communities. This arrangement had continued till 1979, i.e. till four years after the integration of Sikkim with the Indian Union. In October, 1977 the Sikkim Legislative Assembly adopted a Resolution demanding the inclusion of the Nepali language in the Eighth Schedule of the Constitution. Similar Resolutions were taken by the Assemblies of West Bengal and Tripura where a substantial number of Nepalis live. The State Assembly was given powers of enacting laws relating to education, public health, excise, press and publicity, transport, market, forests, public works, agriculture, food supplies, economic and social planning, home and establishment, finance and land revenue.

The Sikkim Sangram Parishad of Mr. Bhandari had asked the Centre to come in a big way to help Sikkim develope in agricultural, industrial, tourism and communication sectors so that this State could catch up with the rest of the developed States of India. Sikkim being a mountainous State, only 12 per cent of the landmass was under agriculture and more and more land needed to be developed for this purpose.

E.

The Indo-Sikkim Treaty was signed in 1950 under the aegis of the Ministry of External Affairs. Both parties agreed on the progressive association of the people with the governance of the State. The issue of the Panchayati raj had also been raised and village panchayats were established all over the State successfully. The Darbar had agreed to curtail the powers of the landlords and the tenants had stopped paying, having been provoked by the Congress Party. The Maharaja agreed to install a five-member interim government with two nominees of his own. The durbar reserved to itself the power to announce the date, time and place of holding the election and it was stipulated that the five candidates who got the highest number of votes would be declared elected to the Panchayat provided no malpractice or irregularity was committed during the election. A Sarpanch or Mukhia used to get elected and no meeting was regarded valid unless at least 4 members were present.

F.

The election processes are complicated; a candidate, in order to get elected, must not only secure the highest number of votes from his/her community, but also a minimum percentage of the other communities' votes. All the political parities except "National Party", are agitating against this system. Besides, there is no permanent Election Commission; there is an ad hoc Committee for every election. Sikkim State Congress is the oldest political party, established in December 1947. The demand for accession to India was first raised by this Party. Elections used to be held even before Sikkim formally became part of India. The two significant dates were 1958 and 1967. The emergence of political parties in the political arena had been the main force in bringing about winds of change in the State. Since its inception in the late forties, the Sikkim State Congress Party had taken upon itself the task of ventilating the grievances of the people and demanding urgent political and social reforms; it demanded Panchayati raj also. Interestingly the feudal class wanted to be relieved of the juridical duties which the notification of 1906 had bestowed upon them.

G.

The demand raised by the Sikkim State Congress in 1947 for the establishment of interim government as a precursor to democracy and a responsible form of government had been the reflection of the desires of the majority of the people; the State Congress was the largest and the most representative party at that time and its membership included all the three major communities of Sikkim, viz. The Nepalis, the Bhutias and the Lepchas. Democracy in India had inspired the educated and the enlightened who could not think of suffering the whims and tyranny of Feudalism. The demand for popular rule continued to grow unabated and it got manifested through the various resolutions adopted by the various political parties at different points of time. The joint convention of a number of political parties held in 1959 reiterated the old demand for "responsible" government and the adoption of a democratic Constitution for the State with universal adult franchise based on joint electorate. Discontent against the Durbar started breeding and growing. The message was sent to the Government of India through the Sikkim National Congress Party. The gradual spread of education, growing contact with the outside world which led to the inflow of modern and new ideas contributed to a steady rise in the awareness and political consciousness of the people. Interestingly, a new political party emerged on the eve of each election and all believed in people's government and democracy. Both the leaders and common people strongly felt the need for a radical change and it came finally in 1975. The elections before that were charged with rigging and the long-standing demands for popular written Constitution, Fundamental Rights and universal adult franchise. The Joint Action Committee urged upon the Chogyal to fulfil their demands failing which it will launch a mass movement. When preparations were on for celebration of the Chogyal's 50th birthday, thousands of people clashed with the police. Hundreds of demonstrators were pouring into Gangtok from different parts of Sikkim. A kind of a Janata Raj got established in the south and the east of Sikkim. Arrest warrants were issued. Chogyal and his Darbar requested the Government of India for help with regard to the discontent of the people and mass movements. The former even requested the latter to take over the administration.

H.

The first general election for a 32-member Assembly was held in April, 1974. As many as 15 seats—almost half—were reserved for the Minority Bhutias and Lepchas. One seat was reserved for Scheduled Caste. Meanwhile, Sikkim National Congress and Sikkim Janata Party got merged into one. This new Party promised to ensure full-fledged democracy, rule of law, clean and efficient administration, social justice, economic progress and protection of the rights of the Minorities. The Sikkim National Congress swept the poll by securing 31 seats and most of the new legislators refused to take oath in the name of Chogyal and they boycotted the lunch hosted by the Chogyal. A unique system of representative self-government existed in two villages of Lachen and Lachung.

On the question of associating people in the system of government, the problem of representation of the different communities came into forefront. In 1951 a system of parity was evolved. There was not only equal distribution of political rights, but also of other social and economic rights and opportunities. Care was taken to see that any law repugnant to any local use or custom was not enacted and those were in consonance with the principles of Equity, Justice and Good Governance. But community-based reservations led to community-based competitions in political, social and economic spheres. The political parties, though non-communitarian could not totally prevent them from being parties to their respective communities. Even though they fought the elections on the Party basis, their share in the government was on the community basis. An Election Commission was established consisting of the Dewan to direct and control the elections. It appointed various officers for various purposes. Candidates had to obtain a certificate of permanent residence in a "fixed habitation" for contesting from a particular constituency unlike what now happens in present India—Manmohan Singh contesting from Assam! The Sikkim National Party, the Sikkim State Congress, Sikkim Rajya Praja Sammelan and Sikkim Scheduled Castes League were the main parties and there was no Bhutia or Lepcha candidate from Sikkim State Congress; that perhaps, is the reason why the Minorities in Sikkim do not vote for Congress. And the Indians, even if settled in Sikkim, were not allowed to take part in the elections—neither as a voter nor as a candidate.

"Fixed Habitation" did not necessarily mean owning land or making a livelihood in Sikkim but more on the termination of nationality or fixed habitation of another country.

In the 1967 election of the Council seats were allotted in the following fashion—

Gangtok town constituency—one Bhutia/Lepcha seat and one Nepali seat & four contestants

East Constituency—one Nepali & two Bhutia/Lepcha seats & three contestants

South Constituency—one Bhutia/Lepcha & two Nepali seats & six contestants

West Constituency—one Bhutia/Lepcha & two Nepali seats & six contestants

North Constituency—one Nepali & two Bhutia/Lepcha seats & four contestants

General constituency—one seat and one contestant.

The following is the number of seats secured by different political parties—National Party got seven, Sikkim National Congress got five, State Congress got four, Sangha got one and an independent got one.

A year before Sikkim's accession to India, the Chogyal prohibited that election meetings on the day of election as well as on preceding day; there was penalty for disorderly behaviour in or near the polling stations, offences relating to disturbance during the election meetings and offences generating enmity between the classes or the communities. Side by side mandate was issued regarding the proper conduct during election meetings and election results.

I.

The anti-merger stand of Prime Minister Morarji Desai led him to face severe criticism and created considerable sensation in Sikkim. A number of parties even demanded the undoing of the merger, which had happened 25 years after the State

Congress had demanded. An anti-India feeling in the State was growing. Kazi Dorji, who had been an undisputed leader for some time, lost his position and the anti-India stance of many Opposition parties led to his decline. He was even accused of functioning as mini-Chogyal, who had deprived the people of the right to freedom of speech and expression.

A split in the ruling Janata Party led to President's rule in Sikkim in August, 1979. The election was supposed to be held in November that year. But, the Parliament itself was adjourned sine die leading ultimately to the dissolution of the Lok Sabha. So, President's rule in Sikkim could not continue and the Election Commission announced October 12, 1979 as the date of election. The tenure of the new government thus became six years instead of five. The electorate comprised of 1,17,640 of which surprisingly the number of the female voters was less (53,374) than that of the male voters (64,266)! There is no evidence of repression of the females or female infanticide/ foeticide though the society is patriarchal with the right to property being with the males only. A record number of nominations (436) had been filed; this was almost 4 times than of what was filed in 1974. The number of those actually contesting was 247. And this was the first time that the Sikkimese living on the plains got the right to vote. Sikkim was the first State in India to have introduced photo-identity cards for the voters. The number of candidates that contested from various Parties is as follows—

Sikkim Prajatantra Congress—31

Janata Party—30

Sikkim Janata Parishad—30

Sikkim Congress (Revolutionary)—26

Indian National Congress (U)—11

CPI (M)—2

Sikkim SC League—1

Here now is the number of votes secured by the candidates from different Parties.

Mr. P. Subba—SJP—31,750

Mr. R. C. Poudyal—SC(R)—11,632

Mr. I.B. Rai—SPC—5,125

Mr. R. P. Sharma—Ind.—1,073

Mr. K. N. Adhikari—Cong (U)—943

Mr. A. K. Subba—Ind.—801

Mr. D. K. Pradhan—Ind.—179

What is to be noted here is that in spite of the Minority Bhutias and Lepchas getting equal status in the elections, the winners are invariably Nepalis and males only and in every constituency except Khamdong and Chakung, the SJP candidate scored the highest vote. Besides, the Parties were more concerned with their victories in the Assembly polls than in the Lok Sabha. In 1979, interestingly, no Party was confident enough to win a simple majority. Though the Parties did not fail to realise that merger with India was an irrevocable fact, none of them had any allegiance to any national party of India. They did not want any supervising by the Central government. Kazi and his Party were exceptions; they always fought against sectarian, regional and communal feelings.

The Constitution of India was made operative ever since the accession of Sikkim to India in 1975. The regional-interest-oriented politics in the State took time to drift towards national-interest-oriented politics.

J.

The study of the pressure groups is considered an important channel towards understanding modern political system; pressure groups are the organised bodies which try to influence the decision-making and the policies of the government in order to promote and preserve their own interests. The process through which demands are made to the decision-makers gives vent to interest articulation. Certain pressure groups often achieve their goals while the others fail to do so. The methods adopted by different groups obviously are not according to a same or similar pattern. All try to impress upon how deserving of attention and response their demands are. Many believe that ethnic imbalances were results of merger of unequal ethnic groups and merger of Sikkim to India. Democracy in Sikkim meant concentration of eco-political powers in the hands of the overwhelmingly Majority Nepalis. The Nepalis did not have too many seats in the Assembly; the number of Bhutias and the Lepchas together was not less than that of the Nepalis. Yet, a prominent section of the former group turned to the Government of India as their saviour vis-a-vis the Nepalis. Similarly parliamentary democracy in Sikkim brought hope to the Nepalis that they will dominate because of their high proportion in the population. They started claiming reservations for themselves also.

The most powerful group was the Kazi—a Bhutia-Lepcha landlord group; Thikadars were their Nepali counterparts. The Kazis were like the upper caste among the Bhutia-Lepchas; they were educated and provided good education to their children because of their good financial condition and they were also the first organised body in Sikkim, who in early thirties, raised their voices against the authority of the ruler and reminded him of their position as feudal barons, which they were earlier. This economically dominant class in feudal, pre-democratic Sikkim had played a dynamic role in both administrative and judicial fields. They were able to impose their wills on all and sundry though the landlord system was abolished as early as in 1949-50. In 1953 the State Council was formed consisting of both elected and nominated members. Some powers got transferred to the Executive Council composed of the elected members only. Yet, the real authority remained with the King and his political clique who had control over the State Council and the Executive Council. The most important, yet the scarcest source of production viz. land, was still in the hands of the landlord class and thus, its influence on the government machinery could not decline. This class, being socially influential and financially strong, influenced the government policies and the development programmes in order to derive maximum benefit for themselves. The changes that were ushering in the arena of Indian politics during the mid-forties had their impact on Sikkim also. An advanced section of the commoners was observing the course of Indian struggle for freedom with interest and was thus nursing the idea of emancipation from the yoke of Feudalism and the consequent agonies due to exploitation. There was an accumulation of grievances among the down-trodden Bhutias, Lepchas and even Nepalis, who had suffered miseries and were denied the most elementary justice; that had become almost unbearable and that is how the urge for merger with Republican, Democratic India had arisen.

The Lamas used to play a dominant role in Sikkim under the Chogyals. Traditionally the Lamas had their allegiance to the ruler like the Brahmins in India had to the Kshatriya kings. Sikkim was a theocratic State with Buddhism as the State religion and thus the High Lamas and the monasteries enjoyed a role in the political policy decisions. The high Lamas had even administrative and magisterial roles. Many of the kings were considered to be the incarnations of high Lamas and/or Bodhisattvas!

K.

Rajya Praja Sammelan, formed by Gobardhan Pradhan and Dhanbahadur Tiwari, stood for accession of Sikkim to India. It also wanted that the Gurkhas of Sikkim should unite with those of Darjeeling/North Bengal. Praja Mandal was formed by Kazi Lehndhup Dorji and was the oldest Party in monarchical Sikkim. This Party stood for the promotion of the welfare of the ryots and protection of their rights. It also sought to promote communal harmony among the three major communities for the unity of Sikkim. It was under Tashi's leadership and in the wake of India's independence a political movement—the first of its kind—had started in Sikkim. The Durbar agreed to the demand for the abolition of landlordism, the process for which had already started. The reasons the National Party gave as to why accession of Sikkim to India was unacceptable were as follows—

(a) Historically, socially, culturally and linguistically Sikkim had been closer to Bhutan and Tibet than to India,

(b) Sikkim had only political relations with India, which were imposed on her,

(c) Being Buddhist and Lamaist, Sikkim was again, quite distinct from India and closer to Tibet and Bhutan.

L.

In 1973 election, the National Party found an unusual increase in Nepali votes in its favour and secured 10 seats while the Sikkim National Congress secured five and the Janata Party only two seats. One seat went to the SC candidate. The last two Parties were accused of rigging the election. Sikkim National Congress and Sikkim Janata Congress formed a Joint Action Council to start an agitation against rigging.

In the fifth general election the powerful victory of the Sikkim National Party confirmed the faith and confidence of the Sikkimese people in this Party. From now onwards the representatives of the people started being called Ministers instead of "Executive Councillors." The Sikkim Congress decided to merge with the Indian National Congress once Sikkim became a part of the Indian Union. One of the ruling Party spokesmen explained that Sikkim had to depend on the Centre for everything and hence the ruling Party would not oppose any government which came to power at the Centre. Political uneasiness was there in Sikkim and it was alleged that the ruling Party was alternately using pressure and purse to maintain the support of the MLAs. Besides, the demand for Nepali language as the official language and its inclusion in the Eighth Schedule (of the Constitution of India) generated considerable tension among the Bhutia-Lepcha people.

All the three major Opposition Parties, viz. Sikkim Janata Parishad, Sikkim Prajatantra Congress & Sikkim Congress (R), are regional Parties and held the Party of Kazi Dorji as their common enemy though all of these professed democracy and socialism as their common goal. Yet they could not establish a common platform wherefrom to fight the Janata Party. Occasional attempts were there to form some sort of united front of the parties. Not just with Sikkim, this is a pan-Indian characteristic and happens in almost all the States.

After the Parliamentary election of February, 1980, when Congress (I) returned to power with overwhelming majority, almost all important leaders from the four major political parties including Mr. N. B. Bhandari and Kazi L. Dorji visited Delhi to feel the direction of the wind. The ruling Sikkim Janata Parishad had the blessings of the then Prime Minister of India.

M.

The Sino-Indian conflict of 1962 led India to fortify its strategic bases on the border areas, a huge communication network was necessary and that needed a huge number of labourers. The number of the Lepchas and the Bhutias was not enough; so a huge number of labourers had to be imported from Nepal, the neighbouring country where a huge population was jobless. These Nepalis did not go back once the work was over; they made Sikkim their homeland. Thus demand for already scarce agricultural land in Sikkim increased thus creating a socio-economic pressure on the kingdom. Nepali migration to Sikkim never stopped and every year at least a thousand of them entered and settled down in Sikkim. They came with work permits to work on the paddy and/or cardamom fields. This huge and ever-increasing Nepali population created a problem for the Durbar. Their numerical strength compared to that of the original inhabitants of Sikkim kindled a desire in their hearts to establish a people's rule and evict the Bhutia King. The Bhutia-Lepcha groups, on the other hand, wanted some sort of safeguard against this continuous Nepali immigration and some sort of security against them. The Nepalis, that is why, wanted democracy by accession to India (they could not have created jobs and democracy in their own land with an autocratic monarch); the Bhutia-Lepchas, on the other hand, wanted their own special identity within their own kingdom since the monarch was benevolent and non-Nepali.

CHAPTER XIII

Achievements of Sikkim Democratic Front

In September 1974, Sikkim became an "Associate State" by an Act of Parliament and it became a part of the Indian Union in April next year as the 22nd State. Earlier it had protectorate status (like Bhutan has now). The new State has an area of 7096 sq. km. with an electorate of 2.5 lakhs. There is a 32-member Assembly and a single Lok Sabha member; both the elections were held in October of that year. Twelve Assembly seats are reserved for the Lepchas and the Bhutias, who are in the minority in spite of being the original inhabitants of Sikkim! The majority Nepali community had migrated into much later. There are two seats reserved for the SCs and one for the Sangha. The last one is a unique case where there is reservation for the Buddhist monks and that is why, this constituency has no boundary or specific area. Both the candidate and the voters are monks, i.e. belong to the Sangha. Before its accession to India, Sikkim was a Buddhist nation with a Buddhist monarchical dynasty. It is not considered a Hindu State even though the Nepalis constitute two-thirds of the total population and they are Hindus; there is no caste discrimination or oppression even though the Nepalis believe in caste.

Indian National Congress was the first political party to rule over Sikkim right in the beginning; Sikkim's accession to India was effected by this party only. But, it started losing strength within five years before the next election though Nar Bahadur Bhandari had stayed in power for three terms, except a brief break when the State was under President's rule; in the 1985 election SSP won 29 of the 32 seats and in 1989 it got all the 32 seats. In 1993, a year before the next election Pawan Chamling broke away from Bhandari's cabinet and formed his own Party called Sikkim Democratic Front. He secured absolute majority in 1994 election and there was no end to that though we had to wait till May 16, 2014 to know if history would repeat itself. He and his Party secured absolute majority—32 out of 32 seats in the Assembly—ever after. Yet, INC did not give up contesting in all the 32 seats—so very conceited it was! Thus there was no Opposition in the Sikkim Assembly and only recently one MLA had come out of SDF and had formed his single-member party called Sikkim Kranti Morcha. In 2014 election, this new party secured as many as 12 seats!

The SDF gave reserved seats not only to the SCs , the Lepchas, the Bhutias and the monks, but also to the Other Backward Castes (OBCs) amongst the Nepalis; those were Newars, Bahuns, Chhetris, Jogis, Sanyasis, Thamis and Chamling himself was an OBC. He and his rule hed become immensely popular because the cross-border trade with Tibet through Nathu La pass (which was stopped by the Government of India after the 1962 attack by China) was re-opened. Cross-border trade and cultural interaction are very important and necessary for all the tribes living on the border; we have seen it in case of Arunachal Pradesh and Himachal Pradesh. The speedy progress of the Teesta Hydel project (for which the State government had to pressurise the Central government a lot) was another reason behind the unmatched popularity of the Chief Minister and his party. Besides, the non-Hindus were rather unhappy with the Government of India formed, at that time, by the Congress, for acceding Sikkim to the

Indian Union. The otherwise peace-loving Lepchas and Bhutias get visibly upset if asked about the reason/s for their dislike of the Congress Party.

The accountability of the democratically elected leaders and the implementation of the policies by the government machinery are the key concerns that are being hotly debated almost all the time by the Chief Minister Dr. Pawan Chamling and his dedicated team because a very large section of our population face social and economic exclusion. The Ministers turn ideas into action and the actions into impact. In December 2012 Sikkim was given the IBN7 award for the best small State or the best State in the otherwise backward North-east of India. Sikkim was adjudged ahead of Delhi, Goa, Himachal Pradesh, etc., which are considered more developed than so many big States. There are a few pockets without electricity or potable water no doubt, but every citizen has a shelter and enough to eat; only a miniscule section is in BPL category. In 1994, Chamling started with only 50 crore in hand; today there is 1,300 crores showing an annual growth rate of 35 per cent. It is a beggar-free and slum-free State! There is an "inclusive growth" with food, water, health, education and livelihood opportunities for almost everybody.

Like in all other States of the North-east, women are not much interested in politics; yet, there is 50 per cent reservation for women both in the Panchayats and the Assembly, while the women's movement in the mainland India is struggling for only 33 per cent reservation in the legislative bodies! This makes governance, both in the urban and rural areas truly functional and effective. There are at least two women constables in each of the police stations, which mostly remain inactive because of the low rate of crimes. I did not come across a single case of murder or rape during my several visits to Gantok and other parts of Sikkim, whereas every morning when I open the newspaper in Hyderabad, I come to know of at least one murder (if not more) and more than one rape cases! The other tribal States of the North-east are not too bad compared to Sikkim; crimes committed there are by the police and the Army and seldom by the marginalised people.

The first thing that the people from other States, particularly from the North-east, notice is the absence of gun-toting police and/or army personnel! I was shocked to enter a Minister's chamber without being stopped and questioned and harassed by the Security men!

The next impressive achievement is the almost total absence of the 'drop-outs' from the schools and for the few who drop out due to disinterest in text-book studies, there are 'livelihood' schools in each constituency which trains them up in different professions so that there is no absence of opportunities for anybody. Besides, the first 10 meritorious students from each government school are picked up and put into English-medium Public Schools so that they can develop confidence in themselves and compete with anybody from the highly educated backgrounds/families. In other States, we have noticed, the SCs, the STs, the OBCs and the other underprivileged do not get a job in spite of 'reservation' because they lack the self-confidence and smartness and the reserved posts remain vacant and then get filled up by the upper castes/classes after a minimum stipulated period. Sikkim is one of the first States to devolve powers related to secondary and primary educations directly to the Gram Panchayat units. Chamling fears that democracy in Sikkim is still fragile and is in the danger of being usurped by the anti-democratic forces if the youth does not share in the democratic values espoused by him and his party.

There are Public Health Centres, popularly known as PHCs in every village however remote it may be from the capital and there are hospitals with all the modern amenities (including scanning, ultrasound, etc.) in every district. The Head of the Population Foundation of India, during a surprise visit, had found the PHCs well-equipped and the doctors and the nurses dedicated—very much unlike in any other part of

India. There are 24 PHCs when only 17 are required and there are 267 nurses and midwives while only 171 would have sufficed. There are as many male nurses also and the strangest thing is that there are 42 doctors when only 24 would have served the purpose. That is why, there is never a long queue in the health centres and even the MLAs and the Ministers go to the same hospitals where common people go. (I have seen a similar situation in Tibet-nobody is a VIP & nobody is privileged. On top, there is the provision of sending difficult patients to All India Institute of Medical Sciences, New Delhi; special monetary assistance is given to these patients and his/her escort. Both birth and death rates have gone down as compared to India's and to what those were before SDF came to power. Infant mortality rate has gone down from 51 to 26—lower than India's average. There are about 30 per cent BPL in India, but in Sikkim it is only 13 per cent and they get as much as 50 kg of rice per month!

Sikkim's GDP is 12.26 per cent—the highest in India! There is complete freedom of press and the Right to Information Act really works there; one does not have to bribe the clerks to get the copies of the required files out. Modernisation of the media has been promoted with the government presenting them computers, digital cameras, printers and other accessories. The Press Club of Sikkim receives an annual grant of Rs. 1 lakh. Computerisation of the land records has been achieved and all the bills can be paid through a single window of the internet. E-governance in Hyderabad during the Chief Ministership of Chandrababu Naidu was much advertised; Sikkim achieved it quietly. Ten bank branches are available per 1,000 sq. km and for 8,252 persons. Not a single block is unbanked.

As mentioned earlier there is 50 per cent reservation for women though most strangely, women constitute only 47 per cent of the total population! In none of the States of the North-east or any tribal State like Jharkhand and Chhattisgarh there is any instance of female infanticide or foeticide or torture of the girls or women; we are not aware of it. Yet, the percentage of women population is less, which goes against Nature. It is asserted by all anthropologists and social workers that if left to Nature, females will be more in number since a female baby can take more hardship and rough handling than the male babies.

As mentioned elsewhere, the MLAs and the MPs are almost always touring the remotest parts of their constituencies; the Chief Minister is no exception to that; his 'village to village' tours are famous and much appreciated. He takes people's representatives and senior bureaucrats with him in order to understand the people's problems and requirements directly and clearly. This is bringing governance to the doorstep. In "Janata Melas," the people come to know directly and hear with their own ears the various plans and programmes of the governments. Many benefits are handed over to the people directly in these 'melas'. An attitudinal change is thus brought over in the minds of the executing officers. Chamling has thus, already achieved what Kejriwal is now trying in Delhi; the latter should have rather gone door to door in the slums and the areas inhabited by the under-privileged instead of calling them over in an open space and getting badly mobbed and then later discard the system attogether.

Barefoot engineers get appointed initially at the gram panchayats levels for minor repair works and for the maintenance of water and sewage systems. The gram panchayats have been authorised to issue or cancel trade licences since 2011. Sikkim was honoured with the third best and the second best State for the implementation of Panchayati Raj in 2007 and 2011 respectively.

No discrimination is made among the poor and the rich, the caste Hindus and the Scheduled castes or Scheduled tribes, women, children and the senior citizens with regard to the amenities and abundant opportunities provided by the State; there is no animosity amongst the Hindus and the Buddhists either. Marriages also take place sometimes between the two communities. All languages and the history of all communities get equal weightage in the syllabi of the schools; not only Bhutia, Lepcha and Limboo languages are taught according to the choices of the students, but a few schools have teachers for Sherpa, Gurung, Newar, Tamang, Mangar, Mukhia and Rai languages also. There is any number of libraries all over Sikkim and in 2002, Rs. 180 lakhs have been allotted for Library Corpus Fund. Public Sikkim Akademi, an autonomous literary body like the Sahitya Akademi in Delhi, has also been established.

Under the Indira Gandhi National Disability Pension Scheme, each differently abled person get a monthly pension of Rs. 600. Pensions for the Senior Citizens have increased from Rs. 100 in 1994 (when SDF had come to power) to Rs. 600 in 2010. Thirty per cent of the government jobs are reserved for women, 3 per cent for physically challenged persons, 3 per cent for ex-servicemen and 2 per cent for sportspersons. It is interesting that all the Ministers are interested in sports and quite a few in reading and music. One-time incentive of Rs. 20,000 is given to the couple going for inter-caste marriage and Rs. 10,000 to the man marrying a widow. There are homes for deserted and destitute women and unmarried girls of 13 and above get Rs. 8,000 as incentive for further studies. Women working even in unorganised sector get two months' maternity leave (which is in no other State of India).

Sikkim's per capita outlay on education is Rs. 1,288, whereas the national average is shamefully only Rs. 65! In healthcare the per capita investment is Rs. 296, which is the second highest amongst the States. Today Sikkim is a polio-goitre-cretinism-free State (though the entire India today is claimed to be polio-free). Sikkim is the first State to launch a free Hepatitis B vaccine programme. Sikkim is the only State in the country to achieve the national norms of establishing one PHC per 20,000 population and one sub-PHC per 3,000 populations. Ninety percent of births and deaths get registered due to computerisation. A 575 bed multi-speciality hospital has come up in Sichey Busty—a must tourist destination. Pure drinking water was available to 94.50 per cent of the households in 2008-9; now it is almost 100 per cent.

Literacy rate has gone up from 56 per cent in 1994 (when SDF had come to power) to 82.2 per cent in 2012; the national average is 74 per cent. All students of the government schools are provided with free textbooks, school-bags, rain-coats, shoes and socks, and healthy mid-day meals; not a single case of mass illness due to stale or poisonous mid-day meals has ever been reported from Sikkim or any other State of the North-east (though all these States may not be providing mid-day meals to all). Per capita consumption of electricity in Sikkim is as high as 850 kwh when it is only 258 in the rest of the States of the North-east and 778.71 on an average in India. There is 100 per cent electrification of the rural households and 50 units are given free to the BPL families (whose number is very less compared to the rest of India). BPL population in entire India is 33.8 per cent. Only 2.50 per cent does not have a sanitary latrine.

Over the last 20 years, the increase in tourists influx into Sikkim has been 7 lakhs from 1,23,000 in 1994. It shows what a sincere effort has been put in the proper and fast development of the infra-structure. There has been a 48 per cent rise in road connectivity and 82 per cent rise in tourists inflow giving an 137 per cent rise in revenue.

Let us now look at the investments in different sectors. In Roads and bridges 591 crores, water supply and sanitation 188 crores, wage employment 315 crores, self-employment 19.40 crores, housing 176.38 crores, etc. For obvious reasons, the investment on roads is highest because it is a mountaneous region and tourism is the main source of revenue.

The Sikkim Democratic Front (SDF) swept the Panchayat polls by winning 103 out of 108 zilla parishad seats 895 out of 987 gram panchayat seats.

Thus, Sikkim is India's fastest growing State and yet, its growth story has not been in the limelight like Gujarat and even Bihar (after Nitish Kumar came to power)! The next question that comes to mind is how could SDF bring about 'development consensus' amongst people, particularly when a major part of the State is rural with a very traditional social structure. In most parts of India, we see the biggest impediments to development are that the locals do not want to give up on land or traditional means of livelihood. Trade with China's Tibet through the Nathu La pass has also contributed to the well being of the people on the border (like in Arunachal Pradesh). The people have faith in the SDF government; they think that if their parents cannot feed them or educate them, their government, with Pawan Chamling as the Head, will do.

Chapter XIV

Political Leaders of Sikkim

A.

Let us now look into the short biographies of some of the important political leaders of Sikkim. That may help us to understand what made the Chief Minister Pawan Chamling and his colleagues/ Party so popular. As mentioned elsewhere, Sikkim's is a unique case where there is Parliamentary Democracy without an Opposition.

1. Dr. Pawan Kumar Chamling was born in 1850 in South Sikkim and joined politics in 1973 and was the Vice-President of District Youth Congress in 1975. Later he served as General Secretary and Vice-President of Sikkim Prajatantra Congress from 1978 to 1984 and was unanimously elected Panchayat Pradhan in 1982. He became an MLA in 1985 and was re-elected in 1989. He started as the Minister of Industry, Information and Public Relations Departments and proved his leadership qualities by forming Sikkim Democratic Front in 1993; he became the Chief Minister the next year itself and continues to be the Chief Minister till today though as a result of the recent Assembly election an Opposition got formed.

Pawan Chamling is also a literateur with several publications to his credit; he also edited journals and founded a well-known publishing house.

2. Shri Thutop Bhutia was born in 1959 in West Sikkim. He studied only up to Class VII and worked as a contractor before joining politics; such a bio-data is not uncommon among the MLAs of so many other States of India. He was also active in social work which helped him to become popular and be successful in politics. He too, like Pawan Chamling, had become Panchayat Pradhan in 1993. He too, became MLA the next year contesting from Sikkim Sangram Parishad Party. Both the bio-data show that social work and work for the rural areas as Panchayat Pradhans help in becoming popular. Unlike in most of the cases in a majority of the Indian States, they must have taken their Panchayat work seriously and thus won people's confidence. He used to take special interest in preserving the environment and formation of co-operatives. He even led the local sports activities and took sports ahead. His special interests were in chess, badminton, trekking, gardening, rearing pets apart from group discussions on serious matters of social work and politics. He has travelled widely in India and South-east Asia.

Bhutia joined SDF or the Chief Minister's Party and got inducted as a Minister after winning the 1999 election.

3. Shri Sher Bahadur Subedi, born in West Sikkim in 1958, too, was not highly educated. He had passed Higher Secondary examination and was in government job before joining politics in 1994 as a candidate from the Gangtok Constituency of the SDF Party. He used to be the General Secretary of the All Sikkim Students' Association. He lost the election with a thin margin and finally won in 1999. In between he had served as the Chairman of the Electricity Advisory Board and later became the Minister for Transport.

Subedi too, was involved in social work, led many awareness campaigns and helped the needy. We must note that all the Ministers have a background of social work or leading the Panchayat thus showing their love for the people unlike with those in the mainland States of India. He too enjoys reading, travelling and watching sports.

4. Shri Narendra Kumar Subba was born in West Sikkim in 1968 and is a graduate. He too, had held the position of Panchayat Pradhan from 1993 to 1997 and was Zilla Adhyaksha too, till 1999. He won the General Election from SDF in 1999. Social work and interests in sports and travelling are also in his background.

5. Shri Tulshi Prasad Pradhan was born in 1939, got elected in 1994 and was inducted in the Ministry as the Minister for Urban Development and Housing.

6. Shri Ongden Tshering Lepcha was born in 1969 and had studied up to Class XII; he worked as a teacher from 1987 to 1998 and was nominated a member of the Central Working Committee of SDF. He got elected to the Assembly in 1999 and became the Minister for Women and Child Development and was later elevated to the Cabinet rank. He has contributed a lot to the promotion of Lepcha language and published many books and essays in various journals.

7. Shri Prem Singh Tamang was born in 1968 and is a graduate in Geography. He is also the co-founder of the Sikkim Democratic Front party. He was elected in 1994 and inducted in the Cabinet as the Minister for Animal Husbandry & Veterinary Services. He held the same portfolio when he won the next election. Tamang's political training was as the Presidents of the Students' and Teachars' Associations. Like others, he too was interested in various types of sports.

8. Shri Ram Bahadur Subba was born in 1952 in West Sikkim (which, till now, seems to be the haven of the successful politicians), is a B.A., LLB and was an advocate in the Sikkim High Court before joining politics in 1984 having formed his own Party, viz. Sikkim Himali Congress; he later merged his Party to Indian National Congress. He could not win any election but became the General Secretary of Sikkim Sangram Parishad—the then ruling Party. He won when, in 1999, he contested from the ruling SDF Party; he then became the Minister for Education and Law.

9. Shri Ram Bahadur Subba, born in 1956, was an active member of Congress (I) during 1984 to 1993. He too, had become Panchayat Pradhan and Zilla Adhyaksha in 1992. He got elected to the Assembly when he contested from the SDF Party and got re-elected in 1999. He was earlier Minister of Forests, Mines & Geology and later Minister for Roads & Bridges+ Parliamentary Affairs.

Sikkim being an under-populated State, the number of MLAs is low and thus one Minister is allotted many responsibilities. We should by now keep in mind that a political aspirant wins only when he contests from the ruling SDF Party—the Party was and is so popular. By now, I hope, my readers have understood why there was no Opposition in the Sikkim Assembly after many elections. The second point to note here is that a majority of the MLAs are from the Nepali community about 80% of Sikkim's population being of Nepali origin.

10. Shri Bhoj Raj Rai, born in 1964, is from South Sikkim. He had passed Higher Secondary and was a teacher before he joined politics. He had not made the mistake of trying to contest from a non-SDF Party and was thus elected every time he contested. And, like so many others he, too, loves sports and travelling and had got engaged in social work. He was a member of the Red Cross and the President of the South-West Taxi-drivers' Association.

11. Shri Dorji Dazom Bhutia was born in 1946 and had passed Higher Secondary before he started working as a teacher. He won the 1994 election by contesting from SDF Party and became Minister for Roads & Bridges and Building and Housing Departments. Next time he was appointed Minister for Health & Family, Science & Technology and Culture. Like all others, he too, was interested in sports and travelling; but, like a few, was interested in reading too. He brought Sikkim in the world of Cricket with the State's affiliation with the Board of Cricket Control of India.

12. Shri Kedarnath Rai was born in 1861and had achieved a rare feat by completing post-graduation in Public Administration. He was appointed Minister of Education, Sports and Youth Affairs; he became the Chief Whip after winning the next election as a member of SDF.

13. Shri Girish Chandra Rai was born in 1954 and is a graduate; we have seen till now that very few Ministers have gone beyond Higher Secondary. Like so many others he was involved in social work and became Panchayat Pradhan also. Though a member of Congress (I), he had contested as an independent candidate and had lost. He won in 1992 after joining the ruling SDF Party. He had become a Minister of State for Rural Development and was later (after winning the next election) promoted to the rank of a Cabinet Minister. He too, has special interest in reading books.

14. Shri Chandra Kumar Mohora was born in 1958 and won the election for the first time in 1985 as an independent candidate. Later, in 1999, he contested on SDF ticket and became Minister of State in Printing & Stationeries, Information & Public Relations and Sports & Youth Affairs. Later he became a Cabinet Minister for Sports & Youth Affairs and Excise departments.

15. Shri G. M. Gurung was born in 1963 in South Sikkim. We are noticing that South and West Sikkim are more advanced in political awareness, and so must be more developed and modern. He too, is a graduate and was a teacher before joining politics. He did not make the mistake of not contesting on SDF ticket and won the election, as expected, the very first time he contested. In 1994 he became the Minister for Agriculture, Co-operation & Tourism and Minister of Agriculture, Horticulture & Irrigation after he won the next election. We must note that once a Minister, he wins again and again; the SDF Party is so popular in Sikkim because the Ministers work for the people sincerely and honestly. Till today no media or social worker could bring any allegation against any minister! This is quite

unbelievable considering the fact that corruption is rampant in the rest of India.

Shri Gurung played active role in bringing in awareness among the masses regarding their Rights and Duties and helping them for organising Self-Help Groups. He paid special attention to Adult Education and Family Planning and like most of his colleagues; he is interested in sports and travelling within and outside the country.

16. Shri Nar Bahadur Bhandari was born in 1940, was a graduate and a teacher (like so many others) before entering politics. He taught in many well-known schools till 1974. He was arrested under MISA and was in jail for a year. His Party, Sikkim Janata Parishad was later merged with Congress; but, his Ministry was dismissed in 1984 due to differences with the Congress-ruled Centre. This happened despite a majority of his Party-members in the Assembly.. He had contested for Lok Sabha in 1984 and had a landslide victory. He won the Assembly election the next year and gave a fitting reply to the high-handedness of the Centre. He had become the Chief Minister of Sikkim for three successive terms. He lost in 1994 and formed the Opposition in the Sikkim Assembly. He too, like the present Chief Minister Dr. Pawan Chamling, is deeply interested in reading and writing and edited and published many books and journals. He is also interested in sports.

17. Shri Karna Bhadur Chamling was born in 1954 in East Sikkim. He lost the first time he contested election in 1979. He lost in 1985 and 1989 also since he contested again and again from Indian National Congress. He realised his mistake and joined SDF and won in 1994. This is a clear case to show that nobody in Sikkim can or could win unless he contested with SDF ticket and also to show why there was no Opposition in Sikkim Assembly. (This point has been noted earlier also).

Mr. Chamling was appointed Chief Whip and later Minister for Welfare & Parliamentary Affairs. When re-elected in 1999, he became Minister for Food & Civil Supplies and Consumer

Affairs Co-operation. Like almost all, his special interests were in sports and visiting places of Natural beauty.

18. Shri Sonam Dorjee was born in 1955 in North Sikkim. We know that a majority of the Bhutias come from North of Sikkim. He was a graduate and government servant before joining politics. He is one of the founder-members of Sikkim Democratic Front. Mr. Dorjee's is a strange case of losing for the Rajya Sabha in spite of contesting from SDF! He then joined Sikkim Sangram Parishad and won the election in 1999. He then reverted back to SDF. This tells us that the MLAs in the Sikkim Assembly do not care for any ideology or a particular path of politics. Their only motto is to win.

Again, like almost all, Mr. Dorjee has interest in sports and travelling. But, strangely, the State has not left any mark in any field of sports!

19. Shri J. K. Bhandari was born in 1959 in East Sikkim and is an M. Com, LLB. He was a practicing lawyer in Sikkim High Court and also in government service before joining politics. He was also Panchayat Pradhan for a while. He contested from SSP Party in 1994 and lost, but got elected (without joining SDF) in 1999! Yet, he joined the ruling SDF Party in 2002. Needless to add, he too has interest in sports and travelling.

20. Shri Gopal Lamichaney was born in 1952 and studied up to Class X. He got elected for the first time in 1994 on SDF ticket and re-elected in 1999. Like all else he has interest in sports but, also in drama and music and the welfare of the scheduled castes having been elected to All Sikkim Scheduled Caste Association and Bishwakarma Kalyan Samiti.

21. Shri Sonam Gyatso Lepcha was born in 1964 in North Sikkim. He had passed Higher Secondary, became a social worker and Panchayat Secretary too. He was elected from Dzongu Reserved Constituency as Sikkim Sangram Parishad Party candidate and yet won in 1999. Yet, he joined SDF the next year. This is inexplicable because people join SDF when

they cannot win election on other Party's tickets. He worked as Panchayat Secretary for 10 long years, which is also rare because all others had given up their Panchayat activities once they became an MLA. He works for the socially backward and the downtrodden, though like others, is interested in sports and travel also.

22. Shri Hishey Langchungpa was born in 1967 and is a graduate. He too devoted his activities to the uplift of the backward and the downtrodden. He was the President of the All Sikkim Students' Association and worked with the Drivers' Union also. He joined SDF in 1990 and became Youth-in-charge and Vice-President of the Party. His tireless work for his Party led to the fall of the Sikkim Sangram Parishad government. He became Minister of Power and Labour and continued to hold the same portfolio when he won the next Assembly election. He too, has special interest in sports and travelling apart from social work and music.

23. Shri Thinley Tsering Bhutia was born in 1957 and has studied up to Class XII. Joined SDF in 1994, contested election, won and became Minister of Food & Civil Supplies. When re-elected in 1999, he became Minister for Public Health, Engineering and Urban & Housing Development.

24. Shri M. Tshering Sherpa was born in 1944 and served as a government servant before joining politics. Had originally joined Rashtriya Congress of Kazi Lhenduup Dorjee. Later he joined Sikkim Sangram Parishad and yet got elected in 1994. He got re-elected in 1999 from the same Party. He is the only one who got elected and re-elected in spite of not belonging to the ruling SDF! He had become the President of a Co-operative and worked for the uplift of the downtrodden.

25. Shri Dorjee Tshering Lepcha was born in 1957 and had studied up to Intermediate from an Army School. He too, got elected from Sikkim Sngram Parishad. Yet, like most others, he joined SDF later perhaps to become a Minister. He was in charge of Forests, Wildlife, Environment and Mines & Geology.

He too, was interested in sports, especially football; but, unlike others, was interested in studies also.

26. Shri K. T. Namgyal Gyaltsen was born in 1961and had completed BA, LLB from Delhi. He was a practicing lawyer before joining politics. He joined SDF in 1993 and became General Secretary of the SDF Legal Cell. He became Officer on Special Duty to the Chief Minister in 1995 and won the 1999 election on SDF ticket. He became Minister of Tourism and Land Revenue. Like all others, he too, has interest in football, volleyball, etc. apart from in painting, debate and Western music. He was the Captain of the State Hockey team and the Captain of the College Soccer team.

27. Shri T. Tashi Bhutia was born in 1962 and holds a Diploma in Civil Engineering. He too, had joined SSP and later got inducted into the Ministry holding the portfolios of Food, Civil Supplies & Consumers' Affairs when his Party later joined SDF. He was also nominated to the post of Chairman, Juvenile Board. He had to fight a lot with the miseries of poverty in his own life and that perhaps, motivated him towards selfless service for the betterment of the poor. But, we cannot forget that there are many Ministers and MLAs who were engaged in social work even when they did not have to struggle under poverty.

28. Shri T. Dorjee Lepcha was born in 1956 in East Sikkim. He is the second post-graduate (among the Ministers), viz. MA, LLB and had served as SDM before joining politics in 1993. He won 1994 and 1999 elections as SDF candidates and became Minister for Building & Housing. He continues to be a social worker and interested in sports too (like most others).

29. Shri Narendra K. Pradhan was born in 1950 and is a graduate. He had won the Gangtok seat in 1994 in spite of contesting from SSP. He got re-elected in 1999 from the same constituency and the same Party and yet joined the ruling SDF in 2002. This shows that every political contestant in Sikkim wants to become Minister or be at least in the ruling Party. That is how there is no Opposition in Sikkim.

30. Shri Palden Lachungpa was born in 1955 in North Sikkim and is another post-graduate—in Buddhist Philosophy and Literature. He was Assistant Education Officer before joining politics in 1985. He served as Chairman of the Scheduled Tribe Welfare Board for a period of five years. In 1999 he was elected the Speaker of the Sikkim Legislative Assembly. He has written books on Buddhism in Bhutia language. He has special interest in social work, reading books, singing and listening to songs apart from travelling to all parts of the State to know the people well. Like so many other MLAs, he has travelled all over the world also.

B.

I was in Gangtok, the capital town of Sikkim, in May 2013 with the purpose of talking to the MLAs and the MPs. First I had decided to visit during the Assembly session so that all the MLAs will be in Gangtok and not far off in their constituencies. They, unlike most of the MLAs of the mainland India, devote a lot of sincere time to the people who have voted them to power and that is why, they tour around their constituencies all the time (except during the Assembly sessions). But, I was advised on phone by their secretaries that the MLAs would be too tired during the session to give me time. So, I better try my luck after the Assembly session. I could meet most of the Ministers at least because they have to stay in the capital through the year. Yet, I could not meet so many Minsters because they did not stop visiting their constituencies even if for a short time. Besides, their work as Ministers demanded their visit to different parts of the State for various different works and duties. This explains why the Ministers get re-elected again and again and why the ruling Party of the Chief Minister has come back to power again and again. West Bengal's Left Front government led by CPI (M) perhaps is the only other example which ruled for so many elections so continuously. But, performance of the ruling Sikkim Democratic Front (henceforth to be known as SDF) is far better than CPI (M) of West Bengal and Tripura because there is no Opposition in the Sikkim Assembly! As Section A showed, very few MLAs won from a Party other than from SDF and nobody could or can win with an Indian National Congress ticket. However much the supporters of the Congress Party believe or say that the people of Sikkim wanted to get rid of monarchy, have democracy and therefore, accede to the Indian Union, to this day the general people of the State—whether Nepali, Bhutia or Lepcha—are not happy with the accession; they wanted democracy, which could have been possible under a like in UK benevolent monarchical dynasty, but not be part of India. They are very disturbed by the immigration of the Biharis, Marwaris, Bengalis, etc., i.e. the non-Sikkimese. The Nepali majority community does not want to join the Gorkhaland Movement nor do they want to merge with the Darjeeling district which has Nepali majority; they do not even have sympathy for the Movement. But, they do not want outsiders from various parts of India. They want Sikkim for the Sikkimese only; in an economically backward State they do not want jobs and businesses, etc. to go to the non-Sikkimese—not even to the Nepalis of Darjeeling! Strangely, the Nepalis of Sikkim have no sympathy for the movement of the Nepalis of Darjeeling! They have become so passionate about this that in the New Development Area, cars with the registration numbers from the other parts of India are not allowed, not a single non-Sikkimese can buy land or build a house or open a shop. Even though no Sikkimese tells it openly, they feel that the so-called "voluntary" accession of Sikkim was like the annexation of Tibet to China.

The peaceful State of Meghalaya now is demanding "inner-line permit" system like in Arunachal Pradesh—for different reasons though. The people of Meghalaya, particularly the Khasis, are very much disturbed due to outsiders marrying Khasi girls and buying land and establishing shops, restaurants, etc. Some day—may be in near future—Sikkim, too, may demand that. But, the total absence of Congress as a political power may work as a deterrent to such demands. In

Meghalaya, on the contrary, there always have been Coalition government, which included Congress. (The present government in Meghalaya is of Congress again). Both the ruling side and the Opposition are coalition, whereas (as mentioned earlier) there was no Opposition at all in Sikkim till the 2014 election!

But, none of the Ministers admit that the people are unhappy being part of India; when asked why then INC cannot win in Sikkim, they keep quiet and try to divert the issue. They try to establish how popular they are because they sincerely and devotedly work for their voters and take care of their minutest complaints or grievances thereby implying that Congress or other all-India parties do not look back towards their constituencies once elected. I feel and I am sure that my readers will also agree with that. That is why, anti-incumbency feeling is not uncommon in quite a few States. Besides, nobody can say that votes are bought or won through threats in the tribal States of India. (Surprisingly, Arunachal Pradesh is an exception; money and power play important roles! Yet, not a single Arunachali I found who wants to accede to China—not even those who have daily barter and interaction with the people from Tibet.)

C.

The questions I usually asked are like the following. (I did not prepare a set questionnaire since all through my research life I have noticed that a set questionnaire makes the interviewed very inhibited and he or she may not even give spontaneous or true answers. The best method is to engage them in casual chitchat and try to get the answers in an indirect way. Yet, let me mention the type of questions I asked.)

Which Party you belong to? The answer, as evident from Section A (of this chapter), was Sikkim Democratic Front. I could not meet all the MLAs I have written about in Section A and all those I could talk to were Ministers and therefore, belonging to the SDF.

Since the focus of this research is on the Lepchas and the Bhutias (the Minorities in Sikkim), I asked the Lepchas and the Bhutias from all walks of life like shop-keepers, taxi drivers, hotel employees, hospital staff, school teachers, college and university students and teachers, etc. about which Party they support and vote for. Except one out of a sample of 50 everybody was all praise for the Chief Minister Shri Pawan Chamling and his Ministers and his Party. What impressed them most was the unassuming behaviour and pro-people attitude of these politicians; they are particularly happy about the health and education facilities though they would have felt happier if the non-Sikkimese were stopped from getting jobs. They were particularly happy about the scheme through which poor meritorious students from the government schools are picked up and admitted in English-medium Public Schools. Correctly they believe that getting a good job depends totally on the confidence and smartness that the Public School students acquire as a contrast to those from the ordinary government schools. How I wish that the other States of India follow this model! I strongly believe that mere intelligence and diligence and good results in the examinations do not help in getting a highly paying job; self-confidence and smart behaviour and ways of talking are very important. Reservation in jobs will become redundant if the Dalits, Adivasis and the other backward communities have self-confidence and smartness. Thus, reservation in good schools is very much essential and not merely in jobs.

I had asked about the role of Opposition while studying two communities from Meghalaya and Assam, but this question was meaningless in Sikkim, where there was no Opposition in the Assembly (till the 2014 election). The role of the Opposition in all States is expected to be constructive—the ruling Party or the ruling Coalition can be oppressive, dictatorial in its absence. Democracy involves the free expression of all kinds of views, opinions and ideologies as well as the freedom of action for the purposes of putting these ideas into reality or for the betterment of the common people. Without Opposition the ruling Party or Coalition can go even anti-people and harmful for the voters. But, Sikkim is such a terrific exception; there are welfare measures for the people and they enjoy better benefits than in a State with an Opposition!

In case of Meghalaya I had tried to find out if Coalition government gives a better voice to the people. The State is known for having both the government and the Opposition of various regional Parties. Is the combination of different views, opinions and ideologies more representative of the voters' voices and opinions and therefore, more democratic? Theoretically, it seems more democratic; but, there is the fear of too many clashes—particularly if it is a coalition only for the purposes of winning the election. People from various walks of life, particularly the teachers and the university students, feel much better development could have taken place and people could have stronger voices if the Parties were not clashing within the Assembly; they feel many beneficial bills cannot be passed easily or not passed at all because it is hard for the various Parties to come to an unanimous decision. But, the government is running quite smoothly in Meghalaya even though the Garos agitate sometimes and the Khasis are demanding the stopping of the buying of lands and marriage, Khasi of girls (who own the land and other properties) by outsiders; they are wanting "inner line permit" like in Arunachal Pradesh.

Since Pawan Chamling's Party was the most popular, I wanted to find out if PDF or the People's Democratic Front was pro or anti Congress and also why it cannot win if it is anti-Congress. I could not get any satisfactory answer either from the voters or from the voted-to-power. Naturally, the question followed was what are causes behind this great success of SDF—is it the Party manifesto or the pro-people work of the Party or the pro-people personality of the Chief Minister? The answers have been more or less discussed under No. 4.

I also wanted to know what are the pro-people work that SDF and the Ministers do and have done. The answers to this also have been discussed under earlier.

1. Do the Lepcha and the Bhutia MLAs raise specific demands? Do they unconditionally support the Chief Minister and do the Bhutias support the Bhutia candidates and the Lepchas support the Lepcha candidates only—like a particular caste voting for the same caste in India? Yes, the trend is not all that uncommon even though the Minorities (the Nepalis being the Majority) do not feel any discrimination; yet, they may (though not necessarily) prefer Ministers from their own community. A small number of Lepchas has formed an association of their own with specific demands of their own. They are the original and the oldest settlers in Sikkim and the Nepalis are the latest; the Lepchas do not like the fact that they have become a minority community, even lesser in number than the Bhutias! I had a long discussion with the President of the Lepcha Association Shri S. D. Lepcha and his associate. He insisted that a separate voice of the Minority Lepchas is necessary, but could not specify the grounds of discrimination or injustice! He did not even ask for a change in the government or the ruling Party. He did not, like all other Sikkimese, want a Congress government; he feared that the situation will be worse.
2. When asked about the role of the Lepcha and the Bhutia MLAs and Ministers, the voters seemed to be having no grudges. The Lepchas are happy with the Bhutia and even the Nepali Ministers (Dr Pawan Chamling is a Nepali) and the Bhutias are happy with the performance of the Lepcha or Nepali Ministers.

One significant indication of this state of mind of the people is that there is no Security system in the Secretariat or the Assembly and the Ministers move around Gangtok and particularly their constituencies without any security force moving with them! This was so even in West Bengal when Late Jyoti Basu was the Chief Minister. If one leader/ MLA or a party does pro-people work sincerely, why should anybody like to attack or kill those in power (from the party)?

3. My next query was if the Lepcha and the Bhutia voters are eager voters and their MLAs are successful? I could not manage to get exact figures, but the people in general are contended and therefore, do not feel the special urge to vote the incumbent out of power; they are quite casual about their voting rights and duties. The Nepalis are much more politically aware and very conscious of their rights. But, as mentioned earlier, they do not want to join the Separation Struggle of the Darjeeling Nepalis, nor do they want the latter to come to Sikkim and settle down! They will not like to join Darjeeling State if it ever gets formed.
4. Do the Lepcha and Bhutia MLAs work only for their own communities or for the general public? The only answer is that the SDF works for all the Sikkimese and does not discriminate between communities and as we know, all the Ministers and the MLAs belong to this single Party.
5. Do the Lepchas and the Bhutias get equal job and education opportunities? No, the Nepalis get a better opportunity since the other communities have remained comparatively backward belonging to the backward areas of North and East Sikkim. My readers must have noticed in Section A that a great majority of the MLAs come from the West and South Sikkim, which are more accessible to the rest of India thus making it easier for the Sikkimese of these areas to come to the developed

States of India. I must remind my readers of the project where the meritorious backward/poor students get an opportunity to study in advanced public schools and thus acquire the required smartness to compete for a good job.

In the Parliamentary election of 2014 there was a powerful urge from the voters for an honest leader like Pawan Kumar Chamling of Sikkim. If Modi boasts of winning 3 elections in a row in Gujarat, Chamling could boast of four and also of freeing Sikkim politics of corruption. In the last election of 2009, But Sikkim krantikari Morcha won as many as 12 seats! Chamling's Party had won 30 out of a total of 32 seats.

Sikkim was a highly corrupt State during the rule of Congress Party's Nar Bahadur Bhandari. Chamling broke away from Congress and formed his own Sikkim Democratic Front on the plank of anti-corruption, pro-people honest government. His opponents have tried to tar his reputation many a times; but, people obviously will always vote for honesty and concern for the weaker sections of the society. Sikkim has flourished economically and socially under Chamling. Its GDP growth in 2007-2012 averaged 9 per cent annually—well above the national average. It has achieved 100 per cent rural electrification and household sanitation. It did not need any Vidya Balan to convince the rural folks for "shauchalaya!" Its economic boom is because of successful tourism, ample hydroelectricity and success in attracting industries like pharmaceuticals.

Like many national regional parties of the North-east, Chamling's Sikkim Democratic Front tends to support whichever party is in power at the Centre; he was with Vajpayee of NDA (though personally not communal at all), then with Manmohan Singh of UPA and both welcomed him! I am yet to know about his attitude to Modi's government at the Centre since I could not meet him after 2014 elections both at the centre & in the State.

Chapter XV

Sikkim—Political Behaviours of the People

A

Though I found an overwhelming majority of the Sikkimese, whatever the community they belonged to, more or less happy with the present government, a few Bhutias expressed displeasure. They could not point out the failures of the government, but wanted a change; they felt that 20 long years' rule of the same party with the same Chief Minister is not good for the political health of a State; there should be change and also a powerful Opposition. (I don't yet know if these Bhutias voted for Sikkim Kranti Kari Morcha in the election of 2014 which brought in an Opposition in the Assembly.)

The Bhandari government earlier had also continued for 20 years in spite of the fact (as mentioned in the preceding chapter) people of the older generation were not happy with Sikkim's accession to India which was mainly engineered by the Congress Party in Sikkim. The King used to be a Bhutia (Buddhist Tibetan & not from Bhutan) and benevolent. Common people did not seem to be unhappy or oppressed (as is generally expected in a monarchy); yet, the Congress government of India could manipulate to create a supposedly public opinion in favour of accession to "democratic" India (from monarchical feudalism). Let me also mention here that the Bhutias were and are far more advanced than the Lepchas (though not as advanced as the Nepalis).

The oldest residents of Sikkim, the Lepchas, were a bit lazy and non-enterprising; the Bhutias were assertive and self-confident (for obvious reasons). The Lepchas are less interested in education. They are very sincere, friendly, docile and non-aggressive and are mainly into agriculture and horticulture. They, like the Bhutias, live mostly in North Sikkim, which is most undeveloped with very bad roads and other communication systems; cultivable land is also very little in this area. In the very beginning the Bhutias used to be proud and a bit arrogant, being the community of the ruling monarch. In the first election there was a tendency of the Bhutias voting for the Bhutia candidates only; but, this trend did not last till the next election. The Lepchas were always very docile and so, they voted for the winning Party always.

In 1975 there was a tripartite agreement among the major three communities of Sikkim—12 out of 32 seats in the Assembly got reserved for the Bhutias and the Lepchas and this was in proportion to their population. There are four lakhs voters and 90 to 92 per cent voting—the highest in India. The State Election Commission is very strict and rules-bound; the mobile numbers of all the members are notified so that any potential voter can complain and seek justice. In the last 10 years there is reservation in the government jobs also for the Bhutias and the Lepchas and even for the various minor clans amongst the Nepalis. Yet, inter-community marriages have started becoming common over the years, though the Buddhists find it difficult to accept marriages with the Hindus. In general, women are more dominating/assertive than men unlike in a major part of the Indian and South Asian societies.

As mentioned in the preceding chapter, the MLAs are so people-friendly that they know each and everybody in their constituencies. They are like Godfathers to their voters! There is no Party politics since there was only one Party for all practical purposes (even though there is Indian National

Congress, Sikkim Sangram Parishad, Sikkim Kranti Morcha, etc.). I came to know of one-member Opposition, which had come up only a year before the 2014 Assembly election. Sikkim Sangram Parishad was formed 20 years back, but has now become defunct. There is no money-power or muscle-power in politics here and no religious conflicts between the Buddhists and the Hindus; the latter is in majority.

B

As mentioned in the preceding chapter, the present Chief Minister is engaged in a lot of pro-people policies and activities; the beneficiaries call such actions "social justice." He does not discriminate at all between the communities and promotes innovative and positive steps particularly for the economically backward. For example, as mentioned earlier, poor meritorious students are selected from the government schools and admitted to renowned public schools. Thus, they develop self-confidence and smartness of the upper class and perform well in the interviews for good jobs even outside Sikkim. If only all other States of India had taken such steps!

Secondly, there are health cards for all the needy, and like in China the government hospitals and the Public Health centres are well-equipped. The patients of the BPL category get Rs. 20,000 in advance. Dr. Chamling has tried to achieve what Nobel Laureate Amartya Sen has prescribed as the three important legs of a table viz. education, health and gender equality.

Thirdly, the government has taken "capacity-building" measures like vocational training in hotel industry (we must remember that Sikkim is a hot spot for tourists), etc.; stipends are given and some of the trainings are even free. The Chief Minister and the other Ministers pay surprise visits to the offices, schools and hospitals on and often in order to ensure that the people are getting justice. They impress upon their voters that the government is "janata ka raj" and the Ministers are the "servants" of the people.

Fourthly, there is 50 per cent reservation for women in the Panchayats and not mere mandatory 33 per cent though in the Assembly there are only four women MLAs out of a total of 32. There are two women Cabinet Ministers. The Speaker was a woman in the earlier session. The reason small member of women in polities is not any deliberate discrimination or biases against them (common in the most States of the so-called mainland India); like in Meghalaya (where too, there is no gender discrimination), women in general, are apolitical and not too keen for political power. They are more interested in social recognitions and advantages; that is how their numbers in the Panchayats are remarkable. Women who have to remain unmarried till the age of 45 are given pensions and there are co-operative banks to help the needy women or the enterprising women. Women are mostly in education and government service, rarely in police or similar jobs.

Fifthly, there is a "10 Minutes to Earth" programme every July 25 when every Sikkimese, including the Chief Minister, must plant trees as many as possible in 10 minutes (even though Sikkim is much greener compared to the States of the Western Himalayas). The goal is that Sikkim must become a complete "organic" State by 2015. Seventy percent of its budget is spent in the rural areas.

Sixthly, the Chief Minister welcomes free interaction with his electorate. Pro-Lepcha or pro-Bhutia issues are rarely raised in the Assembly or in public even though the Nepalis are in great majority. Yet, there are only six lakhs Nepalis in Sikkim, the State is so thinly populated. As a contrast, there are 14 lakhs Nepalis in Darjeeling district of West Bengal. Once Gorkhaland issue was supported in the Assembly, but the Sikkimese Nepalis do not want to join Gorkhaland if it is ever formed.

C.

The anti-incumbency factor thesis, often invoked to explain the defeat of the incumbent party in most States of India, reaches a dead-end in the North-east. What we generally see in this region is a pro-incumbency factor and Sikkim is the most striking example. The 2,81,937 strong electorate of Sikkim is composed of different ethnic groups; the Lepchas (7 per cent) is considered to be the most original group/ tribe; then came the Bhutias (8 per cent). The Nepalis, who compose the overwhelming majority (63 per cent) came the last and they are the ones who wanted accession with India. (May be they thought that they will get a greater weightage in electoral politics because of their number, which they could not have under a Bhutia monarch, however benevolent he may have been. It is believed that the chief reason behind the failure of the Congress Party in Sikkim is because of this accession to India. The other linguistic communities are the Sherpas (4 per cent), Limbu (7 per cent) and the Tibetans (1 per cent). Then, there are Marwaris, Biharis and Bengalis also against whom a lot of resentment is growing up and the Sikkimese want Sikkim only for themselves. The majority (68%) profess Hinduism and the Buddhists are 28 per cent though they appear to be the most conspicuous religious group. There are 3 per cent Christians and 1 per cent Muslims. Bhutia, Lepcha, Limboo and the Tamang are the scheduled tribes.

The ruling party retaining power with as much as two-thirds majority is amazing! The only other example perhaps were West Bengal and Tripura where the Left Front had a continuous rule for 33 years and had an impressive vote share of 53 per cent in 1987. In Udisha Biju Janata Dal was back in power, but with 44 per cent of the votes only, in Andhra Pradesh the Telugu Desham party ruled for consecutive two terms, but with 38 per cent vote share only and in Karnataka the Congress had not fallen a victim to the anti-incumbency factor, with 35 per cent vote share only.

This pro-incumbency trend in Sikkim was there even when Nar Bahadur Bhandari was the Chief Minister; he had ruled for 15 years between 1979 and 1994. The first time he had won under the banner of Samajbadi Janata Party and the next time under Sikkim Sangram Parishad. In 1989 election, his Party came to power in a more convincing manner. While Bhandari did not have much to claim from his 15 years rule other than the inclusion of the Nepali language in the Eighth Schedule of the Constitution, Pawan Chamling has been lauded for his contribution to the expansion of political democracy in the State. The national parties have little hold in Sikkim. Congress had twice come to power, but by co-opting with the regional party. About 60 per cent of the electorate thinks that the regional parties provide better governance than the national parties. The BJP's hopes of making inroads also had failed and even ever-popular Sikkim Democratic Front (earlier an ally of the NDA at the Centre) decided to go alone in the 1994 election. Some of the other parties that contested were the breakaway group of the Sikkim Sangram Parishad, Sikkim Democratic Alliance, Himali Rajya Parishad, CPI (M) and the Sikkim Gorkha Democratic Front and the vote share of the 17 Independent candidates was only 2 per cent. In a survey conducted by CSDS, New Delhi, 53 per cent gave topmost priority to Party, 30 per cent only to the candidate and only 3 per cent gave consideration to caste and community while casting their votes. This is again extremely opposite of what happens in the mainland India, particularly in the Hindi-Hindu heartland. The Chief Minister Chamling had felt "the results of the 7th Assembly polls of Sikkim are indicative of the peoples' disregard for and condemnation of the yellow politics of castes, communalism and opportunism." He further believed that socio-economic and political equality for women, environmental conservation, institutionalisation of democracy and a trouble-free atmosphere are some of the major achievements of his government. Sikkim has indeed recorded several significant gains in the last three decades; infant mortality rate dropped from 60 per 1000 to 51 in 1997, literacy rate went up from 7 per cent to 70 per cent in 2001 and 83 per cent of 6-17 age-group children attend schools. In 1998-99 only 21 per cent children were malnourished as against the national average of 47 per cent. This is lowest among all the States of India. Situations have improved a lot in 2013. As high as 71 per cent are satisfied with their financial condition, and 47 per cent thought that the curbs on corruption and the law and order situation have improved in the last 15 years. According to UNDP, Sikkim has the potential to become the first poverty-free State of India. Of the total of 873 wards in rural Sikkim, the SDF controls 850!

D.

According to the two MPs of Sikkim, whom I met in Delhi when the Parliament session was on, the strength of the ruling party of Dr. Chamling viz. the Sikkim Democratic Front has been gaining in strength with every election, viz. from 20 to 25 and finally to 32, till it became the only party in the Assembly with no Opposition at all! (This is so unique a situation that this phenomenon has been mentioned at quite a few places by me.) It is a pro-poor and welfare-oriented government and this point has been emphasised by all the Ministers, MLAs and even by a large section of the electorate while I was in Sikkim for my field visit; the MPs echoed the same view about the ruling government; they are proud of this and wish that other States of North-east, if not of the entire India, follow this pattern of honest and dedicated work for the people. They believe that there is no issue for the Opposition to raise since the common people do not feel dissatisfied with the performance of the existing party; there is nothing which the people feel that the Opposition could have delivered. Very recently in 2013, one MLA has formed a single-member party called Sikkim Krantikari Morcha. While in Sikkim I could not find a single supporter of this new party; most people were making fun of this party and they believed that it was very narrow personal enmity that has prompted the MLA to form this party. But, the ridiculed party did manage to get seats in the Assembly in the latest election!

The MPs made a very significant observation that the social elite cannot necessarily create the political elite. This is significant because the Congress Party was formed by the social elite of the late 19th century and the situation was/is similar in case of the most other political parties including the Communist parties. The situation was/is that the highly educated and socially privileged and mostly upper caste persons came/come out on the political platform as the leaders. So, obviously, they do not and cannot have a proper idea of the problems and the needs of their electorate (who are mostly poor and deprived, dalits and adivasis). Besides, it is the practice in almost all the States of India that once elected, the people's representatives do not usually look back or visit their constituencies or listen to the people's needs, aspirations and grievances! In Sikkim, it is difficult to find the MLAs in the capital town Gangtok except the Ministers (who too, visit their constituencies every now and then). I had found the MPs of Meghalaya (and other States) mostly living in Delhi (even when the Parliament is not in session); but, the MPs of Sikkim fly back to their constituencies whenever the Parliament was getting adjourned (even if for merely two days) due to the commotion created by BJP and other parties in the Opposition or due to respect paid to Nelson Mandela or to the victims of Uttarkhand disaster and the disastrous cyclones that repeatedly attacked the Andhra and Odisha coasts.

The SDF politicians were sure that their party and the Chief Minister would return to power for the fifth time in 2014. The party focuses on the youth potentiality and youth power and rightly believes in "reservation" in higher education; how can youth from the disadvantaged classes compete for jobs, even if there is the benefit of job reservation, without having the required education, good results, technical training and smartness and confidence that those from the privileged castes and classes have? That is why, in most of the Indian States the reserved posts remain unfilled; the underprivileged students cannot possibly compete with the smart, self-confident, English-speaking ones from the privileged classes, castes and communities. There is 84 per cent literacy in Sikkim—a great achievement for a State which became a democracy so late. In this regard we must not forget that the monarchy of Sikkim was enlightened and modern-minded and not at all anti-people! A good number of Sikkimese believe that the Indian government committed as much folly as China (which had annexed Tibet) by annexing Sikkim; they wanted democracy no doubt but as an independent nation. They even feel that the monarchs were not autocratic and, therefore, Sikkim could have had the status like that of present Bhutan. (We all know that the present Bhutanese king is very democratic and modern).

Strangely, a few upper-class persons and a few (though very little in number) politicians are communal minded in an atmosphere of utter communal and class harmony! A very small section feels that Narendra Modi had done nothing wrong and he is wrongly accused of the massacre of the Muslims in Gujarat. On the other hand, they believe that caste and community make no difference when the people and the government are modern-minded. They are not sure if SDF will refuse if Modi wants to shake hands! This is the view of a very minute section of the Nepalis who are Hindus by religion and constitute the overwhelming majority of the population. They, in general, are broad-minded with love for modernity; when it comes to inter-community marriages, the Buddhists, particularly the Bhutias, are much more conservative and hardly ever agree to such unions. They are much more a-political also and they sometimes miss the rule of their "benevolent" monarchs. We must remember that the demand for joining Indian Union had come from the Hindu Nepalis and not from the Bhutias or the Lepchas; the last two communities were the original inhabitants of monarchical Sikkim and the Nepalis had migrated into long after. The former, therefore, dislike Congress Party a lot and have been welcoming the emergence of Aam Admi Party. SDF was a part of the UPA coalition though not happy with that and believes that the government was following a "flawed model!" It feels that the Prime Minister Manmohan Singh does not understand politics and has no influence over his ministers and that he is a stooge of Sonia and Rahul Gandhis, who were actually ruling from behind. The PM has no capability to take the pro-people correct decisions since he is surrounded by dishonest persons in his Ministry and bureaucracy. (Let me remind my readers that the SDF is doing and has done all those for the welfare of the common people which AAP was and is intending to do if it could come back to power. Not a single Sikkimese I talked to mentioned corruption in the working of the Chamling government or at the Panchayat level).

The SDF supporters felt that the newly formed one-member Sikkim Krantikari Morcha has been instigated by the Gurkha Janamukti Morcha; a few Nepalis of Sikkim may have sympathy for Gorkhaland, but will not like to join Gorkhaland (if it is ever formed); they would like to retain their identity as the Sikkimese.

The people feel that the regional parties are more successful and welcome since, like SDF, they can understand the local/ regional and area/tribe-specific problems better; they give the examples of Telugu Desham Party, Trinamool Congress and DMK of Tamilnadu though, in my opinion, these parties have proved to be as power-hungry and not at all pro-people as the big and traditional national parties are. What specific benefits have the common or poor or under-privileged people derived during the rule of these parties? Besides, if these regional parties were really region-centric, they would not have aligned with the corrupt, bourgeois or communist parties at the national levels. That is why, the Sikkimese feel that the national parties are interested only in power and not regional developments whereas regional/local level developments are of utmost importance in a multi-ethnic, multi-cultural country like India. India can develope as a nation only if the different components of the nation can be and are developed.

Sikkim is such a trouble-free, peaceful nation that there is no arrangements for VIP security and the Ministers are easily accessible. Does AAP of Delhi know that they are not the first to refuse "security," red beacons, etc.? Nobody stopped or questioned me or wanted to see the "Pass" when I went to meet the Ministers in Gangtok!

My favourite question was how can there be "democracy" without an Opposition in the Assembly? In such a situation there is every possibility of the "unopposed" ruling party turning autocratic; besides, criticism is the main plank of democratic or pro-people governance; otherwise, how will the ruling party, however well-meaning and pro-people it may be, know or understand where and in what it is going wrong? Theoretically I was correct; but, in reality, the government without opposition and criticism has done extremely well; it is very successful in feeling the pulse of the people correctly and even guessing what the people need and deserve. Now there is an Opposition and we have to see if this performs constructive or destructive role. I hope the SKM will not be disruptive like the Sangh Parivar was in the Parliament during the two UPA regimes on the congress party is now in the parliament

The latest composition in the Sikkim Assembly provoked me to ask the following questions to the voters from different walks of life—the college and school teachers, college and university students, a few shopkeepers, taxi-drivers, doctors, nurses, tourist-guides and a few politicians and activists. The questions and the answers (clubbed together) were as follows.

Questions:

1. Sikkim was a unique State by having only one party, viz. Sikkim Democratic Front, and no Opposition at all. It had appeared to me by talking to people from different walks of life that people, in general, are very happy with Pawan Chamling's policies and work. Why and how then Sikkim Krantikari Morcha (which was a one-man show when I had visited the State in 2013) manage to get as many as 12 seats in the 2014 election? Did it get invisible support from the BJP or

the voters wanted to experiment with a new party, i.e. the way the voters behaved in almost all States of India?

2. Which community/ies do you think voted for the new party, SKM? Is it the Lepchas? A few Lepchas interviewed during my study in Sikkim in 2013 had wished for a change believing that continuous one-party rule is not good for democracy even though they had no specific grudge against SDF or the Hindu Nepalis. The Nepalis of Sikkim did not appear to be Hindu chauvinists at all.
3. Were the voters influenced by BJP's marvellous success in the Assembly elections of many States before the elections to the Parliament and the Sikkim Assembly took place? Did they want to vote for a winning party—a very common psychology of the voters?
4. Were SDF's pro-people beneficial activities not all that attractive any longer and did the party lag behind in its commitments?
5. Did the electorate seriously start believing that an Opposition is a must for democracy to be successful?
6. What is the age-group, professions and educational qualifications of the voters who voted for SKM or against SDF? Like it has happened in Bengal and in the Centre, voters may not have necessarily voted for an Opposition party; they may have wanted a change and therefore, voted for the party/ies opposing the party ruling for elections after elections?

The answers to these questions can be clubbed together as follows—

1. As we all know SDF has been in power for a very long time—for four terms—as a single majority party with no Opposition at all in the Sikkim Assembly because the party's policies and programmes have always been pro-poor and pro-development. But, with the

overpowering role of Capitalism in India's economy, the number of young unemployed was increasing. This group must have voted for a new party as an experiment.

2. SKM managed to get support from the non-natives of Sikkim (like the Marwaris, the Biharis and the Bengalis) because it promised to give importance to the holders of Aadhar cards, irrespective of the fact of nativity. Most of the seats won by SKM are from East Sikkim (which is more urbanised than the rest of Sikkim); the non-native population is also higher in this part of Sikkim. The new party had given a lot of importance to internet and cyber connectivity and they tried to reach the voters through these modern methods.
3. Like BJP all over India, SKM too, had spread the news through various media that it was going to win the next election. The party even spread false news that SDF had withdrawn from many seats and therefore, it is a cakewalk for SKM.
4. Anti-incumbency too, may have worked; some voters wanted to try a new party even though the ruling party was not anti-people! There is no particular community voting for SKM. The Modi-wave, spread vigorously all over India, may also have been a factor against the ruling SDF. (But, we are not sure if SKM has been influenced by BJP or the Right-minded parties).
5. Unfortunately, the new Opposition is not playing a constructive role; it is behaving like what NDA did while in Opposition at the Centre. They organised students' strikes and provoked them to be destructive. Posters came up in abusive languages against the government. Some fear that this new party was planted by BJP with the sole purpose of disturbing the pro-people government of Chamling.
6. But, the Chief Minister and his team are carrying on with their welfare activities undeterred.

Conclusion

The most significant conclusion I have managed to arrive at is that the social, cultural and the language identities of the tribes I tried to understand are far more important than the political powers they are allowed to wield under the Indian Constitution and the subsequent Laws and Amendments made (over a period of 65 years). They, we must not forget, are "adivasis" i.e. the original inhabitants of this land called India. Like in so many different parts of the world (like in Australia and America, for example), they have been mercilessly displaced by various invading races (like the Aryans in case of India) from outside—far and near. The adivasis of India or the "Aboriginies" of Australia or the Red Indians of North America were basically content with whatever they got from the Nature (without destroying it which the invaders had done) and therefore, they are peace-loving and peaceful. Greed, the worst enemy of human civilisation, was totally absent in their nature and they sang and danced and told stories to their next generations happily; these folklores are a rich part of their civilisation and history. And it is this history and tradition that the present tribes, who have become assertive and are increasingly becoming more and more assertive, are most concerned about. This is because the invaders had not only driven them to the jungles and the hills, they have tried to impose their own history, literature, language and civilisation on the latter, thus trying to wipe out their identities.

The second conclusion I could arrive at was that the adivasis or the tribes learnt violence and the use of weapons against human beings (their crude weapons made of wood and stones were meant for killing ferocious animals in self-defence or for the purpose of eating meat) from the so-called 'civilised' racial and cultural chauvinists from "mainland" India (the word "mainland" or "mainstream" was invented by the successors of the clever Aryans who had slowly invented Vedic religion and the caste-system to force a few economic and social groups away from the fruits of development and civilisation—thereby claiming that all the non-Aryans or the original inhabitants were uncivilised!). Class discrimination also came up side by side with caste discrimination/hatred because the three upper castes happened to control all means of production and thus be rich. The tribes, who were least interested in property, hoarding or making money, produced only that much of food and other things which they needed; they could not think of profits by exploiting and cheating others—not even those who exploited them to become rich and powerful!

My third conclusion follows from my second—the tribes finally learnt to get back what was cheated away from them by the non-tribal people, who wielded both economic and political powers. So they learnt the methods of violence, too. We have witnessed the violent movements by the Nagas, Kukis, the Mizos, etc. and now we are encountering the terrible violence of the Bodos so much so that they are torturing and killing those who are innocent and never tried to dominate over them, viz. the poor Bengali Muslims, who were tortured and deprived in their own land even. Thus, the Bodos are indirectly becoming the friends of the Hindu chauvinists and the present ruling clique. In their heart of hearts they may not be anti-Muslim like the Right-wing parties; it has so happened that the so-called "illegal immigrants" have settled down on the very fertile "char" lands on the Brahmaputra and knows the art of farming very well. So, the Bodos feel economically deprived (by the Bengali Muslims) without realising that the latter are equally poor and hapless and that the duty of development, proper training in agriculture and other methods of income for the Bodos or other adivasis lie with the governments of Assam and India. They do not also realise that the job-reservations given by the Constitution of India to the Scheduled Castes and the Scheduled Tribes have no meaning unless they get proper education and training required for a job or self-employment; they do not also realise that the ruling class of India is, on the contrary, destroying Nature which is and has always been the source of livelihood for these tribes and the other forest-dwellers. They fail to realise that violence against another deprived community cannot provide them with the means of livelihood, not even if they get a State of their own! The experiences of Jharkhand, Uttarakhand and Chhattisgarh have not yet been able to open their eyes to the harsh reality that the upper-caste & upper class clique will go on ruling over them even if separate political entities are granted to them! They also fail to realise that socio-economic powers are the source of political power because independent India has not been able to come out of feudal mode of production and the traditional beliefs of superior and the inferior. Parliamentary democracy that independent India adopted after independence could not be like in UK because of the powerful backward pulls of superstition-based religions and castes; India has not yet experienced the "push" factors of modern thoughts and practises without which democracy does not become the rule of the people and for the people; so, the political power continue to remain in the hands of the economically powerful. The most well-known fact of the politicians spending crores of rupees to win a seat in the legislative bodies proves this hard truth. We are also aware of the huge appeal that caste and religion have in winning the elections in a majority of the Hindi-Hindu States of India. The Dalits and the tribes would not have any representation in the Parliament or the Assemblies if not for the reservation granted to them by the Constitution of India. But the seats they manage to win are too few for exercising any power or say in the matters that concern them or affect them directly. Whatever they get is like alms from the upper caste male Hindus. There is thus very little the tribes get even after having States of their own. The problem was squabbling among the opposing clans of the same tribe or opposing tribes of the same State. The best examples are the endless number of tribal/regional parties that are contesting elections against each other in Meghalaya.

My fourth conclusion thus is the endless inner strifes within the same tribe or among the numerous clans in Meghalaya politics, which is marked by coalition governments as well as coalition opposition in the Assembly elections after elections. The tribes are so deeply conscious of their very special identities that political powers turn out to be less important to them! Besides, almost all the tribes of Meghalaya used to have its own democratic/Panchayat type bodies even before democracy came to India; they used to have more or less egalitarian economic, political and gender structures. This was true about the settlers in Sikkim also. The case of Sikkim, another tribal State of India, was the exact opposite of Meghalaya, i.e. one-party rule elections after elections with not a single member in the Opposition! All the tribes had been united in supporting a single party called Sikkim Democratic Front.

But, the latest Assembly election (which was conducted along with the 2014 Parliamentary election) in Sikkim and the 2013 election of Meghalaya Assembly have reversed the pattern dramatically; there is no coalition government in Meghalaya and an Opposition, though weak, in Sikkim. The Congress party, with the support of two independent MLAs, has returned to power after a long gap in Meghalaya, the Opposition continues to be a coalition of a few regional parties though! And, in Sikkim for the first time there is a party in the Opposition occupying 12 out of 32 seats in the Assembly!

I have to try to understand this complex behaviour of the electorate in these two tribal States. I may be incorrect, but the conclusions I can draw from the unusual behaviour of the voters in these States are (i) Meghalaya is an overwhelmingly Christian State and the Modi-wave in the rest of India must have disturbed the tribes badly. They must have realised the importance of unity in times of a probable crisis. Congress is known to be a secular party even though an overwhelming majority of its members (wielding power) are Hindus. In Sikkim the situation is not clear because none of the activists of the ruling SDF (which comprises of all the three major tribal groups) are clear if the newly launched SKM has appealed to the Nepali Hindu who (who are in majority and wield a lot of political power) voted for the new party. Unfortunately, no election analysis has been conducted by Lokniti (of Delhi). I have a fear that the Modi-wave acted on the minds of the Hindu Sikkimese, who most probably are the powerful and influential Nepalis! But, this kind of surmise is unfair and unwise since nobody knows which is the section of Sikkimese electorate that has voted for SKM.

Bibliography

- H. N. Mota (ed), Parliamentary System in India.
- S. G. Deogaonkar, Parliamentary System in India
- Sundar Ram (ed), Indian Democracy: Prospects & Retrospects
- Hans Raj, Encyclopaedia of Indian Parliament
- M. Bhattacharya & S. Goswami, Assam: Agonies & Grievances
- N. Sengupta, State Government & Politics: Sikkim
- H. G. Joshi, Meghalaya: Past & Present
- S. Bhattacharjee, Politics of Frontier State: Arunachal Pradesh
- S. K. Chaube, Hill Politics in North-east India
- C. Durose, Changing Local Governance, Changing Citizens
- R. Bajpai, Debating Difference: Group Rights & Liberal Democracy in India
- Pradip Kumar, Heterogeneities: Identity Formations in Modern India
- Laila Kabeer, Inclusive Citizenship: Meanings & Expressions
- Csaba, Minority Governments in India
- Rob Jenkins, Regional Reflections
- Chatterjee, Lineages of Politics in Society

- K.M.L. Chhabra, Assam Challenge
- C. Kashyap, Parliament of India: Myths & Realities
- P.S. Datta, Electoral Politics in North-east India
- K.V. Rao, Parliamentary Democracy of India: a critical commentary
- K. Santhanam, Conventions & Proprieties of Parliamentary Democracy in India
- P. Sharma, Working of Parliamentary Democracy in India
- B. K. Tiwari (xxiv) N. G. Jayal (ed), Oxford Companion to Politics in India
- A. Lijphart, Thinking about Democracy: Power-sharing and Majority Rule in Theory & Practice
- B.L. Shankar & V. Rodrigues, Indian Parliament: Democracy at Work
- L. N. Gerston, Public Policy-making in a Democratic Society: a guide to civic engagements
- Bhargava, Bagchi, Sudarshan, Multiculturism, Liberalism & Democracy

Index